S0-FQO-327

DISCARDED

AUDITORY and VISUAL
PATTERN RECOGNITION

AUDITORY and VISUAL PATTERN RECOGNITION

BF
251
A92

Edited by

DAVID J. GETTY
Bolt Beranek and Newman Inc.
Cambridge, Massachusetts

JAMES H. HOWARD, JR.
The Catholic University of America
Washington, D.C.

530670

LEA LAWRENCE ERLBAUM ASSOCIATES, PUBLISHERS
1981 Hillsdale, New Jersey

LAMAR UNIVERSITY LIBRARY

Copyright © 1981 by Lawrence Erlbaum Associates, Inc.
All rights reserved. No part of this book may be reproduced in
any form, by photostat, microform, retrieval system, or any other
means, without the prior written permission of the publisher.

Lawrence Erlbaum Associates, Inc., Publishers
365 Broadway
Hillsdale, New Jersey 07642

Library of Congress Cataloging in Publication Data
Main entry under title:

Auditory and visual pattern recognition.

    Papers of a symposium held at Bolt, Beranek, and
Newman, Inc., Cambridge, Mass. June 28–30, 1978.
    Includes bibliographies and index.
    1. Auditory perception—Congresses. 2. Visual per-
ception—Congresses. I. Getty, David J. II. Howard,
James H. (James Henry), 1947–   . [DNLM: 1. Auditory
perception—Congresses. 2. Visual perception—Congresses. 3. Pattern recognition—Congresses. WV 272 A9117
1978]
BF251.A92   152.1   81-7775
ISBN 0-89859-087-6   AACR2

Printed in the United States of America

LAMAR UNIVERSITY LIBRARY

Contents

    Charles S. Watson and William J. Kelly

    Discriminability of Simple Sounds   *39*
    Perception and Discriminability of Tonal
       Patterns   *43*
    General Conclusions   *56*
    References   *57*

4. **Meaningfulness and the Perception of Complex Sounds   61**
    John C. Webster

    Introduction   *61*
    Factor Analyses   *62*
    Information Analyses   *63*
    Identifying Complex Sounds   *66*
    References   *77*

5. **Speech Perception and Auditory Processing   79**
    A. W. F. Huggins

    Introduction   *79*
    Distinctive Features (A Linguistic Term)   *81*
    Fluent Speech   *85*
    Conclusions   *89*
    References   *89*

PART II: PERCEPTION OF COMPLEX VISUAL PATTERNS

6. **Negligible Symmetry Effects in Dot-Pattern Detection   95**
    William R. Uttal and Thelma E. Tucker

    Method   *96*
    Experiment I   *98*
    Results   *102*
    Discussion   *104*
    References   *105*

7. **A Psychophysical Approach to Dimensional Integrality   107**
    *Robert G. Pachella, Patricia Somers,
    and Mary Hardzinski*

    Historical Precedents   *108*
    The Psychophysics of Integrality   *113*
    References   *126*

Contributors and Participants

The names of conference participants who contributed chapters to this volume are preceded by an asterisk (*). The names of conference participants who presented papers at the conference are preceded by a dagger (†). The list of contributors and presenters includes coauthors and copresenters.

*†**James A. Ballas,** Départment of Psychology, The Catholic University of America, Washington, D.C. 20064

Sidney Berkowitz, David Taylor Naval Ship Research and Development Center, Code 1824, Bethesda, Maryland 20084

*†**Arthur E. Bisson,** David Taylor Naval Ship Research and Development Center, Code 1939, Bethesda, Maryland 20084

Marvin A. Blizard, Office of Naval Research, Code 222, 800 N. Quincy Street, Arlington, Virginia 22217

Louis D. Braida, Massachusetts Institute of Technology, 36-747, Cambridge, Massachusetts 02139

Donald C. Burgy, Department of Psychology, The Catholic University of America, Washington, D.C. 20064

H. Steven Colburn, Massachusetts Institute of Technology, 36-759, Cambridge, Massachusetts 02139

Nathaniel Durlack, Massachusetts Institute of Technology, 36-709, Cambridge, Massachusetts 02139

*†**David J. Getty,** Bolt Beranek and Newman Inc., 50 Moulton Street, Cambridge, Massachusetts 02238

David M. Green, Department of Psychology, Harvard University, William James Hall, Cambridge, Massachusetts 02138

*†**Mary Hardzinski,** Human Performance Center, The University of Michigan, 330 Packard Road, Ann Arbor, Michigan 48104

J. D. Harris, NavSubMedResLab, Submarine Base, Groton, Connecticut 06340

*†**James H. Howard, Jr.,** Department of Psychology, The Catholic University of America, Washington, D.C. 20064

*†**A. W. F. Huggins,** Bolt Beranek and Newman Inc., 50 Moulton Street, Cambridge, Massachusetts 02238

Michael Jones, E. G. and G., Suite 211, 8807 Sudley Road, Manassas, Virginia 22110

James Kadane, NOSC, Post Office Box 997, Kailua, Hawaii 96734

*†**William J. Kelly,** The Boys Town Institute for Communication Disorders in Children, 555 N. 30th Street, Omaha, Nebraska 68131

Jack Kerivan, NavSubMedResLab, Auditory Division, Groton, Connecticut 06340

JoAnn Kinney, NavSubMedResLab, Post Office Box 900, Submarine Base, Groton, Connecticut 06340

*†**Cynthia H. Null,** Department of Psychology, College of William and Mary, Williamsburg, Virginia 23185

John J. O'Hare, Office of Naval Research, Code 455, Arlington, Virginia 22217

*†**Robert G. Pachella,** Human Performance Center, The University of Michigan, 330 Packard Road, Ann Arbor, Michigan 48104

†**Theodosios Pavlidis,** Department of Electrical Engineering and Computer Science, Princeton University, Princeton, New Jersey 08540

*†**Reinier Plomp,** Institute for Perception TNO, 3769 ZG Soesterberg, The Netherlands, (also: Faculty of Medicine, Free University, Amsterdam)

William Robinson, Naval Underwater Systems Center, Fort Trumbull, Code 411, New London, Connecticut 06320

Bernice F. Rogowitz, Harvard University, 906 William James Hall, 33 Kirkland Street, Cambridge, Massachusetts 02139

Joseph Russotti, NavSubMedResLab, Auditory Div., Post Office Box 900, Groton, Connecticut 06340

*†**Patricia Somers,** Human Performance Center, The University of Michigan, 330 Packard Road, Ann Arbor, Michigan 48104

Murray F. Spiegel, Laboratory of Psychophysics, Harvard University, 33 Kirkland Street, Cambridge, Massachusetts 02138

William E. Stephens, 2150 Fields Road, Rockville, Maryland

*†**Joel B. Swets,** Bolt Beranek and Newman Inc., 50 Moulton Street, Cambridge, Massachusetts 02238

*†**John A. Swets,** Bolt Beranek and Newman Inc., 50 Moulton Street, Cambridge, Massachusetts 02238

*†**Julius I. Tou,** Center for Information Research, University of Florida, Gainesville, Florida 32611

*†**Thelma E. Tucker,** The University of Michigan, 3009 ISR, Ann Arbor, Michigan 48106

*†**William Uttal,** The University of Michigan, 3009 ISR, Ann Arbor, Michigan 48106

*†**Charles S. Watson,** The Boys Town Institute for Communication Disorders in Children, 555 N. 30th Street, Omaha, Nebraska 68131

*†**John C. Webster,** National Technical Institute for the Deaf, Rochester Institute of Technology, One Lomb Memorial Drive, Rochester, New York 14623

*†**Frederic L. Wightman,** Department of Communicative Disorders, Northwestern University, 2299 Sheridan Road, Evanston, Illinois 60201

*†**Forrest W. Young,** L. L. Thurstone Psychometric Laboratory, Davie Hall 013-A, University of North Carolina, Chapel Hill, North Carolina 27514

Patrick M. Zurek, Central Institute for the Deaf, 909 S. Taylor, St. Louis, Missouri 63110

Preface

The chapters in this volume represent edited versions of papers presented at a symposium on human pattern recognition and classification. The symposium was held at Bolt Beranek and Newman Inc. in Cambridge, Massachusetts on June 28-30, 1978. The broad objective of the symposium was to consider current issues in the area of human recognition of complex patterns.

The systematic scientific investigation of human perception began over 100 years ago, yet relatively little is known about how we identify complex patterns. A major reason for this is that historically, most perceptual research focused on the more basic processes involved in the detection and discrimination of simple stimuli. This work has progressed in a connectionist fashion, attempting to clarify fundamental mechanisms in depth before addressing the more complex problems of pattern recognition and classification. This extensive and impressive research effort has built a firm basis from which to speculate about these issues. What seems lacking, however, is an overall characterization of the recognition problem—a broad theoretical structure to direct future research in this area. Consequently, our primary objective in this volume is not only to review existing contributions to our understanding of classification and recognition, but to project fruitful areas and directions for future research as well.

In order to develop this overview, related research from several areas is reviewed. Our authors include scientists active in human auditory and visual research and others active in theoretical pattern recognition. It is our hope that this unique combination will provide a broader perspective on the important issues in this area than would be possible with a more narrowly-focused group.

For organizational purposes we have divided the volume into four major sections. This substantive division reflects the primary research interests of the authors and includes separate sections on the perception of complex auditory patterns, complex visual patterns, theoretical approaches to pattern recognition, and multidimensional perceptual spaces.

The first section includes five chapters on human auditory perception. These examine existing work in auditory recognition to identify those issues on which progress has been made or is likely and those on which additional effort is clearly needed. For example, we may ask how an understanding of pitch perception will contribute to a more general theory of auditory classification? What role do higher-order cognitive factors such as selective attention and semantic analysis play in auditory recognition, and how can these factors be incorporated into a theory of auditory recognition? To what extent can our understanding of auditory recognition in general benefit from the extensive literature on human speech perception? Finally, we may ask how our basic understanding of auditory recognition can be used to enhance classification performance in applied listening contexts?

The second section reviews some examples of recent research in visual perception and visual information processing. The contribution of these chapters is to review the theoretical issues and constructs that have proven useful in visual research. To what extent are classification processes similar across the two modalities? Perhaps some common general principles underlie human pattern recognition regardless of modality? In what important ways do auditory and visual recognition processes differ?

Our third section considers work on the development and performance of automatic statistical classification systems. Although these chapters do not explicitly address the processes that underlie human recognition, experience suggests that the ultimate development of formal psychological theory in this area will likely benefit from the concepts and techniques employed in this research. What cues or features have proven optimal in these systems? What is the role of signal structure (i.e., the relations among stimulus components) in aural classification? To what extent are existing statistical and syntactic systems reasonable models of human recognition? To what extent are they unreasonable?

The fourth section includes papers on both auditory and visual information processing. What ties this work together is a common analysis in terms of multidimensional perceptual spaces. Here the psychological representation of a stimulus is viewed as a point or vector in a multidimensional feature space. What advantages and disadvantages does this approach to psychophysical scaling offer? How are we to interpret the abstract stimulus space extracted in a multidimensional scaling analysis? How does this representation relate to an observer's classification performance? What might this research tell us about feature extraction in human pattern recognition?

The symposium was funded jointly by the Engineering Psychology Programs of the U.S. Office of Naval Research and the Naval Ship Research and Development Center. We are pleased to acknowledge the support provided by John

O'Hare and Arthur Bisson, the project managers for the two agencies, respectively. Finally, our special thanks go to John A. Swets for providing an overview of the symposium at its conclusion, and to Mildred Webster for coordinating the planning of the meeting and managing its realization.

David J. Getty
James H. Howard, Jr.

AUDITORY and VISUAL
PATTERN RECOGNITION

PERCEPTION OF COMPLEX AUDITORY PATTERNS

1 Pitch Perception: An Example of Auditory Pattern Recognition

Frederic L. Wightman

INTRODUCTION

Human listeners normally classify sounds on a number of subjective dimensions, among which are loudness, timbre, and pitch. The auditory processes that mediate auditory classifications are quite complex and, because the dimensions are purely subjective, research on these processes is difficult. In the case of loudness and timbre, research is aided by the fact that there are simple physical correlates of the perceptual experiences. Thus, although the exact functional relationship may be very complicated, it is clear that a change in stimulus intensity will generally cause a change in loudness, and alterations of spectral content will usually change the timbre of sound. However, in spite of the obvious relationship between the frequency and pitch of a sinusoid, there is no simple physical correlate of pitch. Although pitch is definitely related to the frequency, or more generally the periodicity of a sound, it has recently been recognized that the relationship is by no means a simple one.

The purpose of this chapter is first to demonstrate that classification of auditory signals in terms of their pitch is an extraordinarily complex process and, second, to argue that the process can conveniently be viewed as a kind of auditory pattern recognition. Finally, with reference to some recent results from my own laboratory, it is suggested that data from listeners with certain hearing impairments may help us to understand in more detail how the auditory system accomplishes this pattern recognition.

THE PROBLEM

The fundamental question motivating all research in psychophysics is: "What is the stimulus?" For the purpose of this chapter, that question reduces to: "What is it about a sound that determines its pitch?" There is an enticing simplicity to the question, but still no satisfactory answer. As early as the time of Pythagoras it was thought that pitch was related simply to the frequency or period of a sound. Pythagoras noted that shorter strings, which vibrate more rapidly when plucked, produced a sound with a higher pitch than did longer strings. For simple sounds such as sinusoids, there is no problem because wave forms with the same period generally do have the same pitch. However, it is relatively easy to produce stimuli that have very different periods yet still seem to have the same pitch. Moreover, the same pitch can be evoked by stimuli of widely varying spectral content (such as those produced by different musical instruments sounding the same note) and by stimuli with very different temporal fine structures (such as those produced by one instrument recorded at different places in a reverberant hall). The main problem, then, which any theory of pitch perception must address, is the invariance of pitch, the fact that many different transformations of the physical stimulus leave its pitch unchanged.

Accounting for invariance of one sort or another is just what most pattern-recognition schemes are designed to do. For this reason, it has proven useful to treat pitch extraction as a kind of auditory pattern recognition. A simple analogy may help to illustrate this point of view. The letter "A" as seen here, has its "A-ness" in common with the same letter printed by hand, in a newspaper, or anywhere else. In every case, it is recognized as the letter "A" in spite of great differences among the various physical representations of the letter (e.g., size, orientation, type style, etc.). Similarly, the musical note "middle c" has the same pitch regardless of the instrument that produces it. In both the visual case and the auditory case, the process of recognition and classification of the stimulus leaves the percept invariant in the face of large intrastimulus variability. Viewed in this way, pitch extraction is clearly a pattern-recognition process.

A BRIEF HISTORY

Subjective attributes of sound are difficult to study because they are not accessible by direct measurement. In contrast, physical features such as intensity and frequency are easily quantified. With modern laboratory gear, we can determine the intensity or frequency of a sound with an accuracy of better than .1%. Pitch however, like loudness and timbre, cannot be measured directly, for it exists only in a listener's head. There is no such thing as a pitch meter. Most listeners can tell us only whether the pitches of two sounds are equal or whether the pitch of one is higher or lower than another. This has led to the use of simple matching procedures to provide at least an indirect measure of pitch.

Matching paradigms require listeners to compare the pitch of the sound in question with that of a reference sound. A pure tone (such as that produced by a sine-wave generator) is a convenient reference because pitch can then be defined in terms of the frequency of the tone. For example, we can say a sound has a pitch of 200 Hz, meaning that its pitch is equal to that of a 200 Hz sinusoid. Matching to a sinusoid is sometimes difficult, however, because many sounds of experimental interest have a rich spectrum, giving them a timbre that is very different from that of a pure tone. In these cases, we use a more complex reference sound, such as a periodic pulse train. Pitch matches between the secondary references and pure tones are usually straightforward. In the discussions that follow, the pitch of a given stimulus is defined as a certain frequency in Hz, implying that the pitch is either directly or indirectly equal to that of a pure tone at the same frequency.

The history of research on pitch perception can be divided into three distinct periods. The first, starting in the early 1840s and lasting almost a century, is characterized both by the completion of the first systematic studies of pitch perception and by the emergence of a simple theory, the familiar "place theory" (von Bekesy, 1960). The second period, from about 1940 to 1970, is distinguished by a number of experiments proving the inadequacy of the simple place theory and by the subsequent development of an alternative, which is sometimes called "fine-structure" theory (Schouten, 1940). By the early 1970s, it had become clear that modern experimental evidence simply could not support the fine-structure theory, and so the third period began with the introduction of three major new theories of pitch perception (Goldstein, 1973: Terhardt, 1974; Wightman, 1973). Each of these theories can be described loosely as a pattern-recognition theory.

Development of Place Theory: 1840–1940

Research during the early years focused on the importance, for pitch, of the lower harmonics of complex tones, specifically the fundamental. This attention to the fundamental was probably motivated by the fact that when we listen to musical tones, which are complex and periodic (or nearly so), and thus contain a number of harmonics, we actually hear just one tone, the pitch of which corresponds to the fundamental. Seebeck (1841) was one of the first to study this phenomenon systematically. He produced periodic stimuli with an acoustic siren, which consisted of a circular disk with holes punched around the perimeter. As the disk was rotated, compressed air was directed at the holes, and as each hole passed by the air source, an acoustic impulse was produced. With the holes regularly spaced around the disk, a stimulus consisting of a periodic sequence of impulses was generated. This stimulus has a spectrum consisting of lines at every integer multiple of the fundamental frequency. The fundamental is of course the reciprocal of the time between impulses. Seebeck noted that the stimulus produced a very strong pitch that corresponded to the fundamental frequency. Moreover, when the number of holes around the disk was doubled, thus halving the time between impulses and doubling the fundamental frequency, the pitch rose an octave. Based on these simple experiments, Seebeck concluded that pitch was determined either by the periodicity of the sound wave or by its fundamental frequency. A later experiment led Seebeck to favor the periodicity position and spawned a celebrated dispute between Seebeck and his contemporary, G. S. Ohm. In this controversial experiment, Seebeck generated stimuli with a disk in which the holes were not equidistantly spaced, but rather one in which the time between air puffs would be alternately t1, t2, t1, t2, etc., with t1 slightly different from t2. The fundamental frequency of the resulting stimulus was of course the reciprocal of its period, t1 + t2. The pitch of the stimulus corresponded exactly to the fundamental frequency. Inasmuch as the spectrum contained very little energy at the fundamental frequency, Seebeck argued that the periodicity of the stimulus, rather than the presence of the fundamental, was the primary determinant of pitch. G. S. Ohm (1843), who firmly believed that a pitch could be heard only if the stimulus contained energy at the corresponding frequency (Ohm's "acoustical law"), suggested that Seebeck's conclusion was inapprorpriate because his stimulus actually did contain some energy at the fundamental. Seebeck replied that the pitch was much stronger than might be expected because the amount of energy at the fundamental frequency was so small. Ohm finally suggested that Seebeck was misled by what he called an acoustical "illusion."

Twenty years later, Helmholtz (1863) offered a possible resolution of the controversy. In his monumental book, *On the Sensation of Tone as a Physiological Basis for the Theory of Music,* Helmholtz strongly supported Ohm's position. He provided both a possible physiological basis for the spectral analysis of sound that Ohm's "law" required and a possible physical explanation of Seebeck's "illusion." First, Helmholtz suggested that the basilar membrane inside the cochlea contained transversely stretched fibers, much like the strings of a harp, with each fiber resonant to a different frequency. Thus, the cochlea would function as a crude spectral analyzer. Second, Helmholtz argued that the transduction of sound from the eardrum to the cochlea was a nonlinear process and that incoming sound waves would be distorted. Distortions such as Helmholtz proposed would introduce spectral components that were not present in the original sound, but which would be analyzed by the cochlea in the same way. With the complex stimuli produced by Seebeck's sirens, the additional components would appear at frequencies given by the frequency difference between the components in the original stimulus. In all the cases studied by Seebeck, most importantly the third controversial case, this frequency is the fundamental. In other words, nonlinear distortion would be expected to add a component to the stimulus, before it was analyzed by the cochlea, at the frequency corresponding to the perceived pitch. Thus, Helmholtz's distortion hypothesis could explain Seeback's "illusion," within the framework of Ohm's "law."

Helmholtz's hypotheses went unchallenged during the next 75 years. But, in 1924, Seebeck's experiments were replicated and extended by Harvey Fletcher using electronic equipment to generate and control the complex stimuli (Fletcher, 1924). Fletcher's results completely corroborated Seebeck's. In fact, Fletcher found that even if the fundamental and several additional lower harmonics were completely removed from the acoustic stimulus, the pitch still corresponded exactly to the fundamental. Fletcher relied on Helmholtz's distortion hypothesis to explain this phenomenon, which was later called "the problem of the missing fundamental."

In the late 1920s, Georg von Bekesy provided firm evidence for the existence of the cochlear spectrum analyzer required by Helmholtz's theory (von Bekesy, 1928, in von Bekesy, 1960). In a series of experiments in which he actually observed the movement of the basilar membrane, von Bekesy showed that the place of maximum vibration of the membrane changed in an orderly way as the frequency of the sound was varied. Low-frequency sound caused a maximum at one end of the membrane, and high-frequency sound produced a maximum at the other end. Although the details of von Bekesy's discovery differed from those originally proposed by Helmholtz, it was clear that the cochlea did indeed perform the spectral analysis required by Helmholtz and Ohm's theory of pitch perception. As this theory required that a corresponding "place" on the basilar membrane be stimulated in order for a pitch to be heard, the theory came to be known as "place theory." It was not until the late 1930s that the inadequacies of the theory were recognized.

Development of Fine-Structure Theories: 1940–1970

The place theory held that a necessary condition for the perception of pitch is stimulation in the cochlea by the corresponding spectral component. In the case of complex tones in which the fundamental was absent from the acoustic stimulus, the corresponding spectral component (the fundamental) was thought to be reintroduced by nonlinear processes in the middle or inner ear. Once reintroduced, the distortion product would be expected to behave just like a simple tone at that frequency.

The demise of place theory was brought about by two simple demonstrations. The first was that the required distortion product was either absent or very weak, and the second was that even if the distortion product was present it could not be the primary mediator of the pitch percept. The early experiments along these lines were conducted in the late 1930s by Jan Schouten and his colleagues in the Netherlands and were truly elegant in their simplicity (Schouten, 1940). In the first, Schouten produced a stimulus consisting of harmonics of a 200 Hz fundamental, with the fundamental component removed. As expected, the stimulus produced a strong pitch corresponding to 200 Hz. Schouten then added a 206 Hz pure tone to the stimulus. He reasoned that if the pitch had been the result of a distortion product at 200 Hz, the addition of the 206 Hz tone would be expected to produce audible beats. No beats were heard.

Schouten's second experiment involved the use of amplitude-modulation techniques to produce so-called anharmonic stimuli. These are complex tones in which the component frequencies are not integer multiples of the frequency spacing between them. They are produced by frequency-shifting each component of a simple harmonic stimulus. As an example, consider a simple three-component harmonic complex, consisting of 1000 Hz, 1200 Hz, and 1400 Hz. Schouten and others showed that this stimulus has a clear pitch of 200 Hz, corresponding of course to the 200 Hz fundamental. When each of the components was shifted up in frequency, for example to 1050, 1250, and 1450 Hz, Schouten found that the pitch shifted upward as well to about 208 Hz, a small but quite noticeable shift. This clearly contradicted the prediction of place theory because the difference frequency, and the frequency of the presumed distortion product responsible for the pitch, remained at 200 Hz. At least a dozen studies of this pitch-shift effect have been reported since Schouten's original experiments, and they have confirmed the salience of this phenomenon (Schouten, Ritsma, & Cardozo, 1962; Smoorenburg, 1971).

Many years after Schouten's pioneering experiments, a third crushing blow to place theory was delivered in the form of a simple masking experiment. Although the experiment has been replicated several times with precise control of the stimulus parameters, J. C. R. Licklider's informal public demonstration of the experiment (1954) is usually regarded as definitive. Licklider first produced a sequence of harmonic complex tones (fundamental removed), each member of which evoked a strong pitch; the change in pitch from tone-to-tone produced a simple melody. Then, Licklider added low-pass noise to the stimulus, at an intensity sufficient to mask any imaginable distortion product. The pitch of each note was unaffected; in spite of the intense low-frequency noise, the melody was quite clear.

Following Licklider's demonstration, it was clear to most researchers in the field that place theory, at least in the form originally proposed by Ohm and Helmholtz, could not account for even the simplest complex-tone pitch. It was Schouten, however, many years before, who provided the theoretical framework of what was to become the most popular alternative to place theory. Schouten's so-called "residue theory" contains all the elements of what I call the "fine-structure" theories. Schouten's theory assumes that an incoming stimulus first undergoes a crude spectral analysis, of the sort performed by the basilar membrane itself. Schouten likened this mechanical spectral analysis to the electrical analysis accomplished by a bank of bandpass filters. Each filter was tuned to a different frequency, and the high-frequency filters were proportionately broader than the low-frequency filters (roughly a constant-Q analysis). Pitch was thought to be extracted by some kind of neural operation on the result of the spectral analysis. More specifically, it was argued (by Schouten and the other fine-structure theorists) that the temporal fine structure (especially the positions of the peaks) of the stimulus wave forms at the output of the first stage analysis was somehow preserved in the temporal patterns of nerve firings, and that pitch was extracted from these temporal patterns. The primary determinant of pitch was assumed to be the time difference between peaks in the stimulus wave form; the inverse of this time difference gives the pitch.

The fine-structure theories predict that given a complex stimulus consisting of a fundamental and all its harmonics, two kinds of pitches will be heard. The low harmonics will be heard out separately, as simple tones, because the spectral analysis at low frequencies is assumed to be relatively complete. On the other hand, because the high harmonics are not separately resolved by the analysis, they interact and produce a complex-tone percept. Schouten used the term "residue" to refer to the percept evoked by the interaction of a number of unresolved harmonics. The pitch of the "residue" was given by the time difference between major peaks in the wave form at the analyzer's output. Thus Schouten, the original proponent of fine-structure theory, emphasized the importance for pitch of the unresolved higher harmonics of a complex tone. This contrasts sharply with place theory's emphasis on the fundamental.

Although later researchers did not agree on which harmonics were most "important" for pitch, fine-structure theories in general were widely accepted until the early 1970s. They can easily account for the pitch of the missing fundamental because the fundamental periodicity of the stimulus is preserved in any group of harmonics. More importantly, the theories could explain the pitch-shift effect quantitatively as well as qualitatively. Figure 1.1 shows how the theory is applied to explain this phenomenon. The major problem with fine-structure theories is that the pitch of a complex tone is thought to be related directly to details of the stimulus wave form or a filtered version of it. It is not difficult to show that a number of very different wave forms, even random wave forms, can lead to the same pitch. For example, scrambling the starting phases of the harmonics of a complex tone can dramatically alter the fine structure of the stimulus wave form, yet it will not affect the pitch in any serious way (Patterson, 1973). Also, adding random noise to a delayed version of itself produces a stimulus with a random fine structure but one which (within limits) evokes a pitch corresponding to the inverse of the delay (Bilsen & Ritsma, 1969). There is even evidence suggesting that the pitch of a complex tone consisting of two harmonics is unchanged if the two harmonics are presented to different ears (Houtsma & Goldstein, 1972). Such dichotic presentations obviously prevent the physical interaction of the two components required by fine-structure theories. Thus, it seems that simple fine-structure theories are also inadequate to explain the vagaries of the pitch percept.

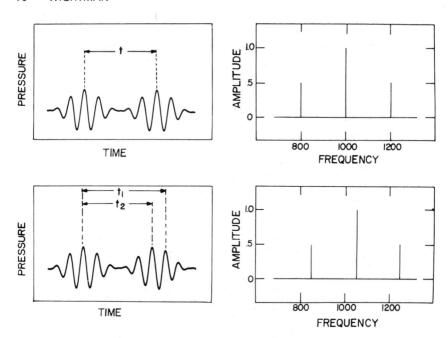

FIG. 1.1.   The "fine-structure" explanation of the pitch-shift effect. The upper panels show the wave form (left) and spectrum (right) of a harmonic stimulus. The reciprocal of the time between major peaks in the wave form (t) equals the fundamental frequency of the wave form (200 Hz). The bottom panels show a similar analysis of an anharmonic stimulus. Note that the frequencies of the components are shifted by 50 Hz relative to the upper panel. The reciprocals of the interpeak times t_1 and t_2 are close to the perceived pitches evoked by the stimulus.

The Pattern-Recognition Theories: 1970–

The third stage in the development of our understanding of pitch perception appears to have begun with the realization, by a number of researchers, that an entirely new approach was needed. The failure of the simple theories, which were based on straightforward place or fine-structure analyses of the stimulus, convinced many of us that the pitch-extraction process accomplished by the auditory system is anything but simple. Within the space of two years in the early 1970s, three new models of that process were proposed. In spite of some obvious differences among them, they are basically similar and are all based on a kind of auditory pattern recognition.

It is difficult to know exactly what stimulated the development of three new theories along such similar lines, but it may well have been the basic pattern-recognition idea described earlier by de Boer (1956). In the same paper in which he proposed developing a temporal fine-structure explanation of the pitch-shift effect, de Boer pointed out that a kind of template-matching model would make the same predictions. He reasoned that the auditory system may be specially "tuned" to harmonic stimuli, because most naturally occurring complex sounds such as those in speech and music are harmonic. Thus, given an anharmonic stimulus, de Boer suggested, the pitch evoked would be the same as the pitch of that harmonic stimulus whose component frequencies most closely matched those of the anharmonic stimulus. In other words, de Boer suggested that the auditory system somehow finds the best fitting harmonic template. For example, the complex consisting of components at 1050, 1250, and 1450 Hz is roughly the same as one consisting of the fifth, sixth, and seventh harmonics of 208 Hz (1040 Hz, 1248 Hz, 1456 Hz). The pitch that most listeners assign to the anharmonic sequence is close to 208 Hz. Of course, de Boer's scheme would predict some ambiguities because the anharmonic complex described earlier is also similar to one consisting of the sixth, seventh, and eighth harmonics of 179 Hz (1079 Hz, 1253 Hz, 1432 Hz), though the match is somewhat poorer in this case. Pitch ambiguity of exactly this sort is characteristic of data on the pitch-shift effect (Schouten, Ritsma, & Cardozo, 1962); the fine-structure theories also predict it (see Fig. 1.1).

The basic pattern-recognition scheme outlined by de Boer has been elaborated and quantified in three new models of pitch extraction. The so-called "optimum-processor" model proposed by Goldstein (1973) most explicitly incorporates de Boer's ideas. Goldstein's "processor" is a hypothetical neural network located in the central auditory system (thus receiving input from both ears) that operates on information received from the periphery. The presumption is that all stimuli are periodic complex tones consisting of adjacent harmonics. The processor estimates the fundamental frequency of a complex in a maximum likelihood way (thus it is "optimum") from the noisy information it receives about the component frequencies. In simple terms, Goldstein's model determines the harmonic sequence that best fits the stimulus spectrum. The principal advantage of the "optimum processor" over other recent models is that it is quantitative. The equations describing the relations between stimulus spectrum and predicted pitch (or pitches) are readily evaluated with only one free parameter, namely the variance of the noisy frequency estimates. More importantly, it is irrelevant for the model exactly how information about component frequencies is encoded. Thus, the model does not specify whether information about those components is encoded by a spectral (place) or a temporal (periodicity) mechanism.

The "learning-matrix" model proposed by Terhardt (1974) is another of the recent pattern-recognition models of pitch extraction. It is similar to Goldstein's in that it does not specify how information about the "patterns" is encoded. However, Terhardt's emphasis on the role of learning places his model apart from the others. Thus, this model might more appropriately be called an association-network model than a pattern-recognition model. Terhardt draws a basic distinction between what he calls "spectral pitch," the pitch of a pure tone, and "virtual pitch," the pitch evoked by a complex-tone stimulus in which a corresponding spectral component is absent. Spectral pitch is thought to be readily explained either by a place or a periodicity theory. Regarding virtual pitch, Terhardt argues that through the process of learning to recognize speech sounds, specifically vowels, the correlations among the harmonically related spectral components of those sounds are recognized and stored. These stored traces are then thought to be the basis of the virtual pitch evoked every time a stimulus consisting of a group of harmonics is presented. Presumably, the stored trace that best matches the stimulus in some way determines the perceived pitch. Terhardt's model, like Goldstein's, is successful in accounting for much of the existing pitch data. However, it has a serious limitation in that its central feature, the influence of early learning, may not be readily subjected to experimental verification.

The author's model of pitch extraction is the so-called "pattern-transformation" model (Wightman, 1973). It is quite explicitly a pattern-recognition model and treats the process of pitch extraction as a sequence of transformations of hypothetical patterns of neural activity. The first transformation is from acoustic stimulus to the so-called "peripheral activity pattern." This is the heart of the model, because the first transformation includes the operation of the entire peripheral auditory system. The "pattern" that is the result of the first transformation is thought to represent the result of a limited-resolution spectral analysis of the incoming stimulus. The resolution is limited by the precision of the cochlear analyzer. In other words, the "peripheral activity pattern" in this model is simply the internal representation of the power spectrum of the stimulus. The next transformation in the model is a Fourier transformation of the peripheral activity pattern. The result is a pattern that has much in common with the autocorrelation function of the stimulus, because the peripheral activity pattern is roughly a power spectrum. Pitch is assumed to be related to the positions of maximal activity in this autocorrelation-like pattern. Two stimuli are predicted to have the same pitch if the maxima in their respective transformed peripheral activity patterns appear in the same places.

One strength of the pattern-transformation model may be that its major component has a readily identifiable physiological bases. This allows the choice of model parameters on much more than an ad hoc basis. For example, our knowledge of the spectral-analyzing characteristics of the cochlea tells us that the model's first-stage analyzer should be proportionally more precise at high frequencies than at low frequencies. The major weakness of the model is due to the fact that it is not specifically formulated as a model of pitch matching. Unfortunately, most data on pitch perception come from matching experiments. Therefore, in order for the model to predict results from pitch-matching experiments a number of ad hoc assumptions must be made, specifically about how the maxima in the transformed peripheral activity pattern are interpreted and about how two transformed patterns might be judged to "match." Without extending the model considerably, it is difficult to formulate an objective rule by which it can generate a pitch-match prediction.

The pattern-transformation model appears to stand apart from both Goldstein's optimum-processor model and Terhardt's learning-matrix model in that it is quite specifically a spectrally based model. Whereas the other models are vague on this issue, the pattern-transformation model assumes that the stimulus information transmitted from the periphery and subjected to the central "pattern-recognition" analysis is spectral, or place-encoded information. Wave-form information, or more generally temporal information, is presumed lost. This distinction between the models is an artificial one for two reasons. First, all the models rely heavily on the notion of a neural representation in the auditory system of the power spectrum of the stimulus. It is this "pattern" that is "recognized" and "classified" in the pitch-perception process. Second, although the pattern-transformation model specifies that its computations are based on place information, it is a well-known property of the type of computations proposed, namely Fourier transformation, that an exactly comparable result could be achieved through computations based on temporal information. Thus, it is only information about the spectrum that is required in all three models. None of the models requires that the information be specifically temporally encoded or spectrally encoded.

From the preceding discussion, it should be clear that there are only minor differences among the three most recent models of pitch perception. All are basically pattern-recognition models, and the pattern that is thought to be processed is some central representation of the spectrum of the stimulus. Moreover, the three models are about equally successful in accounting for the available pitch data, although Goldstein's model does somewhat better quantitatively in certain cases. In general, all the models can explain the major phenomena such as the pitch of the missing fundamental, the pitch-shift effect, and the pitch of noise plus a delayed repetition. Therefore, the author can find no compelling reason at this point to favor one approach over the others.

Hopefully, additional experimental data may allow us to refine the models and perhaps come a little closer to a complete understanding of how pitch is processed by the auditory system. We have recently conducted several preliminary experiments in areas relevant to pitch perception, so a brief summary of the more interesting results seems appropriate here. One series of experiments (Houtsma & Goldstein, 1972) was directed at the possibility that pitch is mediated at a level above which information from the two ears is combined. Several experimental findings support this idea. After our attempts to replicate Houtsma and Goldstein's dichotic complex-tone pitch phenomenon, we became convinced that although pitch can be mediated centrally, there are clear differences between the dichotic and monotic percepts. Some of our most intriguing data have come from experiments with hearing-impaired listeners. With the conventional audiometric measures, all of our hearing-impaired listeners exhibited cochlear impairment, so by studying these subjects we are presumably able to evaluate the relative importance of cochlear processing in pitch perception.

OUR RECENT EXPERIMENTS

Central Mediation of Pitch

As mentioned earlier in this chapter, one line of evidence that simple place or fine-structure theories of pitch are inadequate comes from experiments on the pitch evoked by dichotically presented complex tones (Houtsma & Goldstein, 1972). In a dichotic presentation some components of a complex are delivered to one ear and some to the other. The results of several experiments with these stimuli suggested that the pitch of a dichotic stimulus was the same as the pitch of a comparable monotic stimulus (all components presented to one ear). Physical interaction of stimulus components is required by both place and fine-structure theories and of course was prevented in the dichotic condition. The fact that the pitch appeared to be unaffected by dichotic presentation thus contradicted both place and fine-structure theories. Additionally, the dichotic pitch phenomenon appeared to be strong evidence for the central mediation of pitch. We attempted to replicate the original study, which used two-component complex tones as stimuli, and obtained some provocative results.

Many studies of the pitch of complex tones have used two-component complex tones as stimuli. The usual finding is that a complex tone consisting only of two adjacent upper harmonics of some missing fundamental (e.g., 1000 Hz and 1200 Hz, harmonics of 200 Hz) can evoke a pitch (though it is weak) corresponding to the fundamental (Smoorenburg, 1971). In our attempts to replicate the earlier experiments, in which the pitch appeared to be unchanged if one harmonic was presented to each ear, we uncovered a potential artifact in the procedure. The original paradigm involved recognition of the musical interval (e.g., major second, major third, etc.) represented by the change in fundamental from one two-component to another. Observers were required to choose from eight possible intervals. We found that in the dichotic condition, our highly trained observers could score better than chance by listening to one ear alone (the other headphone was disconnected). Apparently, after extensive practice, given only one upper harmonic of each tone, our observers were able to use some strategy that was unknown to us to extract the fundamental and thus reconstruct the correct interval. This strategy probably had little to do with the perception of the pitch in the comparable monotic condition. In other words, the fact that performance in the dichotic conditions was as good as in the monotic conditions may not reflect an equivalence of the pitch percept in the two cases.

In an effort to uncover potential differences between monotic and dichotic perception (rather than performance), we chose a kind of free-response paradigm. The stimuli were pairs of two-component complex tones, as before, in which the change in fundamental frequency from one tone to the next represented a musical interval. (The component frequencies were in the range of 1500 Hz–2000 Hz, and were randomly selected adjacent harmonics of 200 Hz and 300 Hz.) In addition, simply because of the nature of the stimuli, the changes in the frequencies of the individual components of each note from one to the other also represented musical intervals (in most cases different intervals). Four highly trained musicians were asked to listen to the two complex tones and to respond by indicating what musical interval they heard (within a two-octave range: an octave up to an octave down). At first, the observers were told to listen to each complex tone as a "whole" and not to try to "hear out" the separate components. Surprisingly, only about 5% of the judgments (several hundred in all from each listener) in the monotic condition could be attributed to the listeners' hearing the missing fundamental. In the dichotic conditions, even fewer judgments appear to "track" the fundamental. Even after specific training and instruction to "listen for the missing fundamental," the results suggested that our listeners did not always hear it in the monotic condition and heard it even less often in the dichotic condition. In contrast with previous reports, we were led to conclude that: (1) the pitch percept (corresponding to the fundamental) produced by two-component complex tones is very weak; and (2) there are clear differences between the monotic and dichotic percepts. This is a significant result in terms of its implications for current theories of pitch perception. Although it does not allow us to reject any of the current models, because none absolutely requires that pitch be centrally mediated, it does force us to reevaluate our position regarding the relative importance of peripheral and central processes for pitch perception.

Spectral Resolution in Normal and Hearing-Impaired Listeners

Recent attempts to model the pitch-extraction process as a kind of auditory spectral pattern recognition lead us naturally to consider experimental measures of spectral resolution. The exquisite spectral resolution of the auditory system is the foundation upon which the concept of spectral patterns is built. Many previous experiments, particularly those on the so-called "critical band" (Scharf, 1970) and on auditory filter shape (Patterson, 1974), provided important data on the parameters of auditory spectral resolution. Our recent work on this problem represents an attempt to circumvent some of the problems inherent in the classical procedures. All the experiments have been standard forced-choice masking experiments, in which we measure the intensity of a pure-tone masker needed to just mask a low-level probe tone of fixed frequency. This pure-tone masking procedure is a standard way to assess auditory spectral resolution. The assumption is that the extent to which one tone masks another gives a measure of the degree to which the two tones are resolved. Perfect resolution would imply that only when the two tones are the same in frequency would any masking occur. In our experiment, the two tones—the masker and the probe—are presented successively. The instant the 200 msec. masker terminates, the 20 msec. probe is presented. This nonsimultaneous procedure, called "forward masking," eliminates the confounding influences of nonlinear probe-masker interactions that are known to occur when the two are presented simultaneously. The masking effect of the masker, presumably due to residual neural activity, is diminished in the forward-masking paradigm, though still present. In our experiments, the frequency and intensity of the probe are fixed, and we measure the level of masker required to mask the probe. The necessary masker level plotted as a function of its frequency describes a psychophysical "tuning curve" (Wightman, McGee, & Kramer, 1977). The width of this curve reflects the precision of spectral resolution at the probe frequency. This is perhaps the most important parameter influencing spectral coding in the auditory system. Normal listeners demonstrate very precise resolution (Fig. 1.2). The width of the tuning curve 10 dB above the minimum is typically about $\frac{1}{8}$ of the probe frequency ($Q_{10dB} = 8$). This finding agrees well with the precision of resolution required by most pitch models and also with estimates of resolution obtained in other paradigms (Scharf, 1970).

Several groups of hearing-impaired listeners (presumed cochlear loss) have also been tested in the psychophysical tuning-curve paradigm during the past

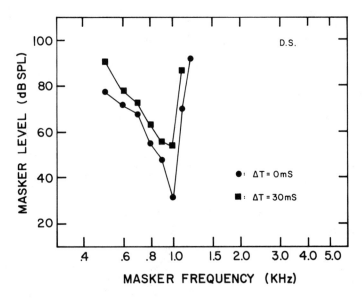

FIG. 1.2.   A representative example of a psychophysical tuning curve obtained from a listener with normal hearing. The probe in this case is fixed at 1000 Hz and 10 dB SL. The parameter Δt is the time from masker termination to probe onset.

year. In general, all tuning curves obtained from the hearing-impaired listeners were broader than normal, implying poorer spectral resolution in these individuals. Even when a tuning curve was measured in a region of normal sensitivity (e.g., a low-frequency tuning curve from a high-frequency loss case), it was broader than normal. The most intriguing result came out of our study of persons with a flat loss (about 40–50 dB at all frequencies) of pure-tone sensitivity. As Figs. 1.3 and 1.4 show, tuning curves from these two cases are broad ($Q_{10dB} = 2$), suggesting poor spectral resolution. However, there is a striking difference in the behavior of the tuning curve from the two hearing-impaired listeners as the delay between masker and signal is lengthened (a forward-masking paradigm is used throughout, recall, to avoid nonlinear probe-masker interaction). In the case of the normal listener (Fig. 1.2), lengthening this delay causes a general (though complicated in detail) upward shift in the curve, reflecting an expected decay of the masker's effectiveness. This is also observed in the data from hearing-impaired listener DM. Note, however, that listener JP's curve does not shift, at least not near the probe frequency. This is highly suggestive of a difference between the listeners in the rate of decay of masking and may indicate general differences in temporal resolution.

The results from just two hearing-impaired listeners should of course only be taken as suggestive. Many experiments (including our own) on hearing-impaired

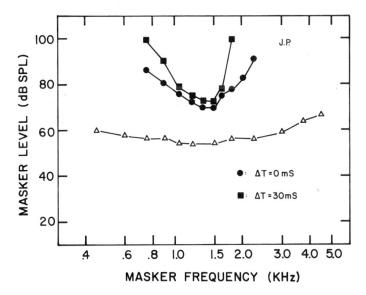

FIG. 1.3. A psychophysical tuning curve obtained from a listener with a hearing loss. The probe was fixed at 1500 Hz and 10 dB SL. The solid symbols have the same meaning as in Fig. 1.2. The open symbols show the unmasked threshold for the probe (ordinate should then read probe level in dB SPL) as a function of its frequency.

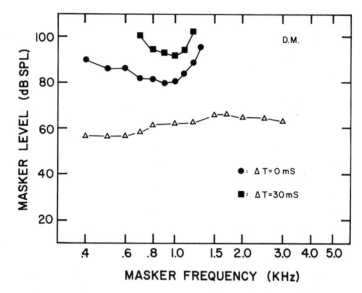

FIG. 1.4.   Same as Fig. 1.3, except that for this listener the probe frequency was 1000 Hz.

listeners show that data obtained from this population are usually highly variable, in spite of efforts to obtain homogeneous groups. The data from JP and DM are illustrative of this point. In terms of the audiometric measures we have taken (pure-tone and bone-conduction audiograms, speech-discrimination scores, special tests), JP and DM are indistinguishable. The data from our resolution experiment, however, suggest dramatic differences. Recognizing that firm conclusions will have to await testing of many more subjects, we tested JP, DM (our extreme cases), and two other hearing-impaired listeners with nearly identical audiometric profiles in a variety of paradigms. Our aim was both to assess these listeners' spectral and temporal resolving power and to measure their basic pitch-discrimination abilities. It was our hope that the performance of the hearing-impaired listeners in these tasks would provide new information on the relative importance for pitch perception of spectral and temporal coding. Whether pitch information is encoded by place (spectral) or periodicty (temporal) mechanisms is perhaps the single question that has most plagued pitch theorists since the time of Seebeck and Ohm.

In terms of spectral resolution, our hearing-impaired listeners were uniformly poor. Tested in the same psychophysical tuning curve paradigm as was described earlier, the two additional hearing-impared listeners produced tuning curves that were basically similar to those from JP and DM (Figs. 1.3 and 1.4). They were quite broad (Q_{10dB} = 1.5, 2.1) and similar in overall shape (only one masker-probe delay condition was tested, t = 0). In fact, among about 25 hearing-impaired listeners (exhibiting a variety of audiometric profiles) tested in our laboratories over the last several years, there is remarkable uniformity in the psychophysical tuning curve. It appears that a broad tuning curve and the impaired spectral resolution it surely reflects is a general characteristic of an individual with a substantial hearing loss.

Lack of intersubject variability is not characteristic of the other data we collected from our four hearing-impaired subjects. Recall that in the original tuning-curve experiment we noted a dramatic difference in the behavior of the tuning curves from JP and DM as the masker-probe delay interval was lengthened. This suggested a difference between the listeners in temporal resolving power and led us to perform an experiment specifically directed at this issue.

Temporal Resolution in Hearing-Impaired Listeners

Our experiment on temporal resolution involved measuring listeners' ability to detect a temporal gap in a burst (400 msec.) of noise. The noises were octave bands centered at 600, 1200, and 3000 Hz and were presented in a wide-band noise background to eliminate spectral artifacts due to the switching. The gap was simply a brief silent period in the temporal center of the noise burst. Listeners were required to discriminate a burst with a zero gap from a burst with a nonzero gap. The smallest gap, which led to 75% correct discrimination, was defined as the gap threshold. Four normal-hearing listeners and the four hearing-impaired listeners were tested. As expected, the results from DM and JP represented the extremes of the results from the hearing-impaired group. Their data are shown along with the data from the normal listeners in Fig. 1.5.

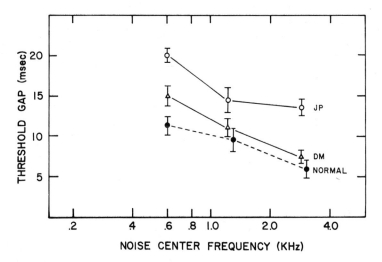

FIG. 1.5. Results from a gap-detection experiment. The solid symbols show the median (and 95% confidence limits) threshold of a group of four listeners with normal hearing. The open symbols show the performance of two hearing-impaired listeners.

Normal listeners detect gaps as short as 12 msec. with the 600 Hz noise and 6 msec. with the 3000 Hz noise. The high-frequency result agrees well with other measures of temporal resolution obtained from normal listeners (Green, 1971). As a group, the hearing-impaired listeners exhibited poorer temporal resolution than the normal listeners. With the low-frequency noise, the mean gap threshold varied from 15 msec. to 20 msec. Performance of these listeners improved at high frequencies, as was typical of the normal listeners, although the hearing-impaired listeners never performed as well as the normals. As suggested by the earlier tuning-curve results (Figs. 1.3 and 1.4), hearing-impaired subject JP consistently exhibited poorer temporal resolving power than subject DM. In the high-frequency condition, JP's gap threshold was two times that of DM. In fact, DM's gap threshold was near normal in that condition.

In order to motivate the final experiments to be described here, those on pitch discrimination, it may be useful to summarize the results from the two experiments discussed thus far. All four of the hearing-impaired listeners that we tested exhibited impaired spectral resolution as measured in the psychophysical tuning-curve paradigm. There was surprisingly little variability among our hearing-impaired listeners in the overall shapes of the tuning curves and their width as defined by the value of Q_{10db}. Such homogeneity was not characteristic of the results from the temporal resolving power (gap detection) experiment. Although gap thresholds were greater for nearly all the hearing-impaired listeners, the range of scores was larger (all the scores lay between JP and DM), and at least one listener, DM, exhibited nearly normal performance in some conditions.

The performance of these same hearing-impaired listeners in the pitch-discrimination experiments should be particularly interesting, in view of our aim of establishing the relative importance of spectral and temporal processes in pitch perception. If spectral information is more important, then the hearing-impaired listeners should be uniformly poor at pitch-discrimination tasks because they all have impaired spectral resolving power. However, if temporal information is more important, there should be a greater range of performance in pitch discrimination, and at least one listener, DM, might be expected to perform normally.

Frequency and Pitch Discrimination in Hearing-Impaired Listeners

Discrimination of a change in the frequency of a pure tone and discrimination of a change in the pitch of a complex tone may or may not be related skills. In fact, most modern theories of frequency discrimination are not easily generalized to theories of pitch discrimination. In spite of this, there is an intuitively appealing similarity between the two tasks. For this reason, prior to the experiment directly aimed at pitch discrimination, we conducted a brief study of the frequency-discrimination abilities of our two "extreme" hearing-impaired listeners, JP and DM. Two normal-hearing listeners were also tested.

We used a standard two-interval forced-choice paradigm to measure frequency-discrimination ability. On each trial, a listener heard two 400 msec. bursts of pure tone presented at about 40 dB SL. The two bursts were of different frequency (f and f+Δf) and were presented in random order. The observer simply had to indicate whether the order was high–low or low–high. The frequency difference, ΔF, was held constant for a block of 100 trials. At least three blocks were completed, with performance in two blocks bracketing 75% correct, before a new frequency (f) was tested. The frequency difference that led to a 75% correct discrimination was interpolated from curves fit by eye to the data points. The median of four determinations of 75% correct was taken as the dependent variable. Before any data were collected, the listeners had practiced at least 10 hours in the frequency-discrimination paradigm.

The results are shown in Fig. 1.6, with results from a comparable study of normal listeners reported by Wier, Jesteadt, and Green (1977). The performance of the normal-hearing listeners is clearly consistant with Wier et al.'s results, giving us some confidence in the general validity of our procedures. Both hearing-impaired listeners performed more poorly than normal in all conditions, although DM's discrimination threshold in the high-frequency condition was only a factor of about 1.5 greater than normal. In most conditions, JP's discrimination threshold was a

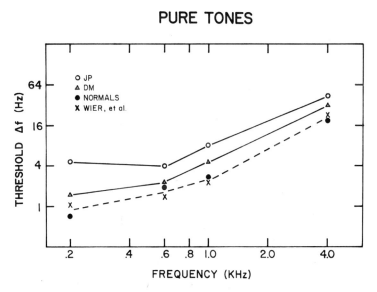

PURE TONES

FIG. 1.6.   Results from a pure-tone frequency-discrimination experiment. The symbols (with the exception of the X's) represent the median of four determinations of "threshold." At least 2400 forced-choice trials contribute to each "normal" point, and 1200 trials contribute to the data points from JP and DM. The X's are data taken from Wier, Jesteadt, and Green's study (1977) of normal listeners.

factor of 2 or 3 greater than the comparable threshold obtained by DM. This is a suggestive result given DM's relatively better scores in the temporal-resolution experiment. However, it almost goes without saying that great caution must be exercised in generalizing from the results of only two subjects.

The pitch-discrimination experiments also used a forced-choice paradigm to measure discrimination threshold. However, in this case, rather than discriminate a change in the frequency of a pure tone, our subjects listened for a change in the fundamental frequency of a complex tone. The complex tones consisted of a group of upper harmonics of the fundamental. In an experiment of this sort, it is important to make certain that the change in fundamental is the only viable cue for the listener. Therefore, stimuli must be constructed so that the changes in frequency signaled by the individual components of each complex tone could not serve as a reliable cue to the change in fundamental frequency. For this reason, stimuli such as those shown in Fig. 1.7 were used in this experiment.

In both intervals of each forced-choice trial a complex tone is presented that is made up of four upper harmonics of some fundamental. The fundamental frequency (fo) in the first interval is fixed, and the fundamental in the second is either Δf Hz higher or lower than in the first. As before, the observer's task is to indicate the direction of change. The specific harmonics used for each stimulus are scrambled from interval to interval, as Fig. 1.7 shows. Thus, the first interval may involve either the fourth, fifth, sixth, and seventh harmonics of f_0 or the

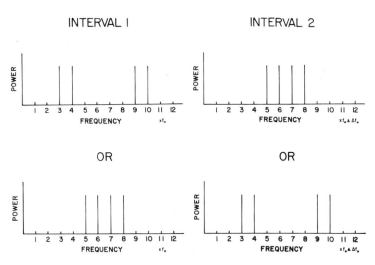

FIG. 1.7. Schematic representation of the spectra of the stimuli used in the pitch-discrimination experiment. Note that in the first interval of the 2IFC paradigm (left panels), the stimulus was made up of harmonics of the fundamental fo (one of two groupings, chosen randomly). In the second interval (right panels), the fundamental was either incremented or decremented by Δfo Hz, and the opposite grouping of harmonics was used.

second, third, eighth, and ninth harmonics of f_0. In the second interval, the opposite group of harmonics is used, and the fundamental is either $f_0 + \Delta f_0$ or $f_0 - \Delta f_0$.

As in the frequency-discrimination experiment, Δf_0 was held fixed for a block of 100 trials, at least three blocks were run for each determination of the threshold Δf_0 (75% correct), and the median of four determinations of threshold was used as the dependent measure. As before, the 400 msec. stimuli were presented monaurally at 40 dB SL, and observers were well-practiced (at least 20 hours) before data collection began.

The results of the pitch-discrimination experiment are shown in Fig. 1.8. The pitch-discrimination thresholds obtained for the normal listeners closely parallel our frequency-discrimination results (Fig. 1.6) and agree well with comparable data reported in the literature. Note that in no case is a pitch-discrimination threshold as small (in terms of Δfo) as a comparable frequency-discrimination threshold, thus highlighting the differences between the two tasks.

The results from our hearing-impaired listeners are somewhat disappointing given our goal of establishing the relative importance for pitch perception of spectral and temporal modes of processing. Listener DM, who performed nearly normally in our temporal-resolution task, fails, in every case, to exhibit normal pitch-discrimination ability. At best, this listener's pitch-discrimination threshold is about two times larger than normal. However, the ordering of the data from our two hearing-impaired listeners is consistent with the hypothesis that temporal

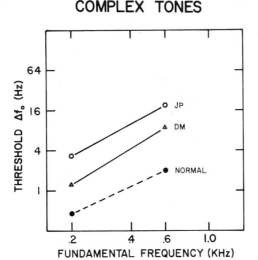

FIG. 1.8. Results from the pitch-discrimination experiment, which used the stimuli diagrammed in Fig. 1.7. The symbols have the same meaning and represent the same number of trials as in Fig. 1.6.

processing is important. Subject JP, who was consistently inferior in the temporal-processing task, was also consistently poorer at pitch discrimination. Thus, our disappointment must be tempered somewhat, both by the ordering of the data and by the fact that such a small sample is represented. At the very least, this experiment will stimulate further work along the same lines.

CONCLUSIONS

In spite of over a century of systematic study, there are many unanswered questions about pitch perception. However, we have come a long way. For example, we can be sure that pitch is not correlated, in any simple way, with stimulus periodicity, spectral content, or wave-form fine structure. It now appears that pitch is extracted in a much more complex fashion, by a kind of auditory spectral pattern-recognition process. Clearly, the features of the spectrum of a stimulus somehow carry the pitch message. Moreover, those spectral "features" appear to be the places in the spectrum where energy is concentrated (e.g., the frequencies of the harmonics of a complex tone). However, the exact way in which the features are encoded and the details of the processing of this information that leads to the pitch percept are still unknown. Several recent models give us alternative ways of viewing the process, but the models are similar enough that experimental data do not yet permit a clear choice among them. Some data we have obtained from hearing-impaired listeners suggests that a temporal encoding scheme may provide the substrate for pitch extraction. However, the data are few, and as the effects are not large, they can only be taken as suggestive.

ACKNOWLEDGMENTS

Preparation of this manuscript and the research described was supported by grants Nos. NS11857 and NS12045 from the National Institutes of Health. Much of the research was actually carried out by my students, Steve McAdams and Pete Fitzgibbons, whose participation is gratefully acknowledged.

REFERENCES

Bilsen, F. A., & Ritsma, R. Repetition pitch and its implication for hearing theory. *Acustica*, 1969, *22*, 63.

de Boer, E. *On the residue in hearing*. Unpublished doctoral dissertation. University of Amsterdam, 1956.

Fletcher, H. The physical criterion for determining the pitch of a musical tone. *Physiological Review*, 1924, *23*, 427–37.

Goldstein, J. L. An optimum processor theory for the central information of the pitch of complex tones. *Journal of the Acoustical Society of America*, 1973, *54*, 1496–1516.

Green, D. M. Temporal acuity as a function of frequency. *Psychological Review*, 1971, *78*, 540–551.

Helmholtz, H. *On the sensations of tone as a physiological basis for the theory of music*. New York: Dover, 1954. (Originally published, 1863.)

Houtsma, A. J. M., & Goldstein, J. L. The central origin of the pitch of complex tones: Evidence from musical interval recognition. *Journal of the Acoustical Society of America*, 1972, *51*, 520–529.

Licklider, J. C. R. Periodicity pitch and place pitch. *Journal of the Acoustical Society of America*, 1954, *26*, 945(A).

Ohm, G. S. Uber die Definition des Tones, nebst daran geknupfter Theorie der Sirene und ahnlicher tonbildender Vorrichtungen. *Annals of Physical Chemistry*, 1843, *59*, 513–565.

Patterson, R. D. The effects of relative phase and the number of components on residue pitch. *Journal of the Acoustical Society of America*, 1973, *53*, 1565–72.

Patterson, R. D. Auditory filter shape. *Journal of the Acoustical Society of America*, 1974, *55*, 802–809.

Scharf, B. Critical band. In J. V. Tobias (Ed.), *Foundations of modern auditory theory* (Vol. 1). New York: Academic Press, 1970.

Schouten, J. F. The residue and the mechanism of hearing. Proc. Kon. Nederl. Akad. Wetenschap. 1940 *43*, 991–999.

Schouten, J. F., Ritsma, R., & Cardozo, B. Pitch of the residue. *Journal of the Acoustical Society of America*, 1962, *34*, 1418–24.

Seebeck, A. Beobachtungen uber einige Bedingungen der Entstehung von Tonen. *Annals of Physical Chemistry*, 1841, *54*, 417–36.

Smoorenburg, G. Pitch perception of two-frequency stimuli. *Journal of the Acoustical Society of America*, 1971, *48*, 924–942.

Terhardt, E. Pitch, consonance and harmony. *Journal of the Acoustical Society of America*. 1974, *55*, 1061.

von Bekesy, G. *Experiments in hearing*, (Ed. and trans. by E. G. Wever). New York: McGraw-Hill, 1960.

Wier, C. C., Jesteadt, W., & Green, D. M. Frequency discrimination as a function of frequency and sensation level. *Journal of the Acoustical Society of America*, 1977, *61*, 178–184.

Wightman, F. L. The pattern-transformation model of pitch. *Journal of the Acoustical Society of America*, 1973, *54*, 407–412.

Wightman, F. L., McGee, T., & Kramer, M. Factors influencing frequency-selectivity in normal and hearing-impaired listeners. In E. F. Evans & J. P. Wilson (Eds.), *Psychophysics and physiology of hearing*. New York: Academic Press, 1977.

2 Perception of Sound Signals at Low Signal-to-Noise Ratios

Reinier Plomp

In studying the recognition and classification of sound signals, one should realize that in many practical situations these signals are heard against a background of noise. Therefore, we have to consider the effect of noise on how the signal is perceived. In general, we can say that noise will reduce the perceptibility of specific properties of the signal, obscuring the dissimilarity between one signal and another. The experimental evidence presented in this chapter illustrates that this perceptual uncertainty may lead to the imagined perception of signals that are actually not present.

PERCEIVED CONTINUITY OF A TONE ALTERNATED WITH NOISE

We consider first the case of signal bursts of, say, 150 msec. being alternated with noise bursts of the same duration. If the noise is loud enough, we do not hear an interrupted signal, but it sounds continuously, right through the noise bursts.

This highly interesting phenomenon seems to have been discovered independently by a number of investigators. Perhaps the earliest description is in a paper by Miller and Licklider (1950) who alternated speech and noise. When the speech bursts were alternated with silent intervals, the voice sounded hoarse and raucous, and the interruptions were quite evident. When noise was introduced in the intervals, the speech sounded continuous, more natural, and uninterrupted. The authors compared the phenomenon with seeing a landscape through a picket fence: The pickets interrupt the view at regular intervals, but the landscape is

27

perceived as continuous behind the pickets. Contrary to their expectation, Miller and Licklider did not find that adding noise in the silent intervals improved intelligibility. Recent investigations with sentences instead of words revealed that the noise does result in significantly higher intelligibility scores (Powers & Wilcox, 1977).

Miller and Licklider observed the same effect with pure tones. This case was studied by Thurlow (1957) who alternated two tones. He found that, under certain conditions, the more intense tone is heard as clearly intermittent, and the less intense tone appears to sound continuously. Thurlow called it "an auditory figure-ground effect." The phenomenon was further explored (e.g., Elfner & Caskey, 1965; Elfner & Homick, 1966; Thurlow & Elfner, 1959; Thurlow & Marten, 1962) and independently rediscovered by Warren, Obusek, & Ackroff (1972) and Houtgast (1972), who used the maximum level for perceiving a continuous tone (the "pulsation threshold") for measuring lateral suppression. Houtgast (1972) proposed the following hypothesis on the physiological background to the continuity effect: "When a tone and a stimulus S are alternated (alternation cycle about 4 Hz) the tone is perceived as being continuous when the transition from S to tone causes no (perceptible) increase of nervous activity in any frequency region. The pulsation threshold, thus, is the highest level of the tone at which this condition still holds [p. 1893]."

The continuity effect is clearest for alternation rates of 2 to 8 Hz. It holds for complex tones as well as pure tones provided the spectrum of the interrupting sound bursts "covers" the spectrum of the tone bursts. This condition is most easily fulfilled if broad-band noise is used for the interrupting sound.

The fact that the continuity effect is not restricted to steady-state signals but is also valid for speech indicates that signal constancy is not essential. This can be nicely demonstrated by an observation explained in Fig. 2.1. A pure tone, gradually shifting from 500 Hz up to 2000 Hz, is alternated with a band of noise between 900 and 1100 Hz (actually the tone shifts much more slowly than the

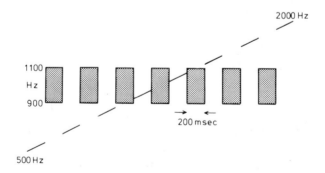

FIG. 2.1. The tone bursts, alternated with band-filtered noise bursts, are heard as an uninterrupted tone with a continuously shifting pitch as long as the tone frequency is within the noise band.

drawing suggests). As long as the frequency of the tone is below about 900 Hz or above about 1100 Hz, we hear a series of tone bursts that increase step by step in pitch. Assuming that the noise is sufficiently intense, the auditory sensation is quite different for the frequency range 900 to 1100 Hz. There, the tone bursts sound as a continuous tone. It is quite interesting that only over this range is the tone heard with *continuously* shifting pitch, right through the noise. The effect of the noise bursts is quite different from that of silent gaps between the tone bursts: The noise bursts *connect* the tone bursts into one continuous tone.

Dannenbring (1974) applied alternately rising and falling frequency glides, centered at 1000 Hz, for investigating the maximum duration of portions of the frequency glide that could be replaced by white noise without affecting the perception of a continuous tone. In the middle of glides taking 2 sec., a gap of about 450 msec. was allowed. The corresponding value appeared to be smaller for a steady-state tone but larger when the gaps were centered at the top or bottom of the glides. No perceptual extrapolation of the incomplete glides occurred beyond the frequency range actually presented.

These results suggest that the perceived continuity of a tone is intensified rather than reduced by varying its frequency. Another interesting signal to be studied is a tone vibrating in frequency more than once over the time intervals in which the signal is replaced by noise bursts. This was explored by the author by means of a 1000 Hz pure-tone frequency modulated with 15 Hz. This tone was either alternated with noise bursts or with silent intervals (see Fig. 2.2). The two conditions result in strikingly different sensations: Modulation within the tone bursts is not very distinct when alternated with silent intervals, but it becomes very prominent and *continuously* audible when alternated with noise. A similar result was obtained with an amplitude-modulated tone. It is of interest that van Noorden (1975) had a similar impression when alternating loud and weak noise bursts of equal durations and with short silent gaps in between. Focusing the attention on the weak bursts, he perceived these bursts with a double frequency, just as if every loud burst covered a weak one.

Other experiments indicated that repetition is not essential for the continuity effect. When a tone burst of 40 msec. is immediately followed by a 300-msec. noise burst, we hear a much longer tone burst, as if it was present during the

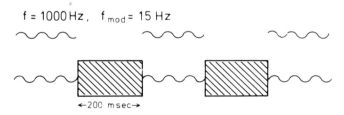

f = 1000 Hz,   f$_{mod}$ = 15 Hz

←200 msec→

FIG. 2.2.   When a 1000-Hz tone, frequency-modulated with 15 Hz, is alternated with noise bursts, an uninterrupted, continuously vibrating, tone is heard.

noise. This can be demonstrated by playing a scale of eight tones of which half are 300 msec. in duration and the other half 40 msec. followed by 260 msec. noise (see Fig. 2.3). We hear a scale of equalduration tones, with four interfering noise bursts.

For demonstrative purposes, it is quite convincing to alternate music with both noise and silent intervals. The difference is dramatic. Alternating speech or music with silent intervals results in such a strong mutilation that we seem to have only separate fragments of sound. Introduction of noise into the silent intervals is experienced as a ''restoration'' of the music into a continuous, be it strongly impaired, stream of sound.

We may conclude from these observations that the hearing system is able to restore sound patterns if the duration of the masked portion does not exceed a few hundreds of msec. The finding that the continuity effect is also operative for sounds varying considerably in time shows that an explanation of the effect in terms of a combined action of forward and backward masking, as has been suggested (e.g., Evans, 1973), is inadequate. It seems obvious that central rather than peripheral processes are decisive.

TRIADIC COMPARISONS OF SIGNALS
PARTLY MASKED BY NOISE

In the previous section, signals that are completely masked for a limited time interval were studied. Let us now consider isolated complex sounds with their spectra partly, but permanently, masked by a band of noise. By comparing such a

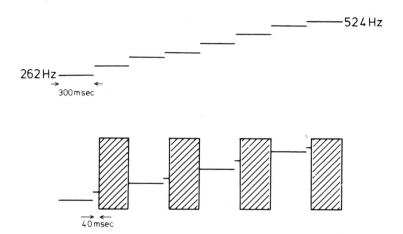

FIG. 2.3.   When the final 260 msec. of half of the tones of a scale of eight 300-msec. tone bursts is replaced by noise, we still hear a series of equal-duration tones.

stimulus with other ones not masked, we can investigate the effect of the noise band on the perception of the stimulus.

It is easy to verify that two complex tones, one with and the other without a partly masking noise band, sound (almost) equal. In 1969, we designed an experiment to investigate the effect of a noise band by means of triadic comparisons. The measurements were performed by Dr. Willard D. Larkin from the University of Maryland, who spent that summer in our institute.

The basic stimulus in this experiment was a steady complex tone with

$$S_0 = \sum_{n=1}^{10} \frac{1}{n} \sin 2\pi n f t,$$

$f = 300$ Hz. The amplitude coefficients, $\frac{1}{n}$, provide a slope of -6 dB/octave. Three other stimuli were derived from S_0 by further attenuating the fourth, fifth, and sixth harmonic components either an extra 5 dB ($= S_{-5}$), 10 dB ($= S_{-10}$), or ∞ dB ($= S_{-\infty}$).

Some of these signals were also presented with a band of noise added, with cut-off frequencies of 1200 Hz and 1800 Hz, thus coinciding in frequency with the fourth, fifth, and sixth harmonics. This noise band was presented at three levels: N_0 just masking a signal consisting of only those three harmonics at the same level as in S_0; N_{-5} attenuating N_0 by 5 dB; and N_{-10} attenuating N_0 by 10 dB. From all possible combinations of signals and noise bands, only the following five were used: S_0N_0, S_0N_{-5}, S_0N_{-10}, $S_{-\infty}N_{-5}$, and $S_{-\infty}N_{-10}$. Together with the four signals S_0, S_{-5}, S_{-10}, and $S_{-\infty}$, we used nine stimuli.

The signals were generated by a digital computer, converted to analog signals, mixed with noise, and presented to the observer via headphones at a sensation level of about 50 dB. The computer also controlled the presentation of the stimuli and processed the responses (for a more detailed description see Plomp & Steeneken, 1969). A triangular response panel, equipped with three push buttons for stimulus selection and three push buttons for response registration, allowed the subject to listen successively to any stimulus out of a subset of three in any order. All 84 possible subsets were compared. The pair of stimuli judged "most similar" was assigned 2 points; the pair judged "least similar" was assigned 0 points; and the remaining pair was assigned 1 point. The subjects were instructed to compare the complex tones and to ignore, as best they could, the noise accompanying some signals.

The responses from 10 observers, accumulated in half a matrix, are given in Table 2.1. Kruskal's multidimensional scaling program (Kruskal, 1964) was applied to these data, and the two-dimensional solution (Euclidean space, 10% stress) is represented in Fig. 2.4.

Figure 2.4 shows that noise, when added to the adulterated complex tone $S_{-\infty}$, creates a tonal percept that migrates, in the scaled space, toward a more complete, or "natural," musical sound. The upward-pointing arrows at the right

TABLE 2.1
Cumulative Similarity Matrix (10 Subjects) for the Signals Described in the Text

	S_0N_0	S_0N_{-5}	S_0N_{-10}	$S_{-\infty}$	$S_{-\infty}N_{-5}$	$S_{-\infty}N_{-10}$	S_{-5}	S_{-10}
S_0	61	51	94	8	46	35	54	18
S_0N_0		98	65	75	101	78	60	61
S_0N_{-5}			107	73	115	62	70	71
S_0N_{-10}				47	72	86	84	65
$S_{-\infty}$					90	116	14	55
$S_{-\infty}N_{-5}$						114	66	91
$S_{-\infty}N_{-10}$							63	90
S_{-5}								58

of the diagram illustrate the kind of perceptual extrapolation possible with sub-masking noise: $S_{-\infty} N_{-5}$ and $S_{-\infty} N_{-10}$ both resemble sounds with attenuated midharmonics (S_{-5} and S_{-10}) to a greater degree than they do with the noise removed ($S_{-\infty}$).

Noise added to S_0 at first has a similar effect. The percept appears to be altered in the direction of the tone complex with diminished middle harmonics when a small amount of noise is added. (Note that S_0, S_0N_{-10}, and S_{-10} are nearly collinear in this scaled space.) There is a new effect, however, when the level of the noise is increased. The greater masking of the middle harmonics produces a tonal percept about halfway between S_0 and $S_{-\infty}$. This terminal stimulus, S_0N_0, does not coincide with $S_{-\infty}$, even though these two stimuli have an identical pattern of audible harmonics. Instead, the perceptual position of S_0N_0 appears to be a compromise between S_0 and $S_{-\infty}$. We have little doubt that a similar

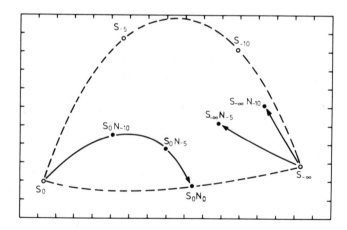

FIG. 2.4. Two-dimensional configuration of points derived by applying MDSCAL on the similarity matrix of Table 2.1.

compromise would have been the end result of mixing higher levels of noise with $S_{-\infty}$.

On closer scrutiny, the perceptual position of S_0N_0 turned out to reflect not a condition of equisimilarity between S_0 and $S_{-\infty}$, but a condition of perceptual ambiguity. The tonal character of S_0N_0 seemed *identical* to S_0 or to $S_{-\infty}$, depending on which of them were offered for comparison. Listening to the stimulus pair (S_0, S_0N_0), or to the pair $(S_{-\infty}, S_0N_0)$, one has the impression that the two stimuli in each pair contain the *same* tonal signal. The perceptual extrapolation, in this case, is completely dependent on the tonal context in which the judgments are made.

SUBHARMONIC PITCHES OF A PURE TONE AT LOW S/N RATIO

As a third example of the strong influence of a biasing signal on our perception of a nearly masked tone, the subharmonic pitches of a pure tone may be mentioned. Houtgast (1976) discovered that, at a low S/N ratio, a single tone with a frequency of nf Hz may suffice to induce a pitch corresponding to f Hz.

This effect may be regarded as the extreme case of the general phenomenon of the low pitch of a group of harmonics. For example, a signal consisting of the three harmonic components 1200, 1400, and 1600 Hz is usually heard as having a pitch equal to the pitch of a tone of 200 Hz (see Wightman's review in Chapter 1 of this volume). Houtgast observed that presenting even the single 1400-Hz component may give rise to the same low-pitch sensation if the subject is biased to hear that pitch and if the level of the signal is only a few dB above its threshold in noise.

In this experiment the subjects were presented with pairs of stimuli. The first (reference) stimulus contained the second, third, fourth, eighth, ninth, and tenth harmonics of a constant (absent) fundamental of 200 Hz. The second (test) stimulus contained, in successive trials, the fifth, sixth, and seventh harmonics, two of these harmonics, one of these harmonics, all multiples of a frequency of either 194 or 204 Hz. The latter two values were randomly chosen, and the subject was requested to decide whether the pitch of the test stimulus was slightly higher or lower than that of the reference stimulus. The results for 50 (naive) subjects are summarized in Fig. 2.5. In the case of a single harmonic being presented, the 50 subjects were unable to respond better than by chance if the signals were presented without noise, but for an S/N ratio of only 6 dB above the masked threshold, the average score of over 80% demonstrated that many subjects were able to perceive the subharmonic pitch correctly. It should be noticed that by presenting subjects first with multicomponent signals their attention was focused on a pitch near to the pitch of a 200-Hz tone. Of course, this biasing is essential because a single frequency component can be a harmonic of various fundamentals.

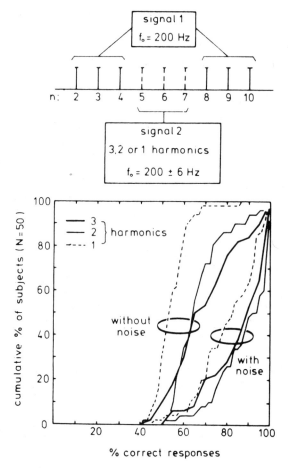

FIG. 2.5. Cumulative scores of 50 subjects in responding to an increment or decrement of the fundamental frequency of a group of three, two, or one harmonics. From Houtgast, 1976.

CONCLUSIONS

The experiments discussed have shown that our perception of sound signals is remarkably resistent against interfering noise. In the case of a sound stream in time, we can miss segments of a few hundreds of msec. before becoming aware of it. Perception is restored as well as possible on the basis of the signal stream as it preceeds and follows the segment masked by noise. In the case of a sound signal of a limited duration, partly masked by noise, our perception of that signal depends on what can be expected in light of earlier sounds presented or signals we are familiar with. It is as if the hearing system tries to find a hypothesis about the mutilated sound signal that best fits all information still available.

In terms of recognition and classification, this means that our perception can be very misleading: We may be convinced we hear a tone of much longer duration when a tone burst is followed by noise, or a low-pitched tone when a higher-pitched tone is only faintly audible, or a tone with a specific timbre when crucial parts of its sound spectrum are masked by noise.

ACKNOWLEDGMENTS

The author wishes to express his thanks to Dr. Willard D. Larkin for performing the experiment explained in the second section of this chapter and for his help in phrasing the results.

REFERENCES

Dannenbring, G. L. *Perceived auditory continuity with gliding frequency changes.* Unpublished doctoral thesis, McGill University, Montreal, Canada, 1974.

Elfner, L., & Caskey, W. E. Continuity effects with alternately sounded noise and tone signals as a function of manner of presentation. *Journal of the Acoustical Society of America,* 1965, *38,* 543-547.

Elfner, L., & Homick, J. L. Some factors affecting the perception of continuity in alternately sounded tone and noise signals. *Journal of the Acoustical Society of America,* 1966, *40,* 27-31.

Evans, E. F. Discussion. In A. R. Møller (Ed.), *Basic mechanisms in hearing.* New York: Academic Press, 1973.

Houtgast, T. Psychophysical evidence for lateral inhibition in hearing. *Journal of the Acoustical Society of America,* 1972, *51,* 1885-1894.

Houtgast, T. Subharmonic pitches of a pure tone at low S/N ratio. *Journal of the Acoustical Society of America,* 1976, *60,* 405-409.

Kruskal, J. B. Nonmetric multidimensional scaling: A numerical method. *Psychometrika,* 1964, *29,* 115-129.

Miller, G. A., & Licklider, J. C. R. The intelligibility of interrupted speech. *Journal of the Acoustical Society of America,* 1950, *22,* 167-173.

Plomp, R., & Steeneken, H. J. M. Effect of phase on the timbre of complex tones. *Journal of the Acoustical Society of America,* 1969, *46,* 409-421.

Powers, G. L., & Wilcox, J. C. Intelligibility of temporally interrupted speech with and without intervening noise. *Journal of the Acoustical Society of America,* 1977, *61,* 195-199.

Thurlow, W. R. An auditory figure-ground effect. *American Journal of Psychology,* 1957, *70,* 653-654.

Thurlow, W. R., & Elfner, L. F. Continuity effects with alternately sounding tones. *Journal of the Acoustical Society of America,* 1959, *31,* 1337-1339.

Thurlow, W. R., & Marten, A. E. Perception of steady and intermittent sounds with alternating noise-burst stimuli. *Journal of the Acoustical Society of America,* 1962, *34,* 1853-1858.

van Noorden, L. P. A. S. *Temporal coherence in the perception of tone sequences.* Unpublished doctoral thesis, Technological University, Eindhoven, The Netherlands, 1975.

Warren, R. M., Obusek, C. J., & Ackroff, J. M. Auditory induction: Perceptual synthesis of absent sounds. *Science,* 1972, *176,* 1149-1151.

3 The Role of Stimulus Uncertainty in the Discrimination of Auditory Patterns

Charles S. Watson
William J. Kelly

Evidence has accumulated in recent years suggesting that the discrimination of complex sounds is not only more difficult than that of simpler sounds, but also that it involves a somewhat different hierarchy of importance in the factors that limit auditory discrimination.

This chapter argues that the limiting factors for discrimination of complex sounds are often *central,* whereas those that limit our hearing of tones, noise bursts, or clicks tend to be *peripheral.* We should probably clarify our use of the central–peripheral distinction. It's obvious that you cannot prove a physiological hypothesis with psychophysical data. Therefore, no literal anatomical or physiological inferences are intended by this distinction. It is merely a convenient way of summarizing some assumptions about the functional sequence of events that must occur as sensory information is processed. These assumptions are: (1) that there is an early stage of auditory transduction that imposes certain fixed limits on the resolving power of the whole system; and (2) that additional limitations on information transmission are imposed at succeeding stages of processing, some of which may not be specific to the auditory system but rather are common to all of the sensory modalities. These are not new assumptions. To them we have added an additional criterion by which some of the postulated central and peripheral factors limiting information processing might be distinguished. It is that those limits on information processing that can be modified by manipulating stimulus uncertainty[1], or by overtraining, are central, whereas those

---

[1] *Stimulus uncertainty,* as used in this discussion, is determined by the size of the set from which samples are drawn, on each trial of a psychophysical procedure. To the degree that sensory resources are differentially employed, depending on the expected nature of the next arriving stimulus, stimulus

insensitive to such modification may not be. This distinction is modest, but we believe it can be useful in summarizing a variety of new research findings.

By *complex stimuli* we merely mean sounds whose spectral and temporal complexity is closer to that of human speech than are the sounds used in the majority of past psychoacoustic experiments. For good reason, most research on human hearing has, over the past hundred years, been focused on the abilities to detect, discriminate, or identify single tones, noise bursts, or clicks. The concentration on the auditory system's ability to cope with such simple sounds was quite understandable given the historical contexts of the law of specific nerve energies, Ohm's acoustic law, Helmholtz's resonance theory of hearing, and finally the early dominance of Titchener's structuralism in experimental psychology. In addition, it is likely that auditory science would have followed many more of the leads of the investigators of visual perception had it not been much more difficult to generate a reliable complex acoustic wave form than to produce a complex but stable picture.

The pressures that maintained a single-tone orientation in psychoacoustic research have been relieved to a considerable degree in the past decade. Computer-controlled function generators and digital synthesis of wave forms now make the production of complex stimuli within the capabilities of most auditory research laboratories. A renewed interest in complex stimuli has also been motivated by the information-processing approach to perception and the ability to characterize psychophysical and physiological responses to simple auditory stimuli in considerable detail. In addition, recent psychoacoustic studies of complex sounds may be partly in response to a gauntlet thrown down by the speech-sciences community in the form of assertions that the most precise processing of complex sounds by the auditory system is that which occurs when those sounds have the form of human speech (e.g., Studdert-Kennedy, Liberman, Harris, & Cooper, 1970). Obviously, research on other sounds as complex as those of speech must be conducted if such hypotheses are to be satisfactorily evaluated.

For these, and probably a variety of other reasons, it is historically accurate to state the last decade has seen a considerable growth of interest in the psychoacoustics of more complex stimuli. In many cases, experimental ventures into the world of complex sounds has meant no more than the study of two tones instead of one. However, even the relatively simple stimulus represented by two tones in sequence, or by a tone and a noise burst, immediately raised the question of temporal interactions, and this quickly became one of the major issues of the psychoacoustics of complex sounds. The focus of the present chapter is entirely on sounds whose components vary in frequency, over time, and on the resulting

---

uncertainty may be expected to be a determinant of psychophysical performance. Studies described in later sections suggest that stimulus uncertainty is a minor factor in the detection and discrimination of simple stimuli but a major factor in the case of complex sounds.

interactions among these components. Complex stimuli produced by the simultaneous generation of two or more components has been widely discussed elsewhere (e.g., Goldstein, 1970) and is not treated here.

DISCRIMINABILITY OF SIMPLE SOUNDS

The discriminability of complex sounds is best appreciated in contrast to that of the simpler sounds from which they may be synthesized, or into which the auditory system may analyze them. A complete review of studies of human listeners' abilities to discriminate between simple sounds would require more space than is available, but the results of a few representative studies gives a reasonably clear picture of the remarkable resolving power of the auditory system.

Single Tones

The simplest case is that of the single "pure" tone, or tone pulse. Longer tones are resolved more accurately in frequency and intensity than brief ones, and there is general agreement that most accurate resolution is achieved for tones in excess of 80–100 msec. (Henning, 1970). For tones in the more sensitive portion of the human auditory range, roughly 300 to 2000 Hz, differences of less than 1% in frequency and slightly less that 1 dB are recognized by trained listeners, if the tones are clearly audible. Below approximately 15-dB sensation level, just-detectable changes in frequency and intensity increase rapidly (Wier, Jesteadt, & Green, 1977). Resolution of duration has not been studied as thoroughly as the other dimensions, but a Weber fraction of roughly 10 to 20% is a useful summary of the just-detectable proportional change in duration for tones ranging from 40–50 msec. to as long as a minute (Creelman, 1961). Resolution of durations of tone pulses much briefer than 40–50 msec. may be accomplished through attention to the associated spectral changes because the frequency range of a tone pulse is roughly the reciprocal of its duration, e.g., a change from 5 to 10 msec. is associated with a reduction in bandwidth from approximately 200 to 100 Hz.

Tone Pairs

After single tones, the next most complex sound that listeners in psychoacoustic research have been asked to discriminate has probably been pairs of tones played either simultaneously or in sequence. This extremely modest venture into the world of complex stimuli produced a variety of results not entirely predictable from studies with single tones. We begin our discussion of the perception of tonal sequences with a brief review of temporal masking.

Temporal Masking.   When a tone is presented that is long enough and intense enough, there is a time of reduced sensitivity to a stimulus presented immediately after it and, somewhat more difficult to understand, immediately before it as well. The former fact is known as stimulus-produced deafness, temporary threshold shift, poststimulatory fatigue, or residual or forward temporal masking, depending on the level and duration of the tone that caused it. For levels below 90 dB and durations less than a few seconds (those of concern in this discussion), the effects apparently reflect minimal temporal diffusion associated with any auditory stimulation. The temporal limits of these very slight reductions in sensitivity are roughly 25–35 msec. prior to the onset of a tone (backward masking) and 40–50 msec. following its offset (forward masking), naturally with greatest reduction closest in time to the tone (Elliott, 1962; Zwicker, 1965). The magnitude of the temporal masking effect depends on the frequency of the masking tone, with greatest loss of sensitivity for stimuli in its frequency region. When a brief tonal signal is both preceded and followed by noise maskers, the temporal separation of those maskers beyond which no further masking is measured, the "critical masking interval," has been found to be 10–20 msec. (Penner, Robinson, & Green, 1972). In general, these experiments on temporal interference show that for sound levels that neither damage nor cause prolonged fatigue, the auditory system is remarkably capable of responding appropriately to sounds even though they are followed or preceded closely by other sounds. For example, a 40 msec., 1000-Hz "signal" tone at 75 dB, SPL, has a sensation level of 65–70 dB for unimpaired listeners. If this signal tone is immediately preceded by an 800-Hz masking tone also at 75 dB, temporal masking will reduce its sensation level to 45–50 dB. This degree of partial masking, in most experiments with highly trained listeners, does not significantly degrade the listener's resolution of the partially masked tone (Leshowitz & Cudahy, 1973). However, several recent studies discussed in following sections have suggested that *under conditions of high stimulus uncertainty* severe reductions in resolution can result from the temporal juxtaposition of two or more such tones.

Temporal Resolution of Brief Sounds

As mentioned earlier, the discriminability of the frequency and intensity of tones is considerably reduced for durations less than 40–50 msec. The fundamental limits of *temporal* resolving power are, however, not discovered until still shorter durations in the 2–10 msec. range are reached. Green (1971) has summarized a variety of experiments that demonstrate accurate discrimination of the temporal details of wave forms as brief as 2 msec., which he convincingly argues to be an estimate of *minimum temporal acuity.* Divenyi and Hirsh (1974, 1975) determined the minimum duration of a sequence of three tones of high, medium, and low frequency, for which their order could be correctly identified to be 6–9 msec. (2–3 msec. per component). Neither Green's listeners nor those of Divenyi and Hirsh probably heard anything they would describe as sounds that were perceptually ordered or distributed in time, but those aspects of conscious experience are not at issue here. Various authors have pointed out (e.g., Broadbent & Ladefoged, 1959) that brief acoustic events are frequently judged by their timbre, or "quality," rather than by subjective duration. The timbre argument is most appealing when stimuli differ in their long-term power spectra. It must be emphasized, however, that both Green's Huffman sequences and Divenyi and Hirsh's three-tone complexes were discriminable at brief durations when their overall power spectra were identical.

Temporal Resolution for Sounds of Longer Duration

In certain other experiments in recent years temporal resolution has been found to be considerably worse than that reported by Green and by Divenyi and Hirsh. Perhaps the best-known example is that of Warren, Obusek, Farmer, and Warren (1969) who asked naive listeners to identify the temporal sequence of several unlike sounds played in a continuing sequence via a tape loop (a hiss, a buzz, a tone, and a noise) and increased the duration of the components until they could do so. The finding that they could not identify the sequence until the components were 200 msec. or more in duration was quite unexpected in light of the data on the discriminability and temporal resolution of simpler sounds. In retrospect, it appears that Warren et al. may have hit on a fortuitous combination of difficult testing conditions, including an uncertain sequence of sounds, the "looped" stimulus presentation, inexperienced listeners, and a broad spectral range of the components. Later experiments have shown that although each of these factors singly has a slightly degrading effect on performance, in combination they can be extremely disruptive of the auditory resolving power that must be prerequisite to the ability to identify sounds. In a later experiment, Warren has reported that the data from his procedure are quite different, with performance improving by as much as an order of magnitude, when trained listeners are employed. Warren's observations with naive listeners had been interpreted as a demonstration that the auditory system is considerably more accurate when judging the temporal order of the sounds of speech than for nonspeech because he had also tested his listeners' abilities to report sequences of spoken digits. The digit sequences were correctly identified at significantly briefer durations than the hiss, buzz, etc., but the fact that listeners are overtrained on speech sounds was not stressed. The importance of training listeners until asymptotic performance is approached has been raised frequently in recent years, especially because training effects are considerably greater for complex than for simple stimuli (Watson, 1979).

Temporal Effects on Frequency Resolution

Another temporal effect on auditory discrimination that has attracted considerable attention in recent years is the reduction in the frequency resolution of a brief (20–40 msec.) tone that sometimes occurs when it is closely followed by a second tone. This backward-maskinglike loss of resolution is quite similar to effects reported in the visual literature under the general rubric of metacontrast (Kahneman, 1968). The auditory case has been described in several papers by Massaro (esp. 1972), who refers to it as a "preperceptual" effect in an allusion to the presumed stage of a processing model within which it might occur. This effect is quite difficult to explain because of the general facts of frequency resolution and temporal masking described in the earlier sections of this chapter, but also because Massaro's results were at variance with the level of performance of listeners tested in a very carefully conducted study by Ronken (1972). In what Massaro calls a "prototype" experiment, the sound to be resolved was a 20-msec. tone, presented at 81-dB, SPL, and followed, at various intervals, by a half-second 81-dB, 820-Hz masking tone. The unexpected result of this experiment was that the ability to discriminate between signals of 770 and 870 Hz approached chance levels as the signal-masker interval was reduced to zero. As discussed earlier, the amount of backward masking expected for this combination of stimuli would be less than 15–20 dB, thus reducing the sensation level of the 20-msec. tone from about 75 to 55–60 dB for normal listeners. It has been clearly established that frequency discrimination for tones is essentially constant for sensation levels above about 20 dB (Shower & Biddulph, 1931; Wier et al., 1977). Massaro's results were sufficiently bothersome to move several investigators to repeat his experiment (Leshowitz & Cudahy, 1973; Loeb & Holding, 1975; Sparks, 1976). Each of these studies failed to replicate Massaro's results, finding instead little or no "recognition masking" *when listeners were overtrained.* Massaro had trained listeners only for a few hours or less, and he presented his stimuli in random sequence, so that from trial to trial the listeners heard samples from a catalog of as many as 64 different sounds (pairs of tone frequencies and signal-masker intervals). These two facts, interpreted together with the results of tonal-pattern experiments described in later sections, are sufficient to explain the discrepancy between Massaro's data and those of other investigations. A point of general disagreement about the preperceptual masking effect, and also about the extremely poor identification of auditory sequences reported by Warren, is that the discoverers of these phenomena insist that what other authors consider flaws in their measurement procedures are in fact critical and valid features. Thus, Warren (1974) insists that only naive listeners can give meaningful reports of their sensations of temporal order, whereas Massaro (1976) argues that the presentation of stimuli from a large catalog, in random order (which he refers to as a "blocked design"), is required if one is to measure preperceptual masking. In support of Massaro it should be mentioned that some studies have obtained preperceptual, or "informational," masking effects similar to those he reported. These include Divenyi and Hirsh (1974), Yost, Berg, and Thomas (1976), and our group (Watson, Wroton, Kelly, & Benbasset, 1975), although we stressed that the effect could be made to disappear if the stimulus order was made less uncertain, and Yost et al. found it to be strongly dependent on psychophysical method. All investigators who have discussed this matter agree that at least early in training the last tone of a two- or three-tone sequence is considerably more salient than the earlier components, a conclusion also strongly borne out by the tonal-pattern experiments presented in the following sections.

PERCEPTION AND DISCRIMINABILITY OF TONAL PATTERNS

"Streaming" in Tonal Patterns

Another series of experiments relevant to the perception of complex auditory patterns has been conducted by Bregman and his colleagues (Bregman & Campbell, 1971; Bregman & Dannenbring, 1973). Bregman's studies have primarily been of tonal sequences and have stressed the Gestalt-like features of auditory perception that are apparent in a rapid sequence of tone pulses. The major conclusion from the first of these experiments was that only the temporal relations among tones within a narrow frequency range are readily noticed and easily discriminated, if altered in a forced-choice task. Inability to resolve temporal differences between tones of widely separated frequencies appears to be related to the emergence of auditory figures, which are most commonly found to be composed of components similar in pitch, loudness, timbre, or mode of attack. This line of investigation has led Bregman to postulate a set of auditory principles quite similar to the Gestalt laws of visual organization. His group continues to conduct studies of the factors that make some sounds "hang together" or form figures, whereas others do not. Although perceptual psychologists have been somewhat neglectful of these issues in audition, several recent studies have dealt with them (e.g., Divenyi & Hirsh, 1978; van Noorden, 1975), and it is likely that the next decade will see a generally accepted set of principles for the generation of auditory Gestalten. However, those interesting issues need not be resolved prior to asking general questions about listeners' abilities to extract information from complex auditory patterns, as we attempt to demonstrate in the following subsection.

Word-Length Tonal Patterns

Among the many questions that may be raised about the way we hear temporal acoustic patterns is the simple one of exactly how well these sounds are resolved by our auditory system. When the word "ballpark" is spoken at a comfortable listening level, and with a reasonably quiet background, most listeners report that they "heard all of it quite clearly." One way to determine the accuracy of listeners' claims is to repeat the word twice, with a subtle change at some point in it, and see whether they are able to notice that change. Many replications of this experiment could yield a picture of the accuracy with which various temporal and spectral portions of the word are resolved. We have conducted such experiments for the past few years but, for several reasons, have used word-length tonal sequences as the test stimuli rather than words. Real speech sounds were rejected in favor of tonal sequences primarily because our interest was in the general capabilities of the auditory system. We also avoided the sounds of real speech because the majority of previous studies of the perception of complex sounds that had been conducted with them had yielded certain results not predictable from psychoacoustic research with simpler sounds. Thus, some investigators (e.g., Studdert-Kennedy et al., 1970) were led to question whether the sounds of speech may not be processed somewhat differently than other complex sounds. Hence, our selection of *non*speech sounds as a complex stimulus was partly motivated by our interest in speech perception because claims that the complex sounds of speech are processed in special ways could not be evaluated without a data base describing the discriminability of similarly complex, nonspeech sounds. Finally, we felt that the history of psychological studies of perception strongly suggests that the processing of complex sounds *with which listeners have had years of auditory and orthographic experience* must be characterized by a prohibitively entangled combination of perception and prediction. We are in complete agreement with those who argue that to understand auditory perception in everyday life we must deal with such overtrained cases as the hearing of connected discourse or of familiar musical passages. We disagree, however, with the trend toward limiting the study of auditory capability to these extremes of auditory experience.

Choice of Tonal Sequences.   This rationale led us to complex, nonspeech sounds but gave little guidance to the selection of specific sounds from the enormous range of possibilities. Clearly, an inappropriate choice could lead to several years of work with little or no general significance. We began with tonal sequences for the following reasons. Most important, the use of single tones as the building blocks of the stimuli meant that a wealth of earlier research could be relied on for estimates of the discriminability of these individual components. The duration of individual components (typically 40 msec.) and of the entire patterns (approximately $\frac{1}{2}$ sec.) were chosen to be similar to those of the shorter phonemes and whole words, respectively. We investigated various frequency ranges, but those most often employed were between 250 and 3000 Hz, representing a compromise between the inclusion of the primary resonances of the vocal tract and the more sensitive portion of the range of normal human hearing.

Terminology.   The following terms recur throughout this discussion with these intended meanings:

Tonal pattern.   Sequence of sinusoidal pulses presented without temporal overlap. The pulses were varied in frequency, intensity, or duration, or in a combination of these.

Target component. The single sinusoidal pulse within a sequence that is experimentally varied on a given trial by the addition of a *signal*.

Signal dimension. Dimension on which target components may be varied. In the experiments discussed here, the signal dimensions are frequency (F), intensity (I), and duration (T).

Signal. Increment or decrement in one of the physical dimensions of a target component (ΔF, ΔI, or ΔT).

Contextual components. Tone pulses other than the target component within a given tonal pattern.

Stimulus uncertainty. General term for the predictability of the tonal pattern to be presented on the next trial in a psychophysical procedure, as determined by the size of a stimulus set from which samples are drawn on a trial-by-trial basis.

Pattern uncertainty. Predictability of entire pattern, which is generally scaled by the size of the set of patterns from which samples are drawn.

Target uncertainty. Predictability of the frequency and temporal position, or both, of a target component within a given pattern.

Signal-dimension uncertainty. Predictability of the physical dimension(s) on which the target component is subject to change. That is, whether the listener must be prepared for a ΔF, ΔI, ΔT, or more than one of these.

Minimal uncertainty psychophysical procedure. "A minimal-uncertainty psychophysical procedure is one which confronts an observer with the lowest possible level of stimulus uncertainty that will permit psychophysical measurement. In such a procedure there is but one signal to be detected and one spectral and temporal context within which that signal may be presented from trial-to-trial. It is thus a 'one-bit' procedure, when the stimuli to be discriminated are presented equally often." (From Watson, Kelly, & Wroton, 1976.)

Psychophysical Methods. The purpose of the initial experiments was to determine listeners' abilities to extract information from the entirety of a word-length tonal pattern. To do this we elected to present a different pattern on each trial of a "same–different" psychophysical procedure. That is, on a randomly chosen half of the trials the same pattern was repeated twice, whereas on the other half the pattern was modified on its second presentation by a slight change in the frequency, intensity, or duration of *one* of its tonal components. This method was intended to force listeners to process the entire pattern, rather than to attempt to "hear out" some specific portion, but ignore the rest. In later experiments, a three-alternative, forced-choice procedure (3AFC) was adopted to avoid the necessity of corrections for response biases. In the 3AFC procedure the increments in frequency, intensity, or duration were added to a single component of a pattern either on its first, second, or third presentation within a single trial.

Interpattern intervals were $\frac{1}{2}$ second in both the same–different and 3AFC procedures, and the listeners were given 1 second in which to respond following the final pattern on a given trial. In the first experiments, patterns were generated by randomly permuting the order of 10 tonal frequencies, generally spaced in equi-log steps. To increase pattern uncertainty still further, in later experiments component frequencies were randomly sampled from each of 10 equi-log frequency ranges, with approximately 3 to 15 Hz spacing of the frequencies from which samples were selected. Tonal components were presented at comfortable listening levels, at 75 dB SPL in the earlier experiments, and with randomly selected levels between 65 and 85 dB in the later experiments. One hundred trials were run in each 5-minute listening block, six or seven such blocks were run per experimental session, and listeners were typically trained for 10 sessions or more before experimental data were collected.

Initial Experiments.   Following several pilot experiments, a group of listeners was trained to asymptotic performance in the detection of changes in the frequency of randomly chosen target components. Each pattern was selected from a catalog of 50 permutations of 10 equi-log spaced frequencies. All components were 40 msec. in duration. Target uncertainty was determined by sampling from four temporal positions (1, 4, 7, or 10, numbered from the first of the 10 40-msec. positions in a pattern) and from five frequencies (frequencies 1, 3, 5, 7, or 10, numbered from lowest to highest in the equi-log spaced set). Just-detectable values (d' = 1.0) of $\Delta F/F$ were estimated from psychometric functions, as illustrated in the bottom panel of Fig. 3.1. The top panel of the figure shows a representative pattern used in one of our first experiments (Watson et al., 1975), together with the just-detectable values of $\Delta F/F$ for four of the tonal components, for each of eight listeners.

Figure 3.2 shows data summarized from two replications of this experiment. The major unexpected result was that frequency resolution of the target components was severely degraded for those components that occurred early in the patterns and also for those of lower frequencies. In these experiments, the frequencies of the 10 components were selected from the range 256–892 Hz (upper solid) or from 500–1500 Hz (lower solid). Thus, the higher frequency components of one pattern were in the lower frequency range of the other, and the dependence of the frequency resolution of the targets on the frequency range of the contextual components is evident. The combined effects of component frequency and temporal position on frequency discrimination, expressed in terms of just-detectable values of $\Delta F/F$, were found to be as large as a factor of 50. Thus, late high-frequency components were resolved with accuracy approaching that for the same duration tones presented in isolation, whereas 30–50% changes in early low-frequency components might go unnoticed.

The same–different procedure was also used to determine listeners' abilities to resolve the intensity of tonal components and, in separate experiments, their

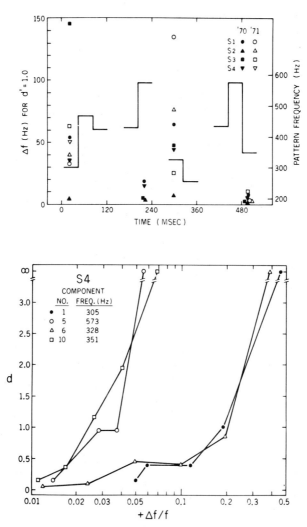

FIG. 3.1. *Top Panel:* One of the 10-tone sequences used in the pattern discrimination experiments. The left-hand ordinate shows just-detectable changes of target component frequency, whereas the right-hand ordinate represents the standard frequencies of those components. *Bottom panel:* Psychometric functions, for one listener, obtained in a same–different psychophysical procedure for four of the components of the tonal pattern shown in the top panel.

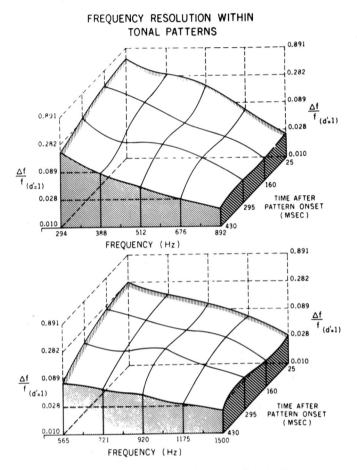

FREQUENCY RESOLUTION WITHIN
TONAL PATTERNS

FIG. 3.2. Detectability of changes in the frequency of single 40-msec. components of 10-tone patterns, as determined by the frequency and temporal position
of the target components, in a high-uncertainty testing condition. The two solids
summarize results for patterns with different ranges of component frequencies and
show that within each range late high-frequency components are resolved 10 to 30
times more precisely than early low-frequency components.

duration. The results again showed poorer performance by highly trained listeners than could be predicted from earlier work on temporal masking. However,
the discriminability of changes in intensity and duration was not as severely
degraded as had been that of changes in frequency (just-discriminable changes of
3–4 dB were obtained in component level and 50–60% in component duration).

Very High Stimulus Uncertainty Experiments.   Comparison between the results described for ΔF, ΔI, and ΔT suggested that the dimension on which the

major variation within a pattern occurs might be the one on which the resolution of target components would be most disrupted by the presence of the contextual components. That is to say, components of the patterns had been varied in frequency but not in duration or intensity, so perhaps that variation primarily acted to degrade the auditory system's frequency analysis. With this hypothesis in mind, another experiment was designed in which the components of each pattern were varied in all three dimensions: frequency, intensity, and duration. In addition, the frequency range was increased to 300 to 3000 Hz. That range was divided into 10 equi-log intervals, with one frequency selected at random from each interval for each pattern, thus avoiding certain problems associated with fixed-frequency catalogs (Wier, 1974). The levels of the contextual components were randomly varied from 65 to 85 dB, SPL, in one-decibel steps, and the durations were randomly varied from 25 to 105 msec. Randomization of the contextual components was further constrained by the following requirements:

1. The total pattern duration was 450 msec., including a 5-msec. period of quieting introduced between each successive pair of components (to reduce audible transients associated with abrupt changes of frequency).
2. In each pattern, one of a set of four 45-msec. target components was randomly selected, the frequencies of which were 534 or 1688 Hz. Those target components occurred at either 90 or 315 msec. after pattern onset and were either the third or eighth components of the patterns. The target components were always presented at 75 dB, SPL.

Thus, the stimulus uncertainty in this experiment compared to that in most psychoacoustic experiments was quite high. From trial to trial the contextual components varied in frequency, intensity, and duration, the target varied in temporal position and frequency, and the signals were randomly selected to be values of ΔF, ΔI, or ΔT. There were thus 12 possible test conditions represented by the combination of two target frequencies, two temporal positions of the targets, and three signal dimensions. A tracking procedure was employed (Levitt, 1971) in which the joint performance of the group of listeners was used to adjust the values of the 12 possible signals on a trial-by-trial basis.

The results of this very high uncertainty experiment are shown in Fig. 3.3 in the form of mean-slope, mean-intercept psychometric functions fitted to data for three listeners, collected after 12–14 hours of training. The functions labeled "1" in the figure are for the very high uncertainty procedure, and those labeled 2, 3, and 4 are for lower levels of stimulus uncertainty, as described later.

Although some listeners were able to do considerably better than others, none could regularly achieve just-detectable ($d' = 1.0$, corresponding to 62% correct in the 3AFC procedure) values of ΔF, ΔI, or ΔT of less than 800 Hz, 7 dB, or 35 msec., respectively. It is clear that this extreme level of stimulus uncertainty resulted in significantly worse performance than the uncertainty level used in

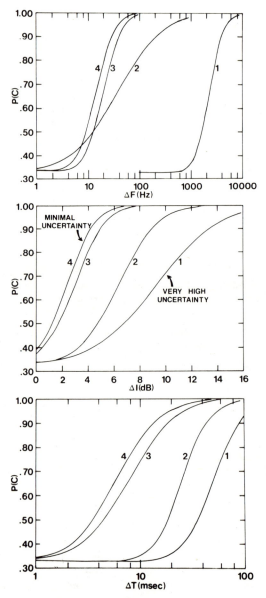

FIG. 3.3. Mean-slope, mean-intercept psychometric functions fitted to pattern-discrimination data collected from three observers after 12 hours of training. Functions labeled *1* are for a very high level of stimulus uncertainty in which the "signals" to be detected were changes in the frequency, intensity, or duration of single components of a new pattern presented on each trial. Those labeled *4* are for a minimal-uncertainty replication of that experiment. Functions *2* and *3* are for intermediate levels of stimulus uncertainty, as described in the text.

those earlier experiments (Fig. 3.2) when component frequency (not level or duration) was varied from trial to trial, there was no signal dimension uncertainty, and a narrower range of frequencies was employed.

The psychometric functions labeled 2, 3, and 4 in Fig. 3.3 represent performance when the level of stimulus uncertainty was reduced as follows: (2) The contextual components were fixed, but the target and signal dimension uncertainties were maintained as in condition (1). Performance improved but was still somewhat worse than that in the earlier experiments. (3) Contextual components were fixed, as in (2), and the target was also fixed at the low-frequency, early position. Performance improved, but a degrading effect of signal dimension uncertainty was still apparent for all signal dimensions. (4) Minimal uncertainty testing; performance approaches that expected for single isolated tones despite the presence of the nine contextual components.

The major differences in the resolution of target frequency, intensity, and duration (Fig. 3.3) are in the degree of improvement in performance between uncertainty conditions 1 and 2. Frequency resolution was improved by a reduction in just-detectable values of ΔF from more than 1000 Hz to approximately 25 Hz. The better frequency-discrimination performance was much closer to that for minimal-uncertainty conditions than were those achieved, in the corresponding conditions, for intensity or duration discrimination. We have no simple explanation for this differential effect of uncertainty on frequency resolution, although it may reflect the unique character of the frequency-analyzing mechanisms of the auditory system.

Our current opinion about the slopes of the psychometric functions is that they do not differ significantly under the various levels of stimulus uncertainty studied in this experiment, despite the two cases of apparently reduced slopes shown in Fig. 3.3 (condition 1 for intensity discrimination and condition 2 for frequency discrimination). The tracking procedure employed in this experiment was primarily designed to yield accurate estimates of stimulus levels associated with performance of 62% correct in the 3AFC task. Its accuracy decreased at the extreme performance levels required to estimate the slopes of psychometric functions because of the low numbers of trials associated with those performance levels.

The experiment just described represents the highest level of stimulus uncertainty we have investigated. We have elsewhere reported the results of several other experiments with various lower levels of uncertainty (Watson, 1976; Watson et al., 1975). Discrimination performance in those studies was intermediate between the results of condition 1 (in Fig. 3.3) and that expected for single tones in isolation.

Minimal-Uncertainty Experiments.   In the experiment just described, highly trained listeners were unable to resolve the frequency, intensity, or duration of target components with anything remotely resembling the precise discrimination performance achieved for isolated tones of similar levels and durations. This degraded performance cannot be readily explained in terms of temporal masking because the other tones in the patterns were typically separated in frequency by a critical bandwidth or more from the target tones, therefore predicting no more than 10 or 15 decibels of temporal masking. The only other likely explanation of the severely degraded performance, if masking and inadequate training are ruled out, is the listeners' uncertainty about the stimulus. Prior experiments on stimulus uncertainty had shown that both the detectability of tones and frequency discrimination are degraded when single tones are varied in frequency from trial to trial. However, the effect of frequency uncertainty on the detection of a single tone in noise is an elevation of its just-detectable level by no more than 2–3 dB (Creelman, 1973; Green, 1961; Johnson, 1978). The just-discriminable difference between the frequencies of two tones is increased only a few Hertz by the introduction of a corresponding level of uncertainty (Harris, 1952). Despite these previous demonstrations of the very slight effects of stimulus uncertainty on auditory discrimination performance, we elected to replicate the pattern discrimination studies under minimal-uncertainty testing conditions. The motivation for these additional experiments was primarily that we could find no stimulus-related explanation for the severe degradation of pattern discrimination in the experiments previously described. The procedure was simply to select representative patterns from among high-uncertainty experiments and repeat the same psychophysical procedures with them. The listeners thus heard the same pattern repeated on each trial, and the same target component was always subject to change. The results, in several different minimal-uncertainty experiments, have always been the same. Listeners can resolve the frequency, level, and duration of 40-msec. components of half-second tonal patterns with accuracy almost as great as can be achieved for the same component in isolation. (This ability is also reflected in the minimal-uncertainty condition of the experimental data shown in Fig. 3.3.)

Figure 3.4 shows the results of a minimal-uncertainty experiment in which listeners were trained to resolve a single target component in each of eight different 10-tone patterns (Spiegel & Watson, 1981). The targets were intentionally chosen from among the early low-frequency components of each pattern, and four or five minimal-uncertainty training sessions were spent teaching the listeners to ''hear out'' the target components in each of the patterns. The level of the target sound was then reduced to determine the level at which frequency discrimination would deteriorate. As shown in Fig. 3.4, this occurred at target levels approximately 35 to 40 dB below the level (75 dB, SPL) of the other nine contextual components. Clearly, given sufficient advance information, listeners have a remarkable ability to resolve specific details of a complex sound, while ignoring contextual components that would completely obscure those details under other testing or training conditions.

Similar minimal-uncertainty experiments have now been conducted on the resolution of target level and target duration, and both of these stimulus dimen-

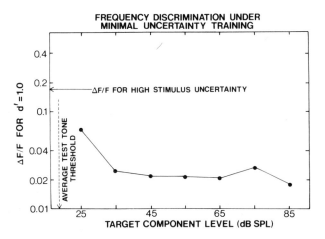

FIG. 3.4. Average just-detectable proportional changes ($\Delta f/f$ for $d' = 1.0$) in the frequency of one target component of each of eight tonal patterns, measured under minimal-uncertainty psychophysical conditions. The levels of the nine contextual (nontarget) components of the patterns were maintained at 75 dB, SPL for all testing conditions, whereas those of the targets were reduced until frequency-discrimination performance was degraded. (Data from Spiegel & Watson, 1981.)

sions are also resolved quite accurately under these conditions (just-discriminable differences of 1–2 dB and 5–10 msec., as shown by condition 4 (Fig. 3.3).

It can be argued that the effects attributed here to stimulus uncertainty might also be the result of prolonged experience with a single stimulus. Two factors lead us to reject this argument, at least in its simplest form. First, precise resolution of a single target in a single pattern can be achieved, under special training conditions (e.g., method of adjustment procedure, described by Watson et al., 1976), after a few minutes of minimal-uncertainty experience, but, after hundreds of presentations of the same stimuli in a high-uncertainty procedure, observers continue to show severely degraded resolution. Second, in several experiments we have fixed the target component while allowing random variation of its context and, although discrimination performance under this condition is considerably more accurate than for random-target conditions, it is still degraded by as much as a factor of 10–15 in just-discriminable $\Delta F/F$, compared to minimal-uncertainty controls.

The auditory system is thus remarkably capable of selectively processing single components of word-length tonal sequences. In addition, in another section of the experiment by Spiegel and Watson, we found that such precision is not restricted to cases in which the same pattern is presented over and over. After the listeners had been separately trained to "hear out" one target in each of the eight patterns, they were retested with the eight patterns presented in random order. Precise discrimination was again obtained for conditions in which the target tones were reduced to 30–40 dB below the context tones. In a final condition, two of the listeners were tested in a remembered standard version of this experiment. Their task was to decide, on each trial, whether one randomly selected pattern of the eight was in its "normal" form or had been changed by a frequency increment of the target tone. They were able to do nearly as well on this task as on the previous minimal-uncertainty conditions, under the same–different psychophysical procedure. This provided a possible hint about the selective mechanism involved in "hearing out" the target tones. Inasmuch as most of the target tones occurred in the early positions of the 450-msec. patterns, within 80–160 msec. of their onset, it appeared unlikely that the listeners were able to identify a given pattern until after the target component contained within it had been presented. This finding pointed directly to a top-down processing scheme (Bobrow & Norman, 1975; Marslen-Wilson & Welsh, 1978), in which the pitch-contour, rhythm, and/or other whole-pattern features can be used as cues selectively to process the stored details of an individual component.

Central or Informational Masking.   The contrast between the very precise resolution of target components under minimal-uncertainty testing and the severely degraded performance under high uncertainty is so striking that the actual audibility of those components might reasonably be questioned under the latter conditions. An explanation of the degraded resolution in terms of contextual (temporal) masking had been rejected earlier when it was found that, under minimal-uncertainty conditions, listeners could resolve target components presented 30–40 dB below the level of the contextual tones. However, that hypothesis was reconsidered when listeners claimed that they *literally couldn't hear the target tones under conditions of very high stimulus uncertainty.* A masking version of the experiment was run in which the 40-msec. target tones were again either 534 or 1688 Hz and were presented with latencies of either 90 or 315 msec. after pattern onset. The contextual tones ranged from 300 to 3000 Hz, varied in duration from 25 to 105 msec., and in level from 65 to 85 dB, as in the previously described high-uncertainty experiment. The method was a 3AFC detection procedure in which the target tone was present only in one out of three otherwise identical patterns on each trial. The patterns that did not contain the target tone had an equal duration (40 msec.) silent gap in its place. Again, a tracking procedure was employed in which each of the four possible targets was maintained at a level that would yield 62% correct decisions ($d' = 1.0$) in the 3AFC psychophysical method.

Results of this detection experiment are summarized in Figs. 3.5 and 3.6. As shown in Fig. 3.5, for the 534-Hz, late target component, none of the four listeners were able to detect the presence of the target at levels less than 55–60 dB, SPL, despite a minimum of 12 hours of training on this task. Similar amounts of "central" or informational masking were measured for each of the other target components. Figure 3.6 shows representative psychometric functions for one listener, for the following conditions: (1) the very high uncertainty

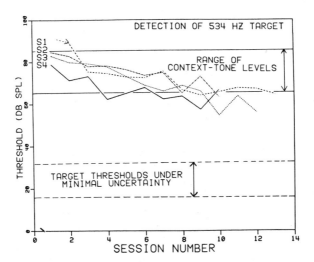

FIG. 3.5. Detection thresholds, obtained in a 3AFC tracking procedure, for a 45-msec. target component presented in the context of a 10-tone pattern. The data are thresholds for four listeners, who were tested under high-uncertainty listening conditions. The dashed horizontal lines show the range of thresholds for the same target tone, when measured under minimal-uncertainty conditions. Solid horizontal lines show the range of levels of the nine contextual (nontarget) components of each pattern.

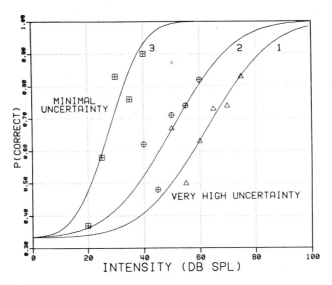

FIG. 3.6. Psychometric functions for the detection of 45-msec. target components of a 10-tone pattern, measured under three levels of stimulus uncertainty: (1) very high uncertainty in which a new pattern is presented on each trial, and the signal to be detected was one of four target tones; (2) same as (1), but with a single target tone (534 Hz, 90 msec. after pattern onset); (3) same target as (2), tested under minimal uncertainty.

condition; (2) detection of a fixed target in the same highly uncertain context condition; and (3) minimal-uncertainty detection of the same target in a fixed context. The data points in the figure were obtained in a tracking procedure (Levitt, 1971) and therefore are estimated from unequal numbers of observations. These points were fit with a cumulative normal probability density function, using the method of probit analysis described by Finney (1964). The masking results obtained under minimal uncertainty clearly cast doubt on an interpretation of this effect as *masking* in the sense of unavoidable stimulus interactions assumed to occur early in the auditory system. However, it is a masking effect in the sense of degraded detection of one stimulus caused by the close proximity of another. These results demonstrate the primary role of stimulus uncertainty in determining the detectability of pattern components as well as their discriminability.

GENERAL CONCLUSIONS

We have conjectured elsewhere about the possible relation between the results of these experiments with tonal patterns and the perception of more familiar sounds, especially those of speech (Watson, 1976), and forego a similar discussion here. The facts seem to be, first, that brief tones *can* be resolved in the context of word-length sequences with accuracy as great as when they are presented in isolation. Second, this remarkable ability to "hear out" a portion of a complex sound only exists when we know that sound quite well. Third, resolution of brief components of word-length complex sounds is severely degraded under high-uncertainty conditions, and, fourth, under those same conditions detectability of the components can be reduced by 40–50 dB. The fact that the sensation levels of the target tones are reduced by these amounts thus makes the degraded resolution of them considerably less surprising, but it is still worse than that expected for equal sensation-level tones presented in isolation (Wier et al., 1977).

The perception of word-length complex tonal sequences, or patterns, is thus severely limited by factors beyond those revealed in experiments with single tones. However, the fact that appropriate forms of training can overcome these limitations implicates central mechanisms, especially those of selective attention and memory, as the source of the limitations on pattern resolution rather than the fixed properties of the peripheral auditory system. The resolution of spectral and temporal components of auditory patterns under conditions of high stimulus uncertainty apparently reflects the typical distribution of auditory attention for unexpected, new sounds. This broadband "unselective" mode of hearing is most often characterized by a major attentional emphasis toward relatively high-frequency, late-occurring portions of single, continuous sounds. Although minimal-uncertainty training can enable a listener to shift his or her auditory attention quite effectively to other temporal or spectral regions, we do not yet know the consequences of such special auditory training for the resolution of all of the portions of a tonal pattern. This is one of several questions that must be answered if the manner in which word-length patterns are perceived, under various levels of uncertainty, is to be incorporated into general auditory theories.

The results of these experiments also underscore the need for better understanding of the role of stimulus uncertainty in auditory detection and of the conditions under which we learn the properties of specific complex sounds. Through such learning, we are apparently able to defeat the otherwise overwhelming effects of stimulus variation, probably through an intermixing of top-down analysis of the immediate input followed, if the task demands it, by bottom-up processing of details stored in an early stage of memory. Thus, we also need to know the limits and nature of the perceptual learning that apparently must precede such multilevel auditory information processing.

ACKNOWLEDGMENTS

The authors gratefully acknowledge the helpful suggestions of their colleagues, Walt Jesteadt, Richard Lippmann, and David Johnson. The research described here was partially supported by grants from the National Institute of Neurological and Communicative Disorders and Stroke and the Division of Research Resources of the National Institutes of Health.

REFERENCES

Bobrow, D. G., & Norman, D. A. Some principles of memory schemata. In D. C. Bobrow & A. M. Collins (Eds.), *Representation and understanding.* New York: Academic Press, 1975.

Bregman, A. S., & Campbell, J. Primary auditory stream segregation and perception of temporal order in rapid sequences of tones. *Journal of Experimental Psychology, 1971, 89,* 244–249.

Bregman, A. S., & Dannenbring, G. L. The effect of continuity on auditory stream segregation. *Perception & Psychophysics, 1973, 13,* 308–312.

Broadbent, D. E., & Ladefoged, P. Auditory perception of temporal order. *Journal of the Acoustical Society of America, 1959, 31,* 1539.

Creelman, C. D. Human discrimination of auditory duration. *Journal of the Acoustical Society of America, 1961, 34,* 582–593.

Creelman, C. D. Simultaneous adaptive threshold estimation with frequency uncertainty. *Journal of the Acoustical Society of America, 1973, 54,* 316.

Divenyi, P. L., & Hirsh, I. J. Identification of temporal order in three-tone sequences. *Journal of the Acoustical Society of America, 1974, 56,* 144–151.

Divenyi, P. L., & Hirsh, I. J. The effect of blanking on the identification of temporal order in three-tone sequences. *Perception & Psychophysics, 1975, 17,* 246–252.

Divenyi, P. L., & Hirsh, I. J. Some figural properties of auditory patterns. *Journal of the Acoustical Society of America, 1978, 64* (5), 1369–1385.

Elliott, L. L. Backward and forward masking of probe tones of different frequencies. *Journal of the Acoustical Society of America, 1962, 34,* 1116–1117.

Finney, D. J. *Probit analysis: A statistical treatment of the sigmoid response curve.* New York: Cambridge University Press, 1964.

Goldstein, J. L. Aural combination tones. In R. Plomp & G. F. Smoorenburg (Eds.), *Frequency analysis and periodicity detection in hearing.* Leiden, The Netherlands: Sijthoff, 1970.

Green, D. M. Detection of auditory sinusoids of uncertain frequency. *Journal of the Acoustical Society of America,* 1961, *33,* 897–903.

Green, D. M. Temporal auditory acuity. *Psychological Review,* 1971, *78,* 540–551.

Harris, J. D. The decline of pitch discrimination with time. *Journal of Experimental Psychology,* 1952, *43,* 96–99.

Henning, G. B. A comparison of the effects of signal duration on frequency and amplitude discrimination. In R. Plomp & G. Smoorenburg (Eds.), *Frequency analysis and periodicity detection in hearing.* Leiden, The Netherlands: Sijthoff, 1970.

Johnson, D. *Attentional factors in the detection of uncertain auditory signals.* Unpublished doctoral dissertation, University of California, Berkeley, 1978.

Kahneman, D. Method, findings, and theory in studies of visual masking. *Psychological Bulletin,* 1968, *70,* 404–425.

Leshowitz, B., & Cudahy, E. Frequency discrimination in the presence of another tone. *Journal of the Acoustical Society of America,* 1973, *54,* 882–887.

Levitt, H. Transformed up-down methods in psychoacoustics. *Journal of the Acoustical Society of America,* 1971, *49,* 467–477.

Loeb, M., & Holding, D. H. Backward interference by tones or noise in pitch perception as a function of practice. *Perception & Psychophysics,* 1975, *18,* 205–208.

Marslen-Wilson, W. D., & Welsh, A. Processing interactions and lexical access during word recognition in continuous speech. *Cognitive Psychology,* 1978, *10,* 29–63.

Massaro, D. W. Perceptual images, processing time, and perceptual units in auditory perception. *Psychological Review,* 1972, *79,* 124–145.

Massaro, D. W., Cohen, M. M., & Idson, W. L. Recognition masking of auditory lateralization and pitch judgments. *Journal of the Acoustical Society of America,* 1976, *59,* 434–441.

Penner, M. J., Robinson, C. E., & Green, D. M. The critical masking interval. *Journal of the Acoustical Society of America,* 1972, *52,* 1661–1668.

Ronken, D. A. Changes in frequency discrimination caused by leading and trailing tones. *Journal of the Acoustical Society of America,* 1972, *51,* 1947–1950.

Shower, E. G., & Biddulph, R. Differential pitch sensitivity of the ear. *Journal of the Acoustical Society of America,* 1931, *3,* 275–287.

Sparks, D. W. Temporal recognition masking—or interference? *Journal of the Acoustical Society of America,* 1976, *60,* 347–353.

Spiegel, M. F., & Watson, C. S. Factors in the discrimination of tonal patterns. III. Frequency discrimination with components of well-learned patterns. *Journal of the Acoustical Society of America,* 1981, *69*(1), 223–230.

Studdert-Kennedy, M., Liberman, A. M., Harris, K. S., & Cooper, F. S. Motor theory of speech perception: A reply to Lane's critical review. *Psychological Review,* 1970, *77,* 234–249.

van Noorden, L. P. A. S. *Temporal coherence in the perception of tonal sequences.* Unpublished doctoral dissertation, Institute for Perception Research, Eindhoven, The Netherlands, 1975.

Warren, R. M. Auditory temporal discrimination by trained listeners. *Cognitive Psychology,* 1974, *6,* 237–256.

Warren, R. M., Obusek, C. J., Farmer, R. M., & Warren, R. P. Auditory sequence: Confusion of patterns other than speech and music. *Science,* 1969, *164,* 586–587.

Watson, C. S. Factors in the discrimination of word-length auditory patterns. In S. K. Hirsh, D. H. Eldredge, I. J. Hirsh, & S. R. Silverman (Eds.), *Hearing and Davis: Essays honoring Hallowell Davis.* St. Louis: Washington University Press, 1976.

Watson, C. S. The time course of auditory perceptual learning. *The Annals of Otology, Rhinology, and Laryngology,* 1980, *89* (5-2), Supp. 74, 96–102.

Watson, C. S., Wroton, H. W., Kelly, W. J., & Benbasset, C. A. Factors in the discrimination of tonal patterns. I. Component frequency, temporal position, and silent intervals. *Journal of the Acoustical Society of America*, 1975, *57*, 1175–1181.

Watson, C. S., Kelly, W. J., & Wroton, H. W. Factors in the discrimination of tonal patterns. II. Selective attention and learning under various levels of stimulus uncertainty. *Journal of the Acoustical Society of America*, 1976, *60*, 1176–1186.

Wier, C. C. *Frequency discrimination in auditory patterns: Effects of time, interpolated stimuli, and decision activity.* Unpublished doctoral dissertation, Washington University, St. Louis, 1974.

Wier, C. C., Jesteadt, W., & Green, D. M. Frequency discrimination as a function of frequency and sensation level. *Journal of the Acoustical Society of America*, 1977, *61*, 178–184.

Yost, W. A., Berg, K., & Thomas, G. B. Frequency recognition in temporal interference tasks: A comparison among four psychophysical procedures. *Perception & Psychophysics*, 1976, *20*, 353–359.

Zwicker, E. Temporal effects in simultaneous masking and loudness. *Journal of the Acoustical Society of America*, 1965, *38*, 132–141.

4 Meaningfulness and the Perception of Complex Sounds

John C. Webster

INTRODUCTION

In recent years computer-aided statistical decision techniques based on electronic and/or visual analyses have proven to be powerful tools for classifying passive sonar signals. Nonetheless, they have not equalled the capabilities of the human auditory system in classifying these complex sounds. This chapter is primarily a review of the author's experimental work over a number of years on human perception of complex sounds and the role of meaningfulness and familiarity in signal identification.

In two early-literature review and summary papers, Webster (1953a, 1953b) looked at the validity of World War II (WWII) sonarman selection test batteries. The general conclusions were that the results of validity studies are very tenuous but that the audiometer and pitch-memory (musical-talent) selection tests are related weakly to sonar operator efficiency (usually assessed by training school grades). It was evident from these papers and a factor-analysis study by Karlin (1942) that auditory thresholds for, and the fine-frequency discrimination of, pure tones in quiet were only two auditory factors among many involved in complex sound perception. Passive sonar listening is a noise-masked task, and the data of other early studies (Webster, Himes, & Lichtenstein, 1950) showed that greater masking occurs in deafened ears than in normal ears. In fact, Webster, Lichtenstein, and Gales (1950) showed that: "mean masked hearing losses increase 1 dB for every increase of 10 dB in absolute hearing loss, as long as the effective noise level is greater than 20 dB . . . (and) . . . people with musical training appear to have lower absolute and masked thresholds than do people with no musical training [p. 489]." These facts may explain the relatively weak but positive relationships between the WWII sonarman selection battery and sonar school grades. However, it was felt that better selection tests could be developed if more were understood about the auditory capabilities or factors involved in complex sound perception. The most common complex sounds are speech, music, and noise. So the first group of experiments to be described are factor-analyses studies of speech and sonar perception. These include studies of Karlin (1942), Hanley (1956), Harris (1957), Solomon, Webster, and Curtis (1960), Harris (1964), and Webster (1964).

A second section of the paper focuses on the role of selective attention in the perception of competing messages. Previous work, summarized in chapter 2 of Broadbent's (1958) book and Garner (1974), found that differences in sound localization, spectrum, intensity, onset time (degree of overlap), and information content aid the auditory system in selectively attending to competing information inputs. One conclusion of these studies is that if speech and sonar signals overlap in time, speech is perceived better when heard in the right ear, and sonar signals are perceived better when heard in the left ear. Inasmuch as interior communications (speech) and sonar signals are wired into the same earphone aboard ships, this result has practical applications.

The third section, the bulk of the chapter, has the most face validity because Royal Navy (RN) rated men served as listeners in a classification task. The experimental work reported in all of section three and some of section two was performed at the Applied Psychology Research Unit in Cambridge, England.

An underlying hypothesis for all studies in which the writer was an author was that familiarity or meaningfulness was important in identifying, classifying, or, in general, perceiving complex sounds.

FACTOR ANALYSES

In one of the first uses of factor-analysis techniques to analyze auditory capabilities, Karlin (1942) identified loudness discrimination, pitch-quality discrimination, memory span, and syntheses analysis as dimensions. Harris (1957), working with sonarmen selection batteries, found that loudness discrimination itself can be subdivided into a pure-tone factor and a more complex loudness factor. He also found melodic memory, sonar performance, complex noise discrimination, pitch, and time intensity factors. Hanley (1956) used college students for subjects in a factorial investigation of speech perception. He identified such dimensions as verbal facility, tonal detection, voice memory, resistance to distortion, resistance to masking, unpleasantness, syntheses, and a separate factor for the Seashore Tests of Musical Talent (STMT). Parts of the STMT were being used for selecting sonarmen. Hanley hypothesized, but did not find, a familiarity or meaningfulness factor, i.e., a relation between verbal facility and resistance (of speech) to masking and/or distortion.

In a study with naval recruits for subjects, Solomon, Webster, and Curtis (1960) used most of Hanley's tests, plus several more, and found most of his factors. However, Solomon et al. also found an additional single factor containing both of Hanley's verbal facility and Seashore factors that had high loadings on speech-perception tests.

The fact that the same test, or series of tests, has high loadings of different auditory factors depending on the background experiences of the listening panels and/or the totality of the tests given in the battery is not unique to the comparison of the results of Solomon et al. and Hanley. In one set of circumstances, Harris (1964) found that the Harvard test of loudness bands was grouped in a detection factor that included sentences, pure tones, and tone bursts all in noise. In another set of circumstances, the Harvard loudness band test stood apart from any complex or simple tone-detection ability and became a pure loudness masking factor. Webster (1964), in commenting on Harris' three detection factors, hypothesized that there might instead be four, namely, tonal/noise, critical band/noise, broad band/noise, and speech/speech or selective attention (distraction) factors.

The results of these studies, the interrelationships between loudness masking and detection abilities, and more particularly, between speech perception, verbal facility (knowledge of vocabulary), and Seashore musical talent measures indirectly lead to much of the work that follows. The motivating idea is that because musical, internal combustion engine, and speech (at least voiced) sounds are very similar in manner of production (physically), their perceptual attributes might also have much in common. And if verbal facility (vocabulary) helps in perceiving distorted or masked speech, perhaps adapting or transferring knowledge of musical or vowel sounds to engine sounds would aid in their identification.

INFORMATION ANALYSES

Webster (1961) studied the fine-grain details of the auditory parameters found useful in the applied studies of selective attention. He assembled a set of four-dimensional, binary-valued sounds that varied in: (1) what was said, either the vowel ah (father) or ee (sea); (2) who said it, male or female; (3) how it was inflected, upward as a question or downward as a statement; and (4) where it was heard, in the left or the right earphone. Four conditions were tested. On each trial two sounds were presented simultaneously. In the ear condition, for example, one sound was presented to each ear with sex, vowel, and inflection randomly determined for each of the sounds. In this condition, the listeners were instructed to listen only to that message in the left (or right) ear and indicate what vowel was spoken, who spoke it, and how it was inflected. In other conditions, the sound pairs were matched by sex of talker, vowel sound spoken, and type of inflection. Four sets of each of the four conditions were tested such that the pairs were presented once every 2.0, 1.33, 1.0, and .67 seconds. If the subject responded correctly with all four attributes of a sound, the amount of transmitted information was 4 bits. As the sounds were presented at different rates, the transmission rate per sound was 2, 3, 4, or 6 bits per second. In this experiment, the average listener's performance did not increase beyond 4 binary decisions per second as transmission rate increased to 6 bits per second. Two of the 12 listeners never could learn the task to criterion levels, whereas one listener was very proficient.

Inflection was always the most error-prone dimension, and often no attempt was even made to categorize it. A final experiment was run to determine if the reason was that the whole syllable had to be attended to before the inflection decision could be reached. The initial consonant sound k and a final consonant t were appended to half the vowels. This increased the "what" dimension from one bit, ah(a) vs. ee(i), to three bits, a, i, ka, ki, at, it, kat, kit. It also allowed the possibility of answering all k's or all t's, i.e., making the decision on the initial or on the final sound of the syllable. All other variables remained as before. The results are shown in Fig. 4.1. They show that: (1) adding the initial and/or final consonants but not using them in any manner in the response did not affect the scores on this test (tests 1 vs. 2 and 3 vs. 4); (2) the average listeners scored higher when responding to the messages in the right vs. the left ear (tests 1 and 2) or the up vs. the down inflection (tests 3 and 4); (3) it made no difference whether the response decision cue occurred at the beginning or the end of the message (syllable); and (4) expert listeners could increase their information rates by two bits if two bits were added to the message (syllable).

Chaney and Webster (1966) used substantially the same experimental paradigm but included sonar sounds in addition to (the same) speech sounds. Other major differences included addition of a fifth bivalued dimension (duration: short = .5 seconds, long = 1.0 second), measurement of reaction time (RT), and use of two groups of listeners (trained vs. untrained sonar operators). The speech sounds were synthesized and the sonar sounds were selected for their physical comparability to the critical dimensions of the speech sounds. In terms of the original Webster study (1961), the dimensions could still be considered appropriate to answer the questions: (1) what (ah/ee, reverberation/whale cry)? (2) who (male/female, octave separation)? (3) where (left/right)? (4) how (rising/falling)? and a new one (5) how long (short/long)?

The results were of three types: reaction time (RT), accuracy, and transmitted information rate. In general, shorter RT's were associated with untrained listeners and with the speech signals. Both trained and untrained groups had shorter RT's for the right-ear response for speech signals and for left-ear response for sonar signals. In addition, they had shorter RT's on the "who" dimension for speech signals. The fast "who-speech" response is probably because in speech an octave separation can be conceptualized as a gender distinction, whereas in sonar it has no meaning per se.

The other possible anomaly in the results is the consistently shorter RT for the longer duration signals. This may be related to the effects of irrevelant informa-

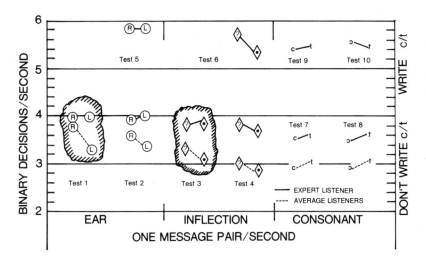

FIG. 4.1.   The results, in correct binary decisions per second (ordinate), of attending to *one* of two simultaneous messages at a one pair per second rate. Tests 1 and 3 are replications of the ear and inflection conditions at the one pair per second rate in the previous experiment before the (k) and (t) sounds were added to the stimulus sounds. Tests 2 and 4 employ messages with a (k) sound before and/or a (t) sound after half of the (a) and (i) messages, but with no difference in response (the k's and t's are not responded to). In tests 5 and 6, the expert listener did respond to the k's and t's. In test 7, 8, 9, and 10 the messages were separated by the initial (k) sound (c) or lack of it (ɔ) and then by the final (t) sound (t) or lack of it (ɟ). All tests except 1 and 3 used new materials with k's and t's added; tests 1, 2, 3, 4, 7, and 8 did not ask for a response to the added k's and t's; tests 5, 6, 9, and 10 did ask for a response to (k) and (t). The choice of which message to attend to was by ear on tests 1, 2, and 5; by inflection on tests 3, 4, and 6; and by (or by lack of) initial or final consonant on tests 7, 8, 9, and 10. Arrows on the ordinate designate 90% correct response. Each data point for each individual listener represents a composite score on 56 items. From Webster (1961).

tion on message reception. Montague (1965) found that signals in the opposite ear interfere more if they had been relevant in other conditions, which was always the case in this study. It seems likely that faster identification of the "long" signal was due to the specific absence of any competing signal during half of its duration.

The major accuracy result was that the trained listeners were significantly better on all dimensions of the sonar signals and on the duration and inflection dimensions of the speech signals. The accuracy results confirm the RT results in showing a right-ear advantage for processing speech signals and a left-ear advantage for sonar signals.

The overall results are probably best summarized in Fig. 4.2, a plot showing the information-transmission rate, a measure which contains both the RT and accuracy results. Note in particular the greater information rate transmitted by

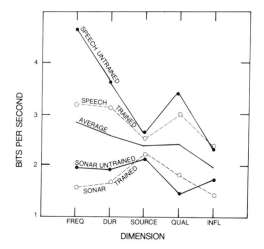

FIG. 4.2. Relation rate of information transmission by dimensions in bits per second, rank-ordered according to average response time. From Chaney and Webster (1966).

speech vs. sonar signals. In summary, the Chaney and Webster results (1966) support the hypotheses: (1) that the perception of various kinds of physically similar multidimensional signals is dependent on the experience the listener has had with each kind, rather than upon the physical properties of the signals per se; and (2) that the relative difficulty of identification of each dimension varies as a function of the kind of signal in which it appears and of the listener's experience. These findings tend to confirm Webster's reported dimensional hierarchy (1961) and are not in agreement with House, Stevens, Sandel, and Arnold (1962), who contend that there is no difference in the information-transmission rate as a function of stimulus dimension.

IDENTIFYING COMPLEX SOUNDS

The following groups of studies were performed using complex signals that had many of the physical characteristics of passive sonar sounds. In most cases, the sounds were synthesized so that the physical characteristics were precisely known. In a few cases, actual musical tones, sustained vowels, and lorry-engine sounds were used. In all cases, steady-state portions of the sounds were used. Beginning and ending transients were purposely removed to more nearly simulate marine-engine sounds. The studies are grouped into four subsections to deal with identification of complex sounds by their harmonic structure, familiarity or meaningfulness, engine speed and type, and formant structure.

By Harmonic Structure

The identification of vowels and musical tones depends on the pattern of the harmonics. How well can complex sounds that are neither speech nor musical tones be identified? This question was addressed in several experiments using a set of buzzlike sounds.

The basic test sounds were prepared by passing the output of a 75-Hz periodic-pulse, or buzz, source through a series of filters. The filters were Wien bridge networks with positive feedback, having symmetrical responses asymptotic to 6 dB/oct. on each side. These filters were ordinarily arranged like comb filters to pass, say, Harmonics 2, 4, 6 . . . or 3, 6, 9 . . . , etc. These selected groups of harmonics were then recombined with the original buzz.

The level at which Harmonics 2, 4, 6 . . . 24 (or 3, 6, 9 . . . 24, etc.) were mixed with the buzz (Harmonics 1, 2, 3 . . . 25) was determined as follows: Two of the experimenters added the selected harmonics to the buzz until they could just tell the difference between the buzz alone (all harmonics) and the buzz plus the emphasized selected harmonics. The selected harmonic complex was then mixed in, 6 dB above this threshold. Nine test sounds (the buzz alone plus the eight complexes) were generated in this manner and then passed through a −6 dB/oct. shaping network.

These nine sounds and other sets of nine, which are discussed later, were assembled into "tests" that consisted of 54 items of four sounds. The duration of each sound and the silent intervals between were each 2 seconds. Five seconds were left between items, i.e., groups of four sounds. The first three sounds within the four-item group were always different sounds, and the fourth sound was always one of the first three. The tests were used in a training paradigm that involved the following succession of tasks: (1) the listeners were asked after each pair of sounds whether they were the same or different and when that task was learned, usually after a single trial; (2) they identified which of the first three sounds the fourth replicated and when that was learned; (3) they identified each sound, usually by a code number.

In the first of two experiments using the sounds and test structure just described, Webster, Carpenter, and Woodhead (1968a) write in summary:

Nine tonal complexes were generated, in which certain groups of harmonics were emphasized. The comparison sound (Sound 9) was a buzz with a fundamental frequency at 75 Hz with equal energy at all harmonic frequencies. All other sounds were a mixture of Sound 9 and complexes based on the same fundamental but with only selected groups of harmonics present. Sounds 2, 3, 4, 5, 6, and 8 emphasized Harmonics 2, 4, 6 . . . ; 3, 6, 9 . . . ; 4, 8 . . . ; etc. Sound 1 emphasized 1, 5, 9, 13, 17, and 21, and Sound 7 emphasized Harmonics 8 and 9. Sounds 1–8 were mixed in phase synchrony with Sound 9, 6 dB above the point where the experimenters could judge that the sound mixtures were just different from Sound 9 alone. Six naive subjects could easily judge pairs of these complexes to be the same or different and whether the fourth sound of a sequence was identical with the first, second, or third sound (72%–85% accuracy), and at least five of the six could identify the sounds by number with greater than 33% accuracy.

The most easily distinguished sounds were those tonal complexes emphasizing Harmonics 6, 12, 18, and 24; 8 and 9; and 8, 16, and 24 [p. 609].

The second experiment by Webster, Carpenter, and Woodhead (1968b) concerned the identification of the three most recognizable sounds when subjected to various conditions of masking, filtering, and fundamental frequency shift. The results of partial masking (a broad band noise 6 dB below the point of total masking) and band-pass filtering (450–900 Hz, a band that passed harmonics 6 through 12) are shown in Fig. 4.3.

Note that partially masking the complexes by thermal noise and reducing the harmonic-to-buzz differential cause correct identification to fall. Bandpassing the partially masked sounds increases scores, but filtering the unmasked sounds is no aid.

When new groups of subjects learned to identify the three sounds at fundamental frequencies of 96, 108, 121, and 150 Hz and were then tested on the original sounds at 75 Hz their performance dropped but as Webster et al. (1968b) state:

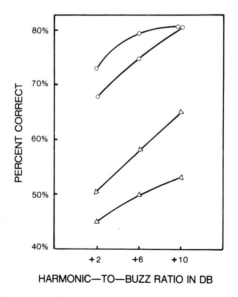

FIG. 4.3. Percentage of correct responses on sounds in quiet (Q), bandpass filtered (QF), partially masked by noise (M), and partially masked and filtered (MF), as a function of the harmonic to buzz ratio. From Webster, Carpenter, and Woodhead (1968).

There is not much question that identifying these meaningless sounds by harmonic structure alone when the fundamental frequency can vary is more difficult than identifying them at the same frequency. But the reasonable standard of performance from listeners to these two-sec tones with relatively short intervals for response shows that this type of identification could be learned if both training time and samples were longer [p. 259].

By Familiarity and Meaningfulness

Corcoran, Carpenter, Webster, and Woodhead (1968) found that knowledge of the physical characteristics of complex (sonar) sounds aided listeners in learning to identify them. Knowledge of the spectra of three (and nine) sounds just discussed did not aid in learning to identify them. Hence, a series of studies were run to determine whether naive listeners could learn supposedly meaningless sounds more quickly if some were indeed sustained vowel and/or musical instrument sounds.

Three sets of nine sounds were used to make three 54-item tests in the format previously discussed. One 54-item test used all sounds with a fundamental frequency of 55 Hz, whereas the second and third tests used frequencies of 110 Hz and 220 Hz. Nine basic sounds were generated: Three were the ones used in the last-mentioned study, except regenerated with a fundamental frequency of 55 Hz. These were considered to be "meaningless" sounds. Three were the vowels /a, i, and u/ phonated by a native British speaker at a fundamental frequency of 110 Hz. The remaining three were sustained clarinet and cello tones and a "tromba" organ stop recorded with a fundamental frequency of 220 Hz. The nine sounds used for the 54-item 55-Hz test were the original three meaningless sounds, the three vowels played (and re-recorded) at half speed, and the three musical sounds at one quarter speed. For the 110-Hz test, the meaningless and musical sounds were played (and re-recorded) at twice and half speed respectively, and the vowel sounds were used as originally recorded. For the 220-Hz test, the meaningless and vowel sounds were quadrupled and doubled in speed respectively, whereas the musical sounds remained as originally recorded at 220 Hz. Each of the three 54-item tests were constructed such that items 1 to 18 were the nine sounds in quiet, items 19 through 36 had a nonsynchronized buzz tone (at the fundamental frequency of the test sounds) with 20 harmonics added to the test sound 12 dB above the point where the buzz was just detectable, and items 37 through 54 had a -6 dB/octave thermal noise added 12 dB above its detection threshold. The test sounds were never truly masked by either the buzz or the noise.

Webster, Carpenter, and Woodhead (1968c) had three groups of six Royal Navy enlisted men listen to and learn to identify the nine sounds. One group always learned the 55-Hz test, a second the 110-Hz test (where the vowel sounds were originally recorded), and the third group the 220-Hz (musical) test. The listeners were told nothing about the stimulus sounds and were asked to identify the sounds by assigning them a numeral from 1 to 9. The group that learned the "real" vowels always made fewer errors in assigning numbers. When all the sounds were shifted up or down one octave, errors among the three classes of sounds were equally divided for the first test session. At the end of one week, there were fewer errors on the vowel-derived sounds shifted down one octave. The musical sounds when stripped of starting and stopping transients were never easy to identify.

In a second paper, Webster, Woodhead, and Carpenter (1970) looked in detail at the effects of buzz and noise masking from the results generated by the same three groups of subjects. The results are shown in Fig. 4.4. In addition to the results previously reported, note from Fig. 4.4 that both vowel-like and music-like sounds resist buzz masking better than thermal-noise masking. Meaningless sounds that gain their identity from harmonic patterning are remarkably resistant to thermal-noise masking and are as easily identified at one octave as another except when masked by buzzes (fundamental and harmonics of both the target tones and the masking buzzes at the same frequencies).

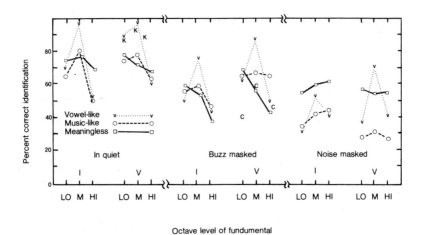

FIG. 4.4.   Correct identification (ordinate) of nine complex sounds as a function of the octave level at which they were played back (abscissa). The three major groupings are the sounds heard "in quiet," masked by a "buzz," and masked by a −6 db octave thermal noise. Within each group are results for the first (I) and last (V) listening session where identification was the task. The parameter is the type of complex sound—vowel-like, musiclike, or meaningless. For the musiclike sounds there were two instances when one of the sounds was identified as significantly different from the other two: The three k's in V, quiet, are where fewer errors were made on the clarinet sounds, and three c's in V, buzz, are where more errors were made on the cello sounds. From Webster, Woodhead, and Carpenter (1970).

If it is assumed that the musical sounds are more speechlike than the meaningless sounds, these results tend to confirm a conclusion of House et al. (1962): "as the stimuli become more like speech there is a deterioration of performance during learning, except when the stimuli are actual speech signals [p. 141]."

It would seem logical that if the listeners knew that sounds 4, 5, and 6 were the vowels and sounds 7, 8 and 9 were musical sounds they could identify them better. So Webster, Woodhead, and Carpenter (1972) picked another group of 17 Royal Navy enlisted men, divided them into three groups, and gave them the same three tests. The differences were in their training instructions. Key phrases for these new groups were: "... three ... are actually vowel sounds, three are ... musical instruments.... The vowels are /a, i, and u/ ... musical tones are ... clarinet, cello, and an electric organ...." For the 55-Hz group: "... played back two octaves lower ... cello may sound like a string bass ... played back one octave lower ... vowels may slightly resemble speech, but ... not ... normal speech..." etc. The results of this experiment, shown in Fig. 4.5, makes the major conclusion evident: Meaningful instructions do not aid listeners in identifying these types of sounds. Qualitatively, the results are even more disturbing because the trends show that although slight improvements were made in vowel scores (in six of nine conditions), musical sounds were less

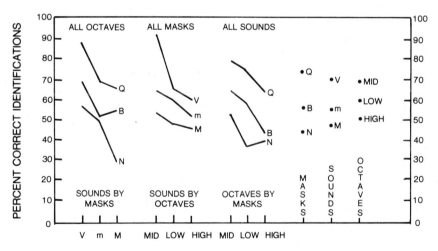

FIG. 4.5. Plot of results of the Webster, Woodhead, and Carpenter (1972) experiment averaged over various parameters. For example, the vowel score in quiet (87.6) is averaged over all octaves, and the single vowel score (71.3) is averaged over all octaves and masking conditions. The resultant scores show the main effects for sounds, musks, and octaves and the three possible two-interaction effects as interpreted from analysis of variance statistical manipulations. Q = Quiet; B = Buzz; N = Noise; V = Vowels; M = Music; m = Meaningless; Low = 55 Hz; Mid = 110 Hz; High = 220 Hz. From Webster, Woodhead, and Carpenter (1972).

well-identified (in eight of nine cases) when knowledge of their origin was known.

A few interpretations of the results should be made in terms of the interaction among the physical parameters of complex sounds, their subjective attributes, and the meaning assigned to them. It appears that once a sound is identified it takes on certain attributes (e.g., jet noises are unacceptable) and can be more easily recognized under adverse conditions (masking). This apparently happened in both of these experiments in the case of vowel-like sounds. They were recognized—although in the first experiment not necessarily identified correctly (because they were identified only by number)—when their acoustic patterning was correct and as such resisted masking very well. When completely identified (by verbal instructions and meaningful responses), they tended to resist noise masking somewhat better, and listeners showed some (though not significant) ability to generalize and identify them better through octave shifts in frequency.

In the case of musical instrument tones, this factor of meaningfulness never surfaced. Not only did the true musical sounds (Hi octave) never become easy to identify—especially when verbally labeled in advance—they lost almost all their identity in thermal-noise masking.

The physical properties of the simulated engine sounds (complex buzzes) were characterized by their ability to withstand thermal-noise masking. They never showed evidence of taking on meaning other than a vague "it's one of those buzzes." However, as they were differentiable by harmonic patterning, they did resist noise masking as well as the transposed vowels and certainly better than the musiclike sounds.

The results support the facts that complex sound identification is partially dependent on acoustic parameters but equally dependent on a true and meaningful identity being established. If a stable identity is established, as in both experiments for vowel-like sounds, recognition is easier and more resistant to certain adverse conditions. Musical sounds (at least the ones chosen) could not be learned even with meaningful verbal instructions, so it must be assumed they are not identifiable in diverse populations of complex sounds as are vowel sounds.

By Engine Speed and Type

One of the problems in identifying engine sounds with the human ear is that the basic firing rate (fundamental frequency) is barely within the lower frequency hearing range. Part of the rationale of the previous work was to show that speeding up (increasing) these low-frequency sounds would aid in identifying them. Unfortunately, speeding the sounds up by factors of two or four and re-recording them always added noise and distortion so the benefits were at the least ambiguous. Nevertheless, the lorry diesel-engine sounds gave another opportunity to try out the speedup concept. Therefore, two 54-item tests were made up such that the second 27 items were made from sounds speeded up and re-

recorded at four times the frequency of the first 27 items. Two more 54-item tests were made by doubling the speed of the sounds in the first tests. That is, the first 27 items of test 1 were made up of nine engine sounds played back at the speed at which they were originally recorded; the second 27 were re-recorded at quadruple speed (all frequencies raised by a factor of four). The first 27 items of test 2 were speeded up by a factor of two; the last 27 by a factor of eight. In actuality, the ×2 and ×4 speedups required one re-recording with associated noise and distortion, and the ×8 required two. Within each half of each test, the first nine items were the engine sounds in quiet, S/N = 20, the second nine at S/N = 10, and the last third at S/N = 6.

Two different sets of experiments were run with these test sounds. In the first (Webster, Woodhead, & Carpenter 1969a), the experimental variables were knowledge of results, amount of cueing, and the meaningfulness of the identifying names. Meaningfulness was varied either by using code names or the real names plus a description of the physical characteristics of the engine.

Where real names were used, identification was more accurate even with frequency multiplication. Engine types were identified better than engine speed (RPM). The accuracy of engine identification decreased as the noise masking increased and as the frequency multiplications changed (nonmonotonically) from ×1 to ×2 to ×8 to ×4. However, when noise masking was absent, engine identification at the ×8 speedup yielded scores equal to ×1 and ×2. The RPM identifications were all equivalent except at ×4 in noise, which always gave the lowest score.

The rationale for the two-, four, and eight-times speedups was that the perception of engine sounds, like vowels or musical sounds, can be due either to patterning among harmonics (for these diesel engines at frequencies below 200 Hz) or to broad resonant formants (above 200 Hz). It was assumed that if the lower frequency components (patterning among harmonics) were an aid to identification, speeding up the frequency of playback by three successive factors of two (i.e., ×2, ×4, and ×8) would make identification easier by shifting the lower frequencies up to better hearing regions of the ear. When identifying engines by their real as opposed to coded names, with no noise masking, the ×8 speedup did give statistically better results than the ×2 or ×1 (original speed) speedup. When masked by a −6 dB per octave noise, which is a form of high passing the engine spectra, the ×1 playback always yielded equal or better engine identification scores than ×2, ×4, or ×8 in either of the +10 or +6 engine-to-noise differential (S/N = +10 or +6) conditions. For the same group of subjects, speedups of ×2 and ×8 always gave equal or higher RPM-identification scores than did the original playback of ×1. The ×4 speedup gave better scores in quiet but considerably lower scores in noise. When all groups were considered, speedups of ×1, ×2, ×4, and ×8 gave roughly equivalent results. The results were therefore inconclusive in regard to the relative importance of the low vs. the high end of the frequency spectrum for identification of lorry diesel engines. The results could only be interpreted to show that, when masked by noise, the high end of the spectrum related better to engine identification than did the lower frequency end of the spectrum. When not masked by noise, the low frequencies in the spectrum were important in identifying either the type of engine or its RPM.

To study the importance of the frequency region more directly, Webster, Woodhead, and Carpenter (1969b) attempted to isolate the frequency region more directly by using frequency selective filters as well as speedup ratios. One group of subjects listened to the sounds bandpassed through a 320–640 Hz lowpass (LP) filter, another through a 640–2560 Hz bandpass (BP) filter, and a final group through a 1280–2560 Hz highpass (HP) filter. In terms of the original spectrum, this isolates a different band of frequencies for the different playback speeds. The results showed that for six of the nine sounds (the Commer and Cummins engines at all speeds) either the judgments were just above chance or were not dependent one way or the other on frequency.

For the Ford at 3000 RPM, all data show the low frequencies to be important, but at 2000 RPM the reverse seems to be true. The recognition of the Ford at slow speed in the absence of masking noise was ambivalent; allpass-speedup data seemed relatively uninfluenced by frequency (speedup), whereas the filter-speedup data seemed to show the importance of low frequencies. In noise, the recognition of the Ford at slow speed seemed to depend more on high frequencies than on the lows.

Concerning the influence of noise on identification: (1) it obviously made identification harder; but (2) when low frequencies were important (Ford at high speed), the speedup of ×8 was unaffected. It appeared that reasoning based on the critical band (shifting the noise but not tonal components out of the critical band) was consistent with the data.

It was apparent from an inspection of the spectra of the engines that the most identifiable engine (Ford) had the most distinguishable spectrum. It is not at all apparent why the low frequencies are more important to the recognition of the fast (and perhaps the slow) speed but not the medium. As in visible speech, there is apparently more to perceiving complex tones than meets the eye.

Webster, Woodhead, and Carpenter (1969b) concluded that:

> It is apparently as difficult to recognize diesel engines sounds unambiguously by their physical spectra as it is to recognize speech sounds or musical instrument sounds from their spectra. Just as different cues are used to recognize different speech sounds so too for engine sounds. There are demonstratable differences between the relative importance of low vs. high frequency regions in recognizing engine sounds but these cannot be predicted from simple spectral analysis schemes.
>
> If low frequencies are important in identifying a particular engine type and/or speed then some scheme for raising these frequency regions to a more discriminable listening region seems to aid identification. Similarly such low-frequency dependent sounds when masked by noise are aided by schemes which enhance the

tone-to-noise differential. This study does not give a clear cut answer as to whether harmonics patterning or formant resonances are the better aids for the identification of diesel engine sounds. Which is the more important is peculiar to the specific sound to be identified and not to the whole class of engine sounds [p. 23].

By Formant Structure

The studies that have been reported did not answer the fundamental question of whether source characteristics (the generation of a complex sound) or resonator characteristics (the shaping of the sound) are more important cues for identifying complex sounds. In some respects this is an irrelevant question because in many situations two questions are asked and not a single one. For example, in singing or speaking there are good (sonorous, penetrating, seductive, sinister) voices and intelligible ones. In music there are good and bad clarinet or cello tones. However, if you must decide which singer is Lily Pons or Barbra Streisand, or which voice is Alistair Cooke's or Eric Sevareid's, you do so on the basis of whatever evidence you have in hand (usually some combination of both types of physical information). This must also be true with complex essentially meaningless sounds.

To get some information on the relative value of harmonic structure vs. formant structure, 16 new sounds were synthesized. These sounds varied in two ways on four physical dimensions, two source dimensions, and two resonator dimensions. These were: (1) the source wave form, containing either all harmonics or odd harmonics only; (2) the fundamental frequency, either 90 or 142 Hz (ratio = 1.6); (3) the number of formants, one or two; and (4) the frequency of the formant(s), either low (600 Hz, or 600 and 1550 Hz) or high (940 Hz, or 940 and 2440 Hz) high/low ratio = 1.6. Webster, Woodhead, and Carpenter (1973) trained 24 listeners to identify these sounds. The results show there was less confusion between pairs of sounds as: (1) the number of dimensions on which they differed increased; and (2) the dimension (single or in combination) changed from formant number to formant frequency region, to fundamental frequency, to source wave form. Listeners appeared to make a generalized classification along a single dimension, which seemed to vary systematically with wave-form complexity and periodicity.

On the assumption that this single dimension was a "complex-pitch" dimension, Webster, Woodhead, and Carpenter (1974) had listeners judge whether the second sound was higher or lower than the first in a paired-comparison paradigm using the same 16 sounds. They concluded on the basis of the results shown in Table 4.1 that there was a complex-pitch dimension based primarily on the frequencies of f_0, f_1, and f_2 and secondarily on the number of formants and/or harmonics (all or odd only).

Howard and Silverman (1976) duplicated the 16 sounds but had listeners judge the similarity of all possible pairs on a one (very dissimilar) to five (very

TABLE 4.1
Judgments of Sounds with 2-Dimensional Differences

predictably MATCHED pairs	Percentage judgments in expected direction Group 1	Group 2	predictably MISMATCHED pairs	Percentage judgments in expected direction Group 1	Group 2
High fundamental + all harmonics vs. Low fundamental + odd harmonics	92%	97%	High fundamental + odd harmonics vs. Low fundamental + all harmonics	66%	73%
High fundamental + high formant(s) vs. Low fundamental + low formant(s)	95%	97%	High fundamental + low formant(s) vs. Low fundamental + high formant(s)	71%	91%
High fundamental + two formants vs. Low fundamental + one formant	94%	98%	High fundamental + one formant vs. Low fundamental + two formants	84%	86%
All harmonics + high formant(s) vs. Odd harmonics + low formant(s)	81%	80%	All harmonics + low formant(s) vs. Odd harmonics + high formant(s)	($p > 0.05$)	73%
All harmonics + two formants vs. Odd harmonics + one formant	80%	86%	All harmonics + one formant vs. Odd harmonics + two formants	66%	76%
Two formants in high position vs. One formant in low position	88%	79%	One formant in high position vs. Two formants in low position	63%	57%
100% = 384 responses			100% = 384		

Notes: 1. Group 2 heard all sounds one octave higher than Group 1.
2. Predicted as high ☐
3. Sound judged as high ⌐⌐⌐

similar) scale. Two analyses were performed on the 16 × 16 matrix of similarity judgments: an individual differences multidimensional scaling (INDSCAL) and a hierarchical clustering. Morgan, Woodhead, and Webster (1976) reanalyzed the Webster et al. (1973) data using the MDSCAL model. Morgan et al. (1976) also had subjects identify the 16 sounds by their visible spectra. The comparison of these finding show that all three studies find psychological dimensions closely correlated with the physical parameters of source wave form and frequency. That is, the 16 sounds group themselves into four quadrants based on all combination of wave form and frequency. In this respect, the only difference is the relative weight given to wave form and fundamental frequency as perceptual attributes. Webster et al. (1973) find wave form to be the best distinguishing attribute closely followed by frequency, whereas Howard and Silverman (1976) found the reverse. This can probably be explained by the task or individual differences, especially because Howard and Silverman tested a number of musically trained subjects. For example, two nonmusical sounds of different wave forms but of the same frequency are more apt to be judged similar than two sounds of the same wave form but at different frequencies, at least by musicians.

The advent of multidimensional scaling techniques for these types of data is most advantageous in the ability to analyze individual differences. The results of Howard and Silverman that musical listeners tend to use either wave form or frequency (pitch) in contrast to nonmusical listeners who tend to use both is useful information. It may say that musically trained subjects are not using all information optimally and may not be the best candidates for sonar-operator training.

ACKNOWLEDGMENT

This chapter was completed as part of an agreement with the Department of Health, Education, and Welfare.

REFERENCES

Broadbent, D. E. *Perception and communication* London: Pergamon Press, 1958.

Chaney, R. B., & Webster, J. C. Information in certain multidimensional sounds. *Journal of the Acoustical Society of America,* 1966, *40,* 447–455.

Corcoran, D. W. J., Carpenter, A., Webster, J. C., & Woodhead, M. M. Comparisons of training techniques for complex sound identification. *Journal of the Acoustical Society of America,* 1968, *44,* 157–167.

Garner, W. R. Attention: The processing of multiple sources of information. In E. C. Carterette & M. P. Friedman (Eds.), *Handbook of perception* (Vol. 2). New York: Academic Press, 1974.

Hanley, C. N. Factorial analysis of speech perception. *Journal of Speech and Hearing Disabilities,* 1956, *21,* 76–87.

Harris, J. D. A search toward the primary auditory abilities. *A decade of basic and applied science in the Navy* (ONR 2). Washington, D.C.: U.S. Government Printing Office, 1957, 244-254.

Harris, J. D. A factor analytic study of three signal detection abilities *Journal of Speech and Hearing Research,* 1964, *7,* 71-78.

House, A. S., Stevens, K. N., Sandel, T. T., & Arnold, J. B. On the learning of speechlike vocabularies. *Journal of Verbal Learning and Verbal Behavior,* 1962, *1,* 133-143.

Howard, J. H., Jr. & Silverman, E. B. A multidimensional scaling analysis of 16 complex sounds. *Perception & Psychophysics,* 1976, *19,* 195-200.

Karlin, J. E. A factorial study of auditory function. *Pychometrika,* 1942, *1,* 198-212.

Montague, W. E. Effect of irrelevant information on a complex auditory discrimination task. *Journal of Experimental Psychology,* 1965, *69,* 230-236.

Morgan, B. J. T., Woodhead, M. M., & Webster, J. C. On the recovery of physical dimensions of stimuli using multidimensional scaling. *Journal of the Acoustical Society of America,* 1976, *60,* 186-189.

Solomon, L. N., Webster, J. C., & Curtis, J. F. A factorial study of speech perception. *Journal of Speech and Hearing Research,* 1960, *3,* 101-107.

Webster, J. C. *A comparison of performance rating and auditory test scores of submarine sonar operators,* (Internal Tech. Memo No. 59). San Diego, Cal.: Navy Electronics Laboratory, February 12, 1953. (a)

Webster, J. C. *History and use of audiometry in the selection of sonarmen for the U.S. Navy during and subsequent to WWII,* (Report No. 381). San Diego, Cal.: Navy Electronics Laboratory, May 1953. (b)

Webster, J. C. Information in simple multidimensional speech messages. *Journal of the Acoustical Society of America,* 1961, *33,* 940-944.

Webster, J. C. Are there three, four, or more signal detection abilities? *Journal of Speech and Hearing Research,* 1964, *7,* 292-293.

Webster, J. C., Carpenter, A., & Woodhead, M. M. Identifying meaningless tonal complexes. *Journal of the Acoustical Society of America,* 1968, *44,* 606-609. (a)

Webster, J. C., Carpenter, A., & Woodhead, M. M. Identifying meaningless tonal complexes, II. *Journal of Auditory Research,* 1968, *8,* 251-260. (b)

Webster, J. C., Carpenter, A., & Woodhead, M. M. Perceiving steady state vowel, musical, and meaningless sounds. *Journal of Speech and Hearing Research,* 1968, *11,* 616-621. (c)

Webster, J. C., Himes, H. W., & Lichtenstein, M. San Diego county fair hearing survey. *Journal of the Acoustical Society of America,* 1950, *22,* 473-483.

Webster, J. C., Lichtenstein, M., & Gales, R. S. Individual differences in noise-masked thresholds. *Journal of the Acoustical Society of America,* 1950, *22,* 483-490.

Webster, J. C., Woodhead, M. M., & Carpenter, A. Identifying diesel engine sounds. *Journal of Sound and Vibration,* 1969, *9,* 241-246. (a)

Webster, J. C., Woodhead, M. M., & Carpenter, A. *Identifying filtered diesel engine sounds* (Technical Publication NUC TP 139). San Diego, Cal.: U.S. Naval Undersea Research and Development Center, May 8, 1969. (b)

Webster, J. C., Woodhead, M. M., & Carpenter, A. Perceptual constancy in complex sound identification. *British Journal of Psychology,* 1970, *61,* 481-489.

Webster, J. C., Woodhead, M. M., & Carpenter, A. Are steady state musical sounds as identifiable as steady state vowels? *Research in the Psychology of Music* (Vol. 8). Iowa City: Univ. of Iowa Press, 1972.

Webster, J. C., Woodhead, M. M., & Carpenter, A. Perceptual confusions between four-dimensional sounds. *Journal of the Acoustical Society of America,* 1973, *53,* 448-456.

Webster, J. C., Woodhead, M. M., & Carpenter, A. Judgment of pitch in complex sounds. *Proceedings of the Eighth International Congress of Acoustics,* 1974, *1,* 149.

5 Speech Perception and Auditory Processing

A. W. F. Huggins

INTRODUCTION

When considering the classification of auditory signals, it is obviously appropriate to include the area in which human auditory-classification skills are most highly and widely developed: speech perception. Even if we consider only those auditory patterns that correspond to words, the number of speech patterns people can recognize is extremely large in comparison to nonspeech patterns. Smith (1941) has estimated that the typical child enters first grade with an aural recognition vocabulary of 10,000 words and leaves high school with some 50,000 words. These figures are increased considerably if inflected forms derived from the same word root are counted as different words. The number of discriminable phrases or sentences is, of course, orders of magnitude larger.

How are words recognized? Do listeners really have separate templates for all the words they know, and must an input word be compared with every template before it can be recognized? Such a scheme can be ruled out immediately if the matching is performed serially, because the process would take far too long for vocabularies of typical size. The alternative, a parallel process, would be possible if each template were an active rather than a passive device, along the lines of Selfridge's "demons" (Selfridge, 1959). A fact favoring a template model is that the 50 most common words represent 60% of all uttered words (Miller, 1951). On the other hand, these 50 most common words are also those that are least precisely spoken and thus present the widest range of acoustic variability to be matched by the template. Like all other models, the template model must address two major problems encountered in speech recognition: those of context- and speaker-normalization. (For a list of listener problems, see Klatt, 1979.) A particular word may be realized as a wide variety of different acoustic patterns, depending on factors such as: its function, its position, and its novelty in the utterance (Fry, 1958; Lieberman, 1963; Umeda, 1975, respectively); the intent and emotion that led to its production (Stevens, Hecker, von Bismarck, & Williams, 1970); and various speaker-dependent variables such as the size and shape of the speaker's vocal tract, the rate at which the speech is spoken, the sex and dialect of the speaker, and even the social context in which the utterance is produced (Fant, 1962; Labov, 1972; Ladefoged & Broadbent, 1957). In addition to the foregoing problems, some of which are more important than others, a template model must somehow address the problem of how new or unfamiliar words are recognized.

A few years ago, template matching methods had been more or less abandoned by speech researchers as inadequate to the task of generalized word recognition. This position is now being reconsidered in view of two recent developments. First, a real-time template matching scheme has been demonstrated that yields very low error rates for continuous speech with a vocabulary limited to about 20 words, and that requires very little training to adapt to a new speaker (Moshier, 1979). It remains to be seen whether such a scheme can be extended to deal with a large vocabulary without requiring inordinate amounts of training for each new speaker. The second is the development of precompiled spectral-sequence networks (cf. Klatt, 1979), which can be regarded as a form of template *sequence* matching.

The most obvious objection to template matching is that it ignores information about the input word that is clearly available to the perceptual apparatus. For example, although it may not always be possible to identify a vowel uniquely, the candidates can be limited to a small class. Yet matching is performed across all words, including all those that do not contain the set of candidate vowels. This is a bit like looking up a word in a dictionary by comparing it with every entry, rather than limiting the search to the words that start with the right letter. Thus speech scientists (as opposed to mathematicians) tend to view template matching as an inefficient, brute-force approach that could be greatly improved by incorporating what is currently known about speech acoustics.

If one were faced with the task of designing a device that would match human word-recognition abilities, it would be very tempting to concentrate on units smaller than words, simply because there are fewer of them. Thus, although there are millions of English words, they contain only about 4000 distinct syllables, and words can be described as fairly constrained sequences of only 40 or 50 phonemes. The reduction of the size of the vocabulary of items to be recognized is bought at the cost of an increased rate of decisions to be made. During conversational speech, speech bursts (uninterrupted by pauses) contain two or three words per second, corresponding to about five syllables per second, or 10–12 phonemes per second. Conceptually, however, the problem is more tractable at the phoneme level than at the word level. As a result, studies of speech perception have tended to concentrate on the cues used to recognize phonemes realized in the simplest possible articulatory units: monosyllabic nonsense syllables spoken in isolation.

Distinctive Features (A Linguistic Term)

Linguists have for some time classified phonemes on the basis of distributional and articulatory properties. Speech consists of an alternating sequence of opening and closing gestures of the vocal tract. The closing gestures correspond to consonants, and the open phases correspond to vowels. Vowels can be classified according to how high the tongue body is held and how near to the lips the point of maximal constriction is. Consonants can be classified according to whether they are voiced (/b, d, g/) or voiceless (/p, t, k/); by their manner of production (stops /p, d/ vs fricatives /f, z/ vs. nasals /m, n/); and by their place of production (labial /p, f, m/ vs. alveolar /t, s, n/). Linguists have tried to develop classification systems based on binary oppositions (Chomsky & Halle, 1968; Jakobson, Fant, & Halle, 1951), mainly because such systems demonstrate great descriptive economy and generate elegant explanations for historical changes in the sound patterns of languages. It is important to stress that these systems of "distinctive features" were first developed by linguists to describe linguistic phenomena, and that they are adequately motivated on these grounds alone, without any appeal to how the sounds are perceived.

Early studies of the cues used in the perception of consonants, and also inspection of spectrograms, showed that there are acoustic differences between consonants, and classes of consonants, that parallel those captured by the system of distinctive features. Much work in speech perception has been aimed at finding the acoustic correlates of the distinctive features. Let us consider, briefly, a typical paradigm for such an experiment, which has come to be known as a "phoneme-boundary" experiment.

The acoustic energy of steady-state vowels is localized at specific frequencies called formants. If the vowel is preceded by a stop consonant, this modifies the start of the formant, introducing a frequency transition. The frequency region that is the starting point for the transition is a main clue to the distinction between, for example, /bɑ/ and /dɑ/ (Liberman, Ingemann, Lisker, Delattre, & Cooper, 1959). A low starting frequency followed, for most vowels, by a rising transition is heard as /b/, and a higher starting frequency with falling transition is heard as /d/. A set of 8 or 10 sounds can be synthesized that are identical except that the frequency from which the second-formant transition begins (F2I) increases in equal steps from a frequency appropriate to a /b/ to one appropriate to a /d/ across the set of stimuli. When these sounds are played to listeners for identification, however, the proportion of /d/ judgments does not increase gradually as F2I increases. Rather, it resembles a step function: The two or three stimuli at each end of the continuum are labeled almost 100% /b/ or /d/, and the switch from one to the other takes place suddenly over a narrow range of two or three stimuli. The stimulus configuration corresponding to the 50% point is called the "phoneme boundary." Stevens (1972) has argued that articulatory patterns used as phonemes by the languages of the world tend to have an acoustic result that is stable despite quite large articulatory perturbations, whereas the boundaries between phonemes correspond to articulatory patterns where the acoustic output changes rapidly in response to only small changes in articulation.

The most interesting aspect of the phoneme-boundary phenomenon occurs when these same /ba–da/ stimuli are used in a discrimination task. In an AX discrimination, two stimuli separated by one or two steps along the continuum are presented, and the subject judges whether they are the same or different. Alternatively, in an ABX discrimination, one member of the pair is repeated as the third stimulus, and the subject must identify the third as being identical to either the first or the second. The discrimination function shows a peak that coincides with the phoneme boundary. Away from the boundary, however, performance is very close to chance levels. That is, subjects are not able to discriminate between stimuli that fall in the same identification category: They can only discriminate between stimuli that they label as different. Perception of stop consonants is "categorical."

This finding contrasts dramatically with results obtained with "simple" acoustic stimuli, such as the pitch or loudness of tones. Only about 10 pitches or loudnesses can be reliably identified in an absolute-judgment task (Miller, 1957). But as the number of dimensions on which the stimuli differ is increased, the ability to identify stimuli that differ on a single dimension declines, until with six or more dimensions, only a binary identification is possible on each dimension. So far, the similarity with speech is apparent. But for tones, many thousands of unidimensional stimuli can be discriminated from each other, and the discriminability on one dimension remains high even when other dimensions are added. Therefore, evidence that speech sounds are no better discriminated than identified lends striking support to the idea that speech sounds are perceived in terms of distinctive features, and that acoustic detail beyond that required for the feature classification is simply not perceived. This view, in turn, has led to the postulation of "feature detectors" specialized for making the acoustic distinctions necessary to classifying speech sounds, and to the view that "speech is special" (e.g., Liberman & Pisoni, 1977). A great deal of recent work has tried to prove the existence of the postulated feature detectors by showing they can be fatigued by repeated presentations of a stimulus from one end of the continuum, for example, the /b/ in the experiment outlined earlier (see Cooper, 1975, for review). Adaptation causes the phoneme boundary to be displaced toward the adapting stimulus. After adaptation with a /b/, fewer stimuli are labeled *b*. Listeners as young as a few months old show equivalent effects, suggesting that the detectors may be innate (Eimas, Siqueland, Jusczyk, & Vigorito, 1971).

Recently, however, evidence of two types has begun to accumulate against the "speech-is-special" view. First, the categorical perception that was thought to be unique to speech has been demonstrated with nonspeech sounds. The sounds used were tones whose onset envelope grows at varying rates, those with a rapid onset yielding a percept of a plucked string, and those with a more gradual onset yielding a bowed-string percept. Using these sounds, Cutting (1978) has demonstrated the sharp identification boundary, the coincident discrimination peak, and the adaptation effects, each of which was formerly thought to occur only in speech. The final, clinching demonstration was that the phoneme boundary between initial /b/ and /w/, which depends on the rise time of the onset envelope leading into the vowel, could be moved around by a *non*speech adaptor such as the plucked or bowed tones (Diehl, 1976).

The second type of evidence conflicting with the view that speech is special involves a demonstration that acoustic detail beyond that necessary to achieving a distinctive-feature classification *is* available to perception. Ingram (1975) had subjects rate the similarity of 12 initial consonants in a triadic comparison task. Nonmetric multidimensional analysis of the results showed that the initial consonants fell into three nonoverlapping categories on the first dimension, with stop consonants (p, t, b, d) at one end, resonants (1, m, n, r) in the middle, and the sibilants (s, z, sh, ch) at the other end. The fact that the sounds fell into three groups, each corresponding to a particular manner of articulation, at first appears to be strong support for an account in terms of distinctive features. Ingram found, however, that the positions of the initial consonants along the dimension correlated .94 with their durations. Duration, a primitive acoustic variable, was able to account for much more of the similarity data than could the distinctive-feature description, which was unable to explain the observed structure *within* each of the three categories.

A recent study by Goldstein (1980) produced additional compelling evidence in the same vein. Goldstein asked whether the fine-structured detail found in any given study performed to establish the reality of distinctive features could also be found in other independently performed studies. He argued that if any pair of studies demonstrated shared detailed structure beyond that implicit in the distinctive-feature description of the stimuli, then this must be evidence that subjects were in fact making finer distinctions than could be explained solely by a model based on distinctive features. He was able to find six sets of confusion data on English consonants to test his theory. Two were sets of production errors (slips of the tongue) collected by Fromkin (1973) and Shattuck-Hufnagel (1975). Two were sets of perceptual confusions between initial consonants, one collected with noise masking and the other in the quiet but at low levels (i.e., masked by "internal" noise). And the final two were parallel sets of perceptual confusions between syllable-final consonants (the latter four sets from Wang & Bilger, 1973). Each of the six sets of data was subjected to nonmetric multidimensional scaling. Following a suggestion by Holman (cf. Goldstein, 1980, p. 1341), the dimensionality of each solution was established by calculating the distances between stimuli in a solution space and rank-order correlating these with the raw distances taken from the paired set of data. That is, modeled interpoint distances for one set of production confusions were compared with raw confusions for the other set of production confusions, and so on. If the correlation increases as a further dimension is added to the solution, then the extra dimension must represent structure that is common to both data sets. If, on the other hand, the correlation does not increase, or even decreases, then the additional structure represents noise that is specific to that data set. For each of the three pairs of data sets, the correlations failed to increase reliably beyond three dimensions in the solution.

After rotation to linguistically plausible configurations, the first dimension divided the consonants into stops vs. fricatives, the second by voicing, and the third by place of articulation. It was possible to subdivide each solution space so that the phonemes fell on one side of the division or the other according to their distinctive-feature descriptors. This was true for all six data sets. Furthermore, the fine-grain detail of the position of individual phonemes *within* each of these subdivisions was highly similar for each *paired* set of data. When position on each of the three dimensions was correlated, within each of the three paired data sets, the smallest of the nine product-moment correlation coefficients was .72, and six were larger than .93 ($p < .001$ for all nine). Furthermore, the correlations remained extremely high within each paired data set when the main effect due to the distinctive features was partialed out. Four of the nine were larger than .88 ($p < .001$), and three more were larger than .62 ($p < .05$). This constitutes strong evidence that differences between the stimuli are reliably detected beyond those necessary to establishing the distinctive-feature classification of the phoneme.

So far, we have considered only the comparisons Goldstein made between matched sets of data (initial consonants with initial consonants, final with final, etc.). The correlations were also high between *unmatched* data sets (e.g., comparing initial with final consonants), but only as long as the distinctive-feature main effect was left in ($p < .001$ for 22 of the 36 correlations, and only two were not significant at $p < .05$). The correlations disappeared completely when the distinctive-feature main effect was partialed out: 28 out of the 36 correlations were not significant, and only one achieved significance at $p < .01$. Furthermore, the two largest were *negative* correlations, showing that the fine detail was in the sense opposite to the main effect. The implication is that different perceptual dimensions are used for recognizing consonants in initial and final position, and that the distinctive features of speech sounds are abstract linguistic properties that are inferred from more primitive acoustic properties, rather than being integrally involved in the perceptual process.

The idea that different acoustic cues underlie the classification of consonants in initial and final position has been pointed out before, at least for some dimensions such as voicing. A major cue for the distinction between unvoiced /p, t, k/ and voiced /b, d, g/ in initial position is the voice onset time, which is the interval between the plosive burst resulting from release of the stop and the onset of vocal cord vibrations. For English voiced stops, voice onset time is usually less than 25 msec., whereas for unvoiced stops it is usually more than 50 msec. (Lisker & Abramson, 1964). Voice onset time is not a useful cue to voicing of stops in final position. Instead (in English) the voicing distinction is carried mostly by the duration of the vowel preceding the final consonant. Vowels preceding voiced consonants are 20% to 50% longer than those preceding unvoiced consonants (e.g., House, 1961). Moreover, this is a learned cue and does not occur in all languages, Danish for instance. In summary, the possibility seems remote that a distinctive-feature description of English consonants can be found that adequately captures the different perceptual effects for initial and final position.

Fluent Speech

What happens in longer sequences? The foregoing discussion has concentrated on recognition of single phonemes and the distinctions that can be made between pairs of similar phonemes. A simple bottom-up approach would describe the recognition process as starting with determination of primitive auditory properties, which are then combined to yield classifications as phonemes, which in turn are combined to form syllables, words, phrases, and so on up. There are several problems with this model, as applied to speech. First, lower level units should be available with shorter latency than the larger units they combine to form. Yet, experimental evidence points in the opposite direction. If subjects listen to a list of nonsense syllables and are asked to press a key when they hear a syllable beginning with a ''b,'' the response is much slower than if they are asked to press when they hear the syllable ''bab,'' even though presentation order is counterbalanced so that the same target operates as a phoneme target for one group of subjects and as a syllable target for a second group (Savin & Bever, 1970). Furthermore, if the subject has to respond to any word that begins with a ''b,'' the response is quicker if the target occurs in a real word such as ''bit'' than in a pseudoword like ''bip'' (Rubin, Turvey, & Van Gelder, 1976). These effects are hard to explain with a strictly bottom-up model (but, see McNeill & Lindig, 1973, who argue that the units of speech perception cannot be identified from phoneme-monitoring experiments.)

A second area of difficulty is the rate at which decisions have to be made if the input phonemes must be individually classified. Miller (1951) has estimated that some 10–15 classifications per second are required in running speech, and the order in which they occur must also be determined. Yet, Warren, Obusek, Farmer, and Warren (1969) have shown that four nonspeech sounds, presented cyclically in a fixed order, must last several hundred milliseconds each before their order can be reliably described. Such temporal order decisions are presumably necessary in speech to distinguish between pairs of words such as ask/axe, pest/pets, and even tops/stop/spot/pots, but the speech sounds last only 80 msec. on the average.

The obvious conflict between Warren's result and the observable facts of speech perception can be resolved in several ways. First, Warren's experiment required subjects to *describe* or *name* the items in the sequence, which presumably is not required *during* speech perception, although the task may require it subsequently (e.g., Savin & Bever, 1970). When naming is not required, subjects are able to compare or discriminate between two nonspeech sequences at much higher rates (Nickerson & Freeman, 1974; Warren & Byrnes, 1975). Second, perhaps the successive events in speech are not treated as disparate, as they were in Warren's experiment. Third, perhaps the decision rate in speech is lower than appears to be required because the perceptual apparatus deals with chunks larger than the phoneme, such as the syllable or word. Fourth, perhaps speech perception is a continuous rather than a discrete process, and we have been deceived into regarding it as discrete by the analogy with written language, which is clearly a more recent development. Some support for this latter view accrues from the difficulties young children have in breaking up the syllables and words they utter into their component speech sounds (Savin, 1972).

If the cyclically presented sounds are made more similar to each other, for example by using excised portions of steady-state vowels, then the minimum duration at which the order can be specified drops to about 125 msec. for natural vowels and 160 msec. for synthetic vowels (Thomas, Hill, Carroll, & Bienvenido, 1970). This is closer to the rate required in speech—the modal duration of syllables in fluent speech is about 150 msec. (Huggins, 1964), and the vowel often accounts for half or more of the syllable. If, in addition, transitions are inserted to make the vowels flow smoothly into each other rather than change abruptly, the maximum rate increases still further.

I argue that the main reason it is hard to determine the temporal order of Warren's sounds is that the sounds are so disparate that they form several separate auditory streams. Bregman and Campbell (1971) have shown that events occurring in different auditory streams are very difficult to interrelate. The sounds of speech, on the other hand, form a single stream within which sequence is easy to follow. Two types of evidence favor this view. First, if a speech sound in a sentence is deleted and replaced by an external sound such as a cough or noise burst, subjects can neither detect the fact that a speech sound has been deleted nor localize the cough in the stream of speech (Warren, 1970). The cough has inappropriate acoustic properties for it to be integrated into the speech, and it is perceived as a separate, extraneous sound in a separate stream (which is just as well!). The result is that its position relative to the speech cannot be determined, and the missing speech is "filled in" by the perceptual apparatus. But, if the same speech sound is replaced by silence instead of a cough, the silence is perceived as an interruption of the speech stream because extraneous silences do not normally blank out an ongoing sound stream. The stoppage can be located in the speech sequence very easily because it has to be treated as part of the speech stream—it stopped and restarted—rather than being regarded as an event extraneous to the speech, like the cough. Given the evolutionary pressures under which the auditory apparatus developed, the different treatment accorded an extraneous noise and a silent interval is not surprising. It is frequently important to attend to one sound in the presence of another, but there is no naturally occurring event that produces a silence in the middle of an ongoing sound. We return to the effects of silence later.

A second source of evidence that streaming is an important perceptual attribute of speech is the failure of attempts to code language into a sequence of sounds that do not form a stream. Some years ago, before the advent of reading machines that convert printed text into speech (e.g., Kurzweil's), there was great interest in more primitive machines that converted text into sequences of arbitrary sounds. The sounds chosen were chords containing up to nine simultaneous tones, which when arranged in ascending frequency, can be regarded as a vertical cursor to be moved from left to right across the line of text. Each tone was turned on or off according to whether the part of the page under the appropriate part of the cursor was inked or blank. Thus, the sounds were closely related morphologically to the letter shapes. In fact, a spectrogram made of the sounds generated from a line of text would reproduce the printed pattern with sufficient accuracy for the text to be read from the spectrogram. But highly motivated subjects, even after years of practice, were not able to read with this machine at a rate of more than 10 words per minute (Freiberger, 1968). A possible reason is that the sounds did not form an auditory stream. Ten words per minute implies a letter rate of about one per second, and at one letter per second, the silence between the printed letters is sufficiently long to destroy any streaming that might have occurred had the sounds been presented faster. It is possible to learn to recognize rapid sequences of nonspeech sounds, whether these be sequences of tones (see Watson, this volume) or artificial analogues of words, presented continuously in an unbroken sequence (Hayes & Clark, 1970).

To go further, the intelligibility of speech can be destroyed by inserting silent intervals to break up its streaming. Miller and Licklider (1950) were the first to demonstrate this by periodically interrupting speech. They used single words as test materials, and the speech that should have occurred during the interruptions was simply discarded, so that listeners on average heard only half of the waveform. Similar results are obtained, however, when continuous speech is used, and all of the speech waveform reaches the listener. A recording of speech can be repeatedly stopped and started again so that the speech reaches the listener in a sequence of speech intervals separated by silent intervals, a type of presentation I have named Temporally Segmented Speech (Huggins, 1975). Speech intelligibility is found to depend both on the duration of the speech intervals and on the duration of the silent intervals. If silent intervals are made long (say 200 msec.) and speech intervals are simultaneously made short (say 30 msec.), the speech is unintelligible, with at most three or four words being identifiable in a 100-word passage (and these are often the result of lucky guesses of "the" or "a"). The intelligibility measure used in these studies was the shadowing score: the number of words in the passage that the listener was able to repeat aloud concurrently with listening to the message.

Intelligibility can be increased either by lengthening the speech intervals or by shortening the silences, as shown by functions A and B in Fig. 5.1. If the silent intervals are held constant at 200 msec., the intelligibility of the speech increases steadily as the speech intervals are lengthened from 30 msec. to 200 msec., where virtually every word is perceived (read function A from left to right). On the other hand, if the speech intervals are held constant at about 60 msec., intelligibility remains low (about 55%) as long as silent-interval duration is longer than about 120 msec. But with further shortening of the silent intervals, intelligibility begins to increase rapidly to almost perfect when the silences last 60 msec. or less (read function B from right to left). I have argued from these results that silent intervals lasting up to about 60–100 msec. do not cause streaming to break down, whereas longer silences do (see Huggins, 1974 for a similar result with pulse trains). Second, when streaming *has* broken down, the acoustic information in each speech interval is essentially processed independently of the

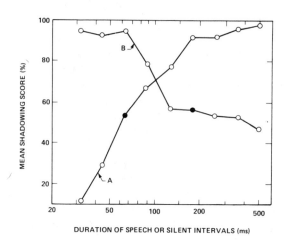

FIG. 5.1.   Function A shows the intelligibility of continuous speech as a function of the duration of the *speech* intervals created by inserting silent intervals of 200 msec. into the speech (i.e., silent intervals constant at 200 msec.; speech intervals vary from 31 to 500 msec.). Function B shows the intelligibility as a function of *silent* interval duration, when silent intervals are inserted into the speech so as to produce speech intervals of 63 msec. (i.e., silent intervals vary from 31 to 500 msec.; speech intervals constant at 63 msec.). Note that the two functions yield similar intelligibilities (as they should) for speech intervals of 63 msec. with silent intervals of 200 msec. (solid points). Adapted from Huggins (1975).

content of adjacent speech intervals, except insofar as linguistic redundancy can be used to complete any mutilated words. (Note that the mutilation consists only of inserting silences: All of the original waveform is presented to the listener, unlike interrupted speech.)

A particularly interesting phenomenological observation is that when continuous speech is broken up into 30-msec. samples by the insertion of 150-msec. silences, it is possible to hear and track the movements of the second formant, especially during vowels. That is, the speech has been reduced to its acoustic elements, which can be perceived as such. Under normal conditions, the phonological and linguistic content of the message preempts all attentional resources, and the purely acoustic aspects of the speech signal are perceived only subconsciously.

CONCLUSIONS

Although (linguistic) distinctive features provide a ready explanation for many of the observed facts of speech perception, close inspection suggests that there may always be primitive acoustic variables that can provide even better explanations. For the most part, however, there has been relatively little success in specifying acoustic invariances that are valid across different speakers and contexts (but see Stevens & Blumstein, 1978, for an exception).

Identification of the temporal order of speech sounds is dependent on speech forming a coherent auditory stream. Insertion of silent intervals into running speech can be used to destroy this streaming, which results in the speech being treated as a sequence of unrelated acoustic events from which the message cannot be extracted.

REFERENCES

Bergman, A. S., & Campbell, J. Primary auditory stream segregation and perception of order in rapid sequences of tones. *Journal of Experimental Psychology,* 1971, *89,* 244–249.

Chomsky, N., & Halle, M. *The sound pattern of English.* New York: Harper & Row, 1968.

Cooper, W. E. Selective adaptation to speech. In F. Restle, R. M. Shiffrin, N. J. Castellan, H. Lindman, & D. B. Pisoni (Eds.), *Cognitive theory* (Vol. 1). Hillsdale, N.J.: Lawrence Erlbaum Associates, 1975.

Cutting, J. E. There may be nothing peculiar to perceiving in a speech mode. In J. Requin (Ed.), *Attention and performance VII,* Hillsdale, N.J.: Lawrence Erlbaum Associates, 1978.

Diehl, R. Feature analyzers for the phonetic dimension stop vs. continuant. *Perception & Psychophysics,* 1976, *19,* 267–272.

Eimas, P., Siqueland, E., Jusczyk, P., & Vigorito, J. Speech perception in infants. *Science,* 1971, *171,* 303–306.

Fant, C. G. M. Descriptive analysis of the acoustic aspects of speech. *Logos,* 1962, *5,* 3–17.

Freiberger, H. (Ed.). *Reading machines for the blind* (V.A. Report No. R-660127, 1968). Summary of the sixth technical session held at Veterans Administration Central Office, Washington D.C., Jan. 27–28, 1966.

Fromkin, V. A. (Ed.). *Speech errors as linguistic evidence.* The Hague: Mouton, 1973.

Fry, D. B. Experiments on the perception of stress. *Language and Speech,* 1958, *1,* 126–152.

Goldstein, L. Categorical features in speech perception and production. *Journal of the Acoustical Society of America,* 1980, *67,* 1336–1348.

Hayes, J. R., & Clark, H. H. Experiments on the segmentation of an artificial speech analogue. In J. R. Hayes (Ed.), *Cognition and the development of language.* New York: Wiley, 1970.

House, A. S. On vowel duration in English. *Journal of the Acoustical Society of America,* 1961, *33,* 1174–1178.

Huggins, A. W. F. Distortion of the temporal pattern of speech: Interruption and alternation. *Journal of the Acoustical Society of America,* 1964, *36,* 1055–1064.

Huggins, A. W. F. On perceptual integration of dichotically alternated pulse trains. *Journal of the Acoustical Society of America,* 1974, *56,* 939–943.

Huggins, A. W. F. Temporally segmented speech. *Perception & Psychophysics,* 1975, *18,* 149–157.

Ingram, J. C. *Perceptual dimensions of phonemic recognition.* Unpublished doctoral dissertation, University of Alberta, Edmonton, Alberta, 1975.

Jakobson, R., Fant, C. G. M., & Halle, M. *Preliminaries to speech analysis.* Cambridge, Ma.: The M. I. T. Press, 1963.

Klatt, D. H. Speech perception: A model of acoustic-phonetic analysis and lexical access. In R. Cole (Ed.), *Perception and production of fluent speech.* Hillsdale, N.J.: Lawrence Erlbaum Associates, 1979.

Labov, W. *Sociolinguistic patterns.* Philadelphia: University of Pennsylvania Press, 1972.

Ladefoged, P., & Broadbent, D. E. Information conveyed by vowels. *Journal of the Acoustical Society of America,* 1957, *29,* 98–104.

Liberman, A. M., Ingemann, F., Lisker, L., Delattre, P., & Cooper, F. S. Minimal rules for synthesizing speech. *Journal of the Acoustical Society of America,* 1959, *31,* 1490–1499.

Liberman, A. M., & Pisoni, D. B. Evidence for a special speech-perceiving subsystem in the human. In T. H. Bullock (Ed.), *Recognition of complex signals.* Berlin: Dahlem Konferenzen, 1977.

Lieberman, P. Some effects of semantic and grammatical context on the production and perception of speech. *Language and Speech,* 1963, *6,* 172–187.

Lisker, L., & Abramson, A. S. A cross-language study of voicing in initial stops: Acoustical measurements. *Word,* 1964, *20,* 384–422.

McNeill, D., & Lindig, K. The perceptual reality of phonemes, syllables, words, and sentences. *Journal of Verbal Learning and Verbal Behavior,* 1973, *12,* 419–430.

Miller, G. A. *Language and communication.* New York: McGraw-Hill, 1951.

Miller, G. A. The magical number seven, plus or minus two. *Psychological Review,* 1957, *63,* 81–97.

Miller, G. A., & Licklider, J. C. R. The intelligibility of interrupted speech. *Journal of the Acoustical Society of America,* 1950, *22,* 167–173.

Moshier, S. Talker-independent speech recognition in commercial environments. *Journal of the Acoustical Society of America,* 1979, *65,* Supplement No. 1, S132.

Nickerson, R. S., & Freeman, B. Discrimination of the order of the components of repeating tone sequences: Effects of frequency separation and extensive practice. *Perception & Psychophysics,* 1974, *16,* 471–477.

Rubin, P., Turvey, M. T., & Van Gelder, P. Initial phonemes are detected faster in spoken words than in spoken nonwords. *Perception & Psychophysics,* 1976, *19,* 394–398.

Savin, H. B. What the child knows about speech when he starts to learn to read. In J. F. Kavanagh & I. G. Mattingly (Eds.), *Language by ear and by eye.* Cambridge, Mass.: MIT Press, 1972.

Savin, H. B., & Bever, T. G. The nonperceptual reality of the phoneme. *Journal of Verbal Learning and Verbal Behavior*, 1970, *9*, 295–302.

Selfridge, O. G. Pandemonium: A paradigm for learning. In D. V. Blake & A. M. Uttley (Eds.), *Proceedings of the symposium on mechanization of thought processes*. Natl. Phys. Lab., Teddington, England, London: HMSO, 1959, pp. 511–529.

Shattuck-Hufnagel, S. R. *Speech errors and sentence production*. Unpublished doctoral dissertation, MIT., Cambridge, Mass., 1975.

Smith, M. K. Measurement of the size of general English vocabulary through the elementary grades and high school. *Genetic Psychology Monographs*, 1941, *24*, 311–345.

Stevens, K. N. The quantal nature of speech: Evidence from articulatory-acoustic data. In E. E. David & P. B. Denes (Eds.), *Human communication: A unified view*. New York: McGraw-Hill, 1972.

Stevens, K. N., & Blumstein, S. Invariant cues for place of articulation in stop consonants. *Journal of the Acoustical Society of America*, 1978, *64*, 1358–1368.

Stevens, K. N., Hecker, M. H. L., von Bismarck, G., & Williams, C. E. Manifestations of task-induced stress in the acoustic signal. *Journal of the Acoustic Society of America*, 1970, *44*, 993–1001.

Thomas, I. B., Hill, P. B., Carroll, F. S., & Bienvenido, G. Temporal order in the perception of vowels. *Journal of the Acoustical Society of America*, 1970, *48*, 1010–1013.

Umeda, N. Vowel duration in American English. *Journal of the Acoustical Society of America*, 1975, *58*, 434–445.

Wang, M. D., & Bilger, R. C. Consonant comparisons in noise: A study of perceptual features. *Journal of the Acoustical Society of America*, 1973, *54*, 1248–1266.

Warren, R. M. Perceptual restoration of missing speech sounds. *Science*, 1970, *167*, 392–393.

Warren, R. M., & Byrnes, D. L. Temporal discrimination of recycled tonal sequences: Pattern matching and naming of order by untrained listeners. *Perception & Psychophysics*, 1975, *18*, 273–280.

Warren, R. M., Obusek, C. J., Farmer, R. M., & Warren, R. P. Auditory sequence: Confusion of patterns other than speech or music. *Science*, 1969, *164*, 586–587.

Williams, C., & Stevens, K. N. Emotions and speech: Some acoustical correlates. *Journal of the Acoustical Society of America*, 1972, *52*, 1238–1250.

II

PERCEPTION OF COMPLEX VISUAL PATTERNS

6 Negligible Symmetry Effects in Dot-Pattern Detection

William R. Uttal
Thelma E. Tucker

Gestalt, information theory, and autocorrelation models (Uttal, 1975) of form perception all predict that pattern recognition should be enhanced by increases in the degree of symmetry of visual stimuli. Indeed, previous findings on the subject have been clear-cut when memorial tasks are utilized. Schnore and Partington (1967) have shown effects of symmetry on recall of patterns, as did Attneave (1955) using dot patterns. In Attneave's experiments, symmetry was found to have no effect only when other means (e.g., varying the number of dots) were used to maintain a constant information content of the utilized stimuli. When the number of dots in his patterns remained constant, however, then symmetry had a strong effect in both recall and reproduction tasks. Adams, Fitts, Rappaport, and Weinstein (1954) found essentially the same substantial effect of symmetry with figures composed of angles and lines.

However, in one of the experiments (Experiment IX) reported in a recent monograph (Uttal, 1975), symmetry of line spacing was found to have a negligible effect in a target-detection task in which dotted forms had to be extracted from dotted visual-noise fields. The discrepancy between the recognition and reproduction tasks, on the one hand, and the target detection task, on the other, represents an important clue to the fact that the two tasks differ in fundamental ways.

In the earlier work (Uttal, 1975), a model incorporating multiple stages of visual form perception, separately assayable by appropriate selection of the experimental task, was presented. Although it would be inappropriate to recapitulate the full rationale for that model here, briefly, it was suggested that the recall and recognition tasks were assaying the characteristics of what was referred to as a Stage 4 pattern-recognition process especially sensitive to the symbolic aspects of the stimulus, whereas the detection task assayed the effects of a precursor Stage 3 process that was especially sensitive to factors of stimulus organization.

Further support for the notion of separately assayable levels of form perception would be obtained if the finding that symmetry does not affect form detection is determined to be robust and generalizable to other stimulus classes. The purpose of the present study is to test for the presence or absence of a symmetry effect in parallel lines with a greatly expanded data base and to perform a similar test with a different stimulus set composed of regular and asymmetrical snowflake-like patterns.

METHOD

Subjects

Undergraduate students at the University of Michigan were used as subjects in the experiments. Each was paid a fixed stipend for a daily 1-hour session, and none reported any evidence of visual abnormalities, although some wore corrective lenses. All subjects became highly trained and served for at least one entire academic semester during which they participated in several experiments. Subjects were always highly familiar with the target stimuli prior to the collection of the experimental data.

Apparatus

Stimuli were generated on the face of a cathode ray oscilloscope under the control of a small digital computer. Each stimulus was composed of a dotted target pattern varying in some aspect of symmetry and embedded within variable amounts of randomly positioned masking dots. A sample stimulus is shown in Fig. 6.1.

Target stimulus patterns were prepared in advance by the experimenter and then stored in the computer for recall as requested by the experimental control program. A random number algorithm was used by this control program to counterbalance the number and order of the stimuli to be presented within each subject's hourly session. The pattern of random-masking dots was recalculated after each trial. The computer also controlled all response acquisition and data-analysis procedures.

The subject viewed the CRT screen from a distance of 33 cm. The viewing region on the face of the oscilloscope on which the random-masking dots were presented was 5.6 deg. by 5.6 deg., and stimulus patterns were smaller, typically subtending an angle of about 3 deg. by 3 deg. The luminance of each plotted dot

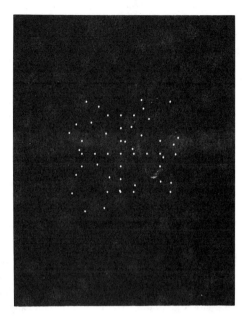

FIG. 6.1. Sample stimulus showing pattern 4 from Fig. 6.2 embedded
in 30 masking dots.

was about .1 candelas/m². Otherwise, the compartment in which the study was conducted was dark and soundproof.

The subject's head was constrained in a fixed viewing position by a chin rest, and a forehead switch. Unless this forehead switch contact was closed, two hand-held response switches were inactive, and no responses could be entered into the computer.

Stimuli were plotted using an intensification pulse with a duration of 8 μsec. to the z-axis input of the oscilloscope. However, the actual physical duration of each dot was determined more by the persistence of the P-15 phosphor of the oscilloscope cathode ray tube than by this electronic pulse. According to the manufacturer's specifications, the P-15 phosphor has a persistence such that the light output is reduced to .1 of 1% of its initial brightness after 50 μsec. The apparent persistence of this briefly illuminated spot, of course, is even further elongated by the properties of the observer's visual system. However, the total physical duration of each stimulus was defined by the number of masking and target dots involved and varied between 1 and 5 msec.

Procedure

The experimental procedure involved was a two-alternative, forced-choice paradigm in which the subject was required to specify (by depressing one or the other of the two hand-held switches) which of two sequentially presented stimuli (separated by 1.0 sec.) contained one of the target patterns as well as the randomly positioned dotted visual-masking dots common to both stimuli. The non-target stimulus contained, in addition to the common masking-dot pattern, a number of randomly placed dots equal to the number in the target pattern scattered over the same 3 deg. by 3 deg. region in which the target pattern was placed to equate overall brightness and dot numerosity.

Following the depression of either one of the response switches, the subject received information concerning the correctness or incorrectness of the choice by means of a plus or a minus sign plotted on the oscilloscope screen. This feedback signal, which lasted for .5 sec., also served as a fixation cue; there was no other fixation cue, other than the stimulus itself, present in the intertrial or interstimulus intervals. The depression of the response switch and the presentation of the feedback signal was automatically followed by the presentation of the two stimuli of the next trial. Pacing, therefore, was a function of the rate at which the subject responded.

All performance was measured as the percentage of the total number of presentations for which the target was correctly detected. A score of 50% represents chance performance in this two-alternative task. These data were accumulated for each subject and punched on a paper tape at the end of each session. At the end of the day, a secondary data-analysis program was used to summarize the results from all subjects. Because very large numbers of trials are pooled in each "percentage correct" score, the conventional tests of significance are not meaningful in the context of the present experiment. The large sample sizes and small intercondition variances, therefore, speak without the intervention of descriptive statistics to the conclusions drawn.

EXPERIMENT 1

Experiment 1 tested for symmetry effects by using a set of snowflake-like patterns that varied in radial, rather than spacing, symmetry. Samples of the target patterns used in this experiment are shown in Fig. 6.2. Other equivalent stimuli (same shape but with different orientation) brought the total number of patterns used in this experiment to 25, and the patterns were presented in random order each day. The masking-dot densities used were 50, 75, 100, 125, and 150. Each of these values was used on all 5 days in the ascending order indicated. The order was then reversed, and the masking densities were used in descending order for 5 additional days. Inasmuch as every stimulus type was presented approximately 150 times to each of three subjects during two sessions, every data point in Fig. 6.4 represents the results of approximately 900 trials. Where the data for all masking-dot densities were pooled, as in Fig. 6.5, each point represents 4500 trials.

1

2

3

4

5

6

FIG. 6.2. Samples of the patterns used in Experiment 1. Other patterns comparable in form, but oriented in different directions, were also used to make up a total of 25 different patterns.

7

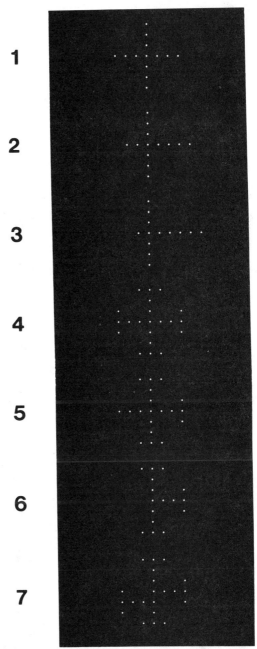

Experiment 2

As is seen later, the results of Experiment 1 did indicate a small but reliable dependence of detectability on the symmetry of the target patterns. Because of this positive outcome, slight though it was, it was decided to replicate the earlier experiment (Uttal, 1975, Experiment IX) in which symmetry of parallel-line spacing had been shown to have no effect. This was done with the set of stimuli shown in Fig. 6.3, but, in this case, the number of trials was also increased far beyond that used in the original experiment. By raising the number of sample

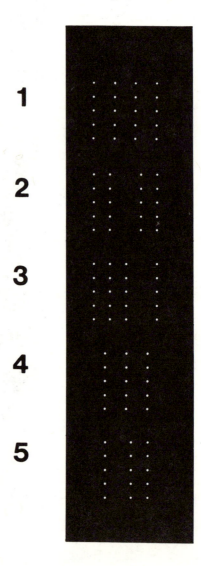

FIG. 6.3.   Samples of the patterns used in Experiment 2. Other patterns comparable in form, but oriented in different directions, were also used to make up a total of 14 different patterns.

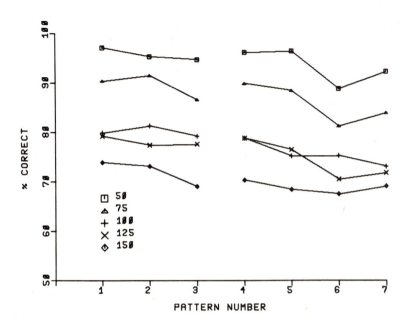

FIG. 6.4. The results of Experiment 1. The effects of symmetry for the two kinds of "snowflake patterns" (1–3 and 4–7) are relatively small, although there does appear to be a slight effect (see text). The family of curves is parametric with the number of masking dots.

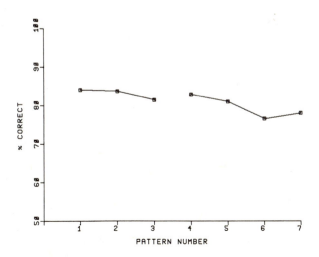

FIG. 6.5. The results of Experiment 1 with all data for all masking-dot densities pooled.

trials available to the data analysis, it was hoped that it would be possible to answer more definitively the question of whether or not there was a small symmetry effect that might have been obscured by the experimental design and sample size used in the original experiment.

In this experiment, masking-dot densities of 50, 75, 100, 125, and 150 were used. These densities were set at the beginning of each daily run and presented in this ascending order for 5 days, then in the reverse order for 5 more days. Inasmuch as every stimulus was presented approximately 75 times to each subject in each hourly session, and each of the three subjects ran in each condition for 2 days, approximately 450 trials have been pooled for every data point in Fig. 6.6. Further pooling of the data for all masking-dot densities resulted in Fig. 6.7 in which each point represents an approximate sample size of 2250 trials.

RESULTS

Experiment 1

The results of the first experiment, in which the effect of figural symmetry of the snowflake-like patterns was examined, are displayed in Fig. 6.4 for each masking-dot density. Once again, the major effect of altering the masking-dot density is observed: a progressive decline in detectability with increased density.

Figure 6.5 shows a summary average of all data pooled from all masking-dot densities for both groups.

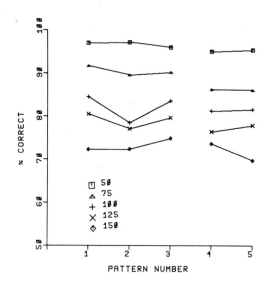

FIG. 6.6. The results of Experiment 2. Little effect on detectability of parallel line spacing occurs at any level of masking-dot density. The family of curves is parametric with the number of masking dots.

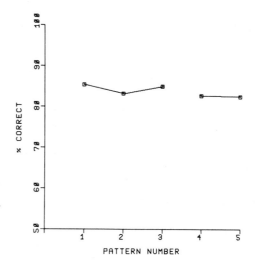

FIG. 6.7. The results of Experiment 2 with all data for all masking-dot densities pooled. For groups of four parallel lines (1–3) and three parallel lines (4–5), there is virtually no effect of spacing symmetry.

Within the confines of this more general effect, however, secondary effects of form are small. The results for the two different kinds of stimuli, those numbered 1–3 and those numbered 4–7 in Fig. 6.2, should be considered separately.

The first group (1–3) consisted of three different kinds of simple crosses. Symmetry was varied in this case by displacing one of the arms of the cross either one or two dot separations from the center. The effect of this increasing assymetry is quite small in comparison with the effects of other dimensions reported in the earlier work (Uttal, 1975). In the same figure, the second group of stimuli (4–7)—made up of the more elaborate multiarmed crosses—also displays a slight sensitivity to the symmetry of the target forms. The complete and symmetrical cross of pattern 4 is more detectable than the asymmetrical cross of pattern 7. Deleting one of the secondary cross members (pattern 5) reduces detectability very slightly, whereas deleting a major cross member (pattern 6) produces a more substantial effect. However, both patterns 5 and 6 also have fewer dots, and thus comparing them with patterns 4 and 7 is confounded. The results of this experiment, we have concluded, exhibit only a weak symmetry effect in terms of the relative performance levels of patterns 1, 2, and 3 and patterns 4 and 7, respectively.

Experiment 2

The results of the second experiment, in which an expanded attempt was made to detect any symmetry effect for groups of parallel lines, is shown in Fig. 6.6 for the five masking-dot densities used. Once again, there is clear evidence of the general effect of masking-dot density, but the more or less flat shape of the family of curves for the two stimulus conditions 1–3 (the four parallel lines) and

4–5 (the three parallel lines) suggests that the effect of spacing symmetry of this sort is very weak, if present at all. The grand average of these data, shown in Fig. 6.7, strengthens this conclusion. Symmetry of straight-line spacing, whatever role it may play in other kinds of form perception, plays little or no role in dotted line detection. Patterns 1 and 3, the two patterns differing most in symmetry, do not differ at all in detectability.

In sum, the results of both Experiments 1 and 2 indicate that symmetry plays only a small role, at best, in the detection of dot patterns as compared to many of the robust results reported in Uttal (1975). Indeed, the only difference that was at all notable—the relative performance levels of patterns 4 and 7 in Experiment 1—may be accounted for in terms of the degradation of the straight-line components of the pattern. This factor has long been known (Uttal, 1969) to be a strong determinant of the detectability of patterns in a dotted mask.

DISCUSSION

The results of these two experiments add further support to the observation that target symmetry is not a strong determinant of the detectability of a dotted form in a field of random masking dots, even though symmetry does play a significant role in tasks involving memorial processes. Many other factors of the organization of a dotted form have been shown to be effective in determining detectability, including some general organizational factors and some that are better described as the microstructure of individual segments of a curve (see Uttal, 1975).

Though it is not fully possible to explain the reasons for the differences in the effect of symmetry on performance with the two tasks at this time, these findings do make it clear that the tasks of recognition and reconstruction, on the one hand, and detection, on the other, do exhibit quite different sensitivities to this stimulus dimension. That much is an empirical fact. Therefore, we may further speculate that the two tasks assay essentially distinct psychological processes, one of which is sensitive to symmetry, whereas the other is not.

If it is the case that the two tasks assay relatively distinct and, at least, partially independent psychological processes, what difference in the properties of the two mechanisms could account for this perplexing discrepancy in performance? A preliminary answer to this question may lie in the fact that the recognition and reconstruction processes involve storage of the pattern information, whereas the detection task does not. Information storage may not be mediated by an isomorphic form of representation. That is, the long-term memorial storage of stimuli that are to be recognized or reconstructed at some later time may be based on certain symbolic properties or intrastimulus relationships that transcend the actual geometric attributes of the stimulus pattern. In this context, symmetry may be an important attribute in the specification of the symbolic representation by which the image will be stored.

In the detection task, on the other hand, the process is much more immediate and depends on first-order geometric properties, such as the linearity or periodicity of the dots that make up the stimuli, as well as certain organizational properties of the lines of dots that make up the stimuli. In this context, isomorphic representation of the stimulus is critical. The information contained in the stimulus pattern, therefore, may be dealt with in a detection task in a far more direct and immediate manner than one in which intermediate memorization is required. More general factors, such as that one we have called symmetry, may not be needed or might be unavailable to the processing mechanism at the detection level that is so heavily dependent on the actual geometry of the stimulus. In this context, the attribute of symmetry would significantly differ from more primitive factors, such as straightness. Symmetry may be a higher order attribute that can be usefully utilized only at later and more complex stages of processing of the visual information.

Although this interpretation is merely speculative, the important conclusion to which we are led by these data is that the empirical discrepancy between the results obtained with the two tasks strongly supports the perspective that pattern perception is a complex of several subskills and that these subskills can be assayed by different psychophysical procedures. Such a conclusion makes non-sensical any question of the generic form—*What is the effect of variation of dimension X on pattern perception?*—unless the particular stage of pattern perception that is being assayed is also specified.

ACKNOWLEDGMENTS

This research was supported by a research grant from the National Institute of Mental Health (1 R01 MH24016) and by an NIMH Research Scientist Award (5 KO5 MH29941–03) to the first author.

REFERENCES

Adams, O. S., Fitts, P. M., Rappaport, M., & Weinstein, M. Relations among some measures of pattern discriminability. *Journal of Experimental Psychology,* 1954, *48,* 81–88.

Attneave, F. Symmetry, information, and memory for patterns. *American Journal of Psychology,* 1955, *68,* 209–22.

Schnore, M. M., & Partington, J. T. Immediate memory for visual patterns: Symmetry and amount of information. *Psychonomic Science,* 1967, *8,* 421–422.

Uttal, W. R. Masking of alphabetic character recognition by dynamic visual noise (DVN). *Perception & Psychophysics,* 1969, *6,* 121–128.

Uttal, W. R. *An autocorrelation theory of form detection.* Hillsdale, N.J.: Lawrence Erlbaum Associates, 1975.

7

A Psychophysical Approach to Dimensional Integrality

Robert G. Pachella
Patricia Somers
Mary Hardzinski

The purpose of this chapter is to define dimensional integrality and to present a theory of integrality that explains the manner and conditions under which integrality operates. The term integrality, like many pieces of contemporary psychological jargon, has both intuitive and technical meanings. Intuitively, integrality refers to the phenomenological coherence of stimulation. That is, it refers to the degree to which several aspects of complex stimulation are perceivable as a unitary entity. The opposite of integrality, separability, refers to the extent to which each of several aspects of complex stimulation can be independently perceived. As such, integrality, or something like it, represents a core problem within several broad areas of perceptual research such as form perception, pattern recognition, selective attention, information processing, and multidimensional scaling. Furthermore, the issues raised about integrality from within these areas vary widely in their generality. Thus, integrality concerns issues as broad and as fundamental as the definition of the stimulus and as esoteric as the appropriate scaling metric for describing similarity judgments. Consequently, the problems of integrality can be addressed from many different perspectives and discussed in different levels of discourse.

With regard to technical meanings, the multifaceted nature of integrality makes its definition a complicated matter because different areas of research have specified different operations and phenomena as essential for its understanding. For example, Gestalt psychology attempted to discover directly and introspectively those aspects of stimulation that were most closely associated with phenomenal unity. In contrast, modern information-processing research, relying on behavioral or performance-based data, has focused on the processes within the organism that are responsible for the ability to attend to various aspects of stimulation selectively. This particular difference in perspective represents one of the primary questions with regard to the study of integrality: Is integrality a property of stimulation, or is it a function of processes within the organism? Undoubtedly, both factors will need to be incorporated into some ultimate definition of integrality. However, as research strategies, these two questions are not equally propitious. Stimulation is directly observable and can be objectively defined. Processes within the organism can only be studied indirectly through chains of inference. Furthermore, in the face of finite behavioral data bases, mental processes can never be uniquely defined. Therefore, as a research strategy, the present work starts with an objective examination of stimulation with the goal of taking this approach as far as it can go. Mental events can then be hypothesized to account for any residual phenomena that still need to be explained.

The theory of integrality to be discussed below has a purely psychophysical base. Integrality is defined as a property of the mapping of a *physical* specification of complex stimulation into the multidimensional *psychological* characteristics of the stimulation as perceived. This psychophysical mapping serves as the criterion for deciding whether or not the stimulation in a given situation can be termed integral. This definition of integrality is then validated against data obtained from standard information-processing tasks involving speeded classification.

This account of integrality is incomplete in at least two ways. First, only one of several psychophysical properties is explored, and other potentially important, but untested, properties are suggested in the concluding section. Thus, the research to be reported is only a first step in what will have to be a broader program of inquiry. Second, it is clear that certain aspects of performance need explanations that have to go beyond a simple psychophysical theory. These are also noted in the concluding section. Nevertheless, the present theoretical framework indicates the direction that additional research will need to take.

HISTORICAL PRECEDENTS

Gestalt psychology is, of course, well-known for its account of the phenomenological unity of figures in the perceptual field. With regard to the concepts to be developed below, two aspects of the Gestalt approach are of particular importance. First, the Gestalt laws represent an attempt to arrive at a phenomenologically based description of the experience of stimulation. That is, each Gestalt law describes some aspect of experience that tends to be perceived as a unitary whole (i.e., as Gestalten). It is important to note that these laws (Figure-Ground, Closure, Prägnanz, etc.) do not constitute explanations of phenomena, but rather are merely descriptions. The Gestalters' physiological model, now rarely discussed, and their beliefs about physical Gestalten (e.g., the tendency toward equilibrium of forces in physical fields) were the explanations for perceived experience. Nevertheless, these descriptions of experience emphasize that figural coherence is the result of the overall organization of the perceptual field and the complex relations among its perceivable components.

Second, Gestalt psychology placed a great emphasis on the primacy of perceptual attributes. Theories of perception should *begin* with phenomenological accounts. To begin accounts of perception with arbitrary physical descriptions of stimulation, as many of the early Structualists did, was thought to be a mistake. Physical descriptions of stimulation should only follow once the important attributes of experience had been identified. One could conceive of many different physical specifications of stimulation, but the only one that mattered was the one that corresponded to the psychological Gestalten. Of course, the psychological Gestalten were thought to be isomorphic to the underlying physiological Gestalten, and these in turn were thought to correspond to physical laws of organization. Thus, because of these isomorphisms, these levels of discourse are sometimes confused. However, within the Gestalt system phenomenology was primary.

This tradition from Gestalt psychology was further developed by Gibson (1960, 1966), and the research described below is an obvious application of Gibsonian principles. Central to Gibson's approach is the notion of perceptual psychophysics: Once a particular perceptual phenomenon has been identified (e.g., monocular depth perception), the study of perception should proceed by finding the physical description of the stimulation that directly corresponds to, or is perfectly correlated with, the phenomenon (e.g., texture gradients). In many cases this description of physical stimulation may be very complex, entailing higher ordered or temporal relations among the simple physical variables. However, the goal of perceptual research is the direct specification of this psychophysical mapping.

Strategies of this type have often been pursued in perceptual research. For example, in the area of speech perception there has been a long search to find those characteristics of the physical speech signal that are correlated with the units of perceived speech, the phonemes. Phonemes have certain invariant perceptual characteristics that do not correspond in a simple way to any low-level physical measures of speech. Thus, the search has been to find that combination or transformation of the simple physical characteristics of speech that will correlate reasonably with the stimulation as it is perceived. Similarly, the research discussed below examines transformations of the physical measures that underlie particular classes of geometric patterns in an attempt to find those transformations that correspond to the perceived characteristics of the forms.

Multidimensional scaling is a third area of research that is antecedent to the present one. The distinction between integral and separable stimulus dimensions came into prominence with the realization that the psychological distances between pairs of stimuli in a multidimensional space are not necessarily Euclidean.

When subjects are asked to judge the similarity of pairs of multidimensional stimuli, their judgments will depend not only on the physically defined differences between the stimuli, but also on the rule or metric that is used to combine the differences on the several dimensions of the stimuli. Torgerson (1958) suggested that when the several dimensions of a stimulus pair are not obvious (that is, when the dimensions are integral), the Euclidean metric is the appropriate combination rule. This makes intuitive sense because distance in Euclidean space remains invariant with rotations of the axes of the space; each pair of stimuli thus defines an attribute through the space. For example, the color space invariably has been found to be Euclidean. Each pair of colors, when judged for similarity, seems to define a unique difference between them. In contrast, when the differences among the stimuli are obvious and compelling (that is, when the dimensions are separable), the city-block metric seems more appropriate. Distance in a city-block space is simply the sum of the distances on each of the "obvious and compelling" dimensions. Thus, in arriving at a judgment, the subject simply notes the difference on each separable dimension and aggregates them linearly.

This idea of assigning different metrics to integral and separable stimulus dimensions is an important one because it suggests that a multidimensional psychophysical property can be used to define integrality. This suggestion is consistent with the concepts developed later, although the present research argues that the scaling metric itself is not an adequate criterion.

Previous research in multidimensional scaling has also motivated the present project in another, more fundamental way. Multidimensional scaling depends heavily on subjects making direct subjective estimations of the similarity between pairs of perceived objects. Similarity judgments thus represent a mode of responding in which subjects can directly code a particular property of their perceptual experiences. As Shepard and Chipman (1970) have noted:

> It is a fact of inadequately appreciated significance that, despite the practically unlimited range and diversity of possible internal representations, we can readily assess within ourselves the degree of functional relation between any two by a simple, direct judgment of subjective similarity. Moreover, we can do this even though (a) we have never before compared the two representations in question, and even though (b) we may be unable to communicate anything about the absolute nature of either of the two representations taken separately.... One could even turn the matter around and argue that it is primitive, internal assessments of similarity of this sort ... that mediate every response we make to any situation that is not exactly identical to one confronted before [p. 2].

The psychophysical theory presented below takes as axiomatic this ability of subjects to estimate the similarity of pairs of stimuli directly. As a psychophysical theory, the description of a psychological space is essential. Consequently, the theory must contain some aspect of subjectivism. However, not only is the subjective component completely identifiable, it is also limited to this primitive ability to assess similarity. Furthermore, whereas the Gestalt approach had to rely on a belief in a first-order isomorphism between properties of stimulation and properties of perceived experience, similarity judgments entail only the notion of second-order isomorphism (Shepard & Chipman, 1970). That is, it is not necessary that object properties themselves be preserved isomorphically in the internal representation of experience, but only that the *relations* among the object properties be isomorphically preserved. Thus, it is not necessary to discuss the nature of a given experience itself, rather only the relation of that experience to other experiences, and it is these relations that are directly designated with similarity judgments.

Garner's Converging Operations

The first attempt to produce a systematic theory about the nature and operation of integrality was made by Garner (summarized in Garner, 1974). Garner's approach entails the use of converging operations and their associated phenomena as the definition of integrality. Three of these converging operations are of particular importance. First, for the reasons previously outlined, integral dimensions should be best fit by the Euclidean metric when used in similarity scaling. Second, when used in speeded classification or choice reaction time tasks, integral dimensions should produce interference when filtering of one dimension from another is required. For example, if a subject is asked to sort a set of stimuli as fast as possible, where one of two integral dimensions is relevant to the sorting and the other is irrelevant, the inability to separate the dimensions should lead to slower reaction times. By inference, information processing should be slowed. Third, if a subject is asked to sort a set of stimuli composed of integral dimensions, again as quickly as possible, and the values of the stimuli are correlated across stimuli (that is, if the two dimensions are redundant), reaction time should be facilitated.

A set of stimulus dimensions that produce these three results in these converging tasks would be termed integral. Conversely, a set of dimensions that would be better fit by the city-block metric, that would yield no filtering interference and no gain as a result of redundancy, would be defined as separable. Again, there is by inference the linkage of these results to the subject's internal information-processing mechanisms: Separable dimensions should not tax the organism's attentive capacity, and information processing should not slow down or speed up in the presence of irrelevant or redundant information, respectively.

There are two sets of problems that arise with regard to this definition. These problems are for the most part more pragmatic than theoretical, but nevertheless they severely limit the usefulness of the definition. First, there is a set of essentially statistical problems associated with determining the appropriate dimensionality and scaling metric for similarity data. Contemporary scaling techniques utilize computer algorithms that require the experimenter to set a priori the value of the number of dimensions and the scaling metric to be fit to the data. The experimenter then runs the data through the program a number of times, each with a different combination of dimensionality and metric. On each run a measure of goodness of fit, usually referred to as stress, is computed. By comparing these stress values, the experimenter supposedly can determine the appropriate parameters for the data. The problem in this, however, is that stress is a monotonic decreasing function of the number of dimensions used to fit the data. Therefore, the experimenter cannot simply look for the minimum stress value. Rather, the function relating stress to the number of dimensions must be examined with the hope that an unambiguous breaking point or "elbow" can be determined. The number of dimensions associated with this elbow is taken to be the dimensionality of the perceptual space for the stimuli in question. The stress value for each metric for this number of dimensions can then be compared, with the better fitting metric chosen as the appropriate one.

Three difficulties, however, can render this solution uninterpretable: There may be no obvious elbow; the elbows for each of the metrics may occur at different dimensionalities; and there are no reasonable statistics that assess how big a difference in stress values is reasonable. Often more than one of these problems exist for the same set of similarity judgments. Consider the data presented in Fig. 7.1. These data, from Hardzinski and Pachella (1977), are based on similarity judgments for 32 simple ellipses that varied in their size and shape and in their spatial position and orientation on the viewing screen. All 496 pairs of the 32 stimuli were judged for similarity, and these judgments were analyzed with the scaling program MINISSA (Guttman, 1968; Roskam & Lingoes, 1970). It is clear from Fig. 7.1 that neither curve has a sharp elbow. Further, even though the Euclidean metric yields a better fit for each value of dimensionality, the difference between the curves is not impressive. Thus, it is not obvious whether the differences for these stimuli should be called integral or separable. Even more to the point, the scaling configuration of the stimulus points in their respective spaces (i.e., Euclidean vs. city block) and their interpoint distances did not differ much. Effectively, the scaling solutions were identical. Hardzinski and Pachella (1977) worked with numerous types of stimulus forms (ellipses, irregular polygons, schematic faces, etc.) and found the situation described here to be the rule rather than the exception. Thus, the determination of the appropriate scaling metric is often the result of an entirely subjective judgment on the part of the experimenter.

A second problem with the converging-operation definition of integrality is the fact that when the operations used to define the concept do not converge, the result is a proliferation of theoretical terms, each corresponding to a different pattern of results. That is, the multiple-operation definition of integrality, with integral dimensions defined by one combination of results and separable dimensions defined by another combination, leaves open the possibility of various

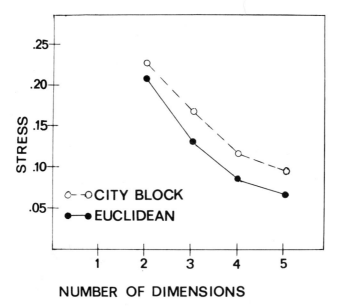

FIG. 7.1. Stress values for multidimensional scaling configurations of similarity judgments of pairs of ellipses differing on five dimensions, as a function of number of dimensions fit for both Euclidean and city-block metrics.

intermediate results that are at best difficult to interpret. For example, at least one example exists of phenomenally integral dimensions that are best described by the city-block metric. In another case, Garner and Felfoldy (1970) found that dimensions that should be compellingly Euclidean (vertical and horizontal position in the Euclidean plane) yielded the expected facilitation of reaction time when the dimensions were redundantly varied across stimuli but surprisingly little interference when filtering was needed to perform a speeded classification task. Such intermediate results have led to a burgeoning taxonomy of integrality types that include "configural dimensions" (Pomerantz & Garner, 1973) and "asymmetric integral dimensions" (Pomerantz & Sager, 1975). This taxonomy thus serves simply to label the different combinations of results without specifying their logical or perceptual relationships.

THE PSYCHOPHYSICS OF INTEGRALITY

The proliferation of types of integrality might lead one to question the unitary nature of integrality as a theoretical concept. An alternative approach to the problem, however, can point out the source of this difficulty. The goal of much previous research has been to discover the property of physical dimensions that leads to their being integral or not. Alternatively, however, attribute perception might be assumed to be invariant. That is, a theoretical account might begin with the assumption that any set of stimuli is definable by an independently identifiable (i.e., separable) set of psychological attributes. What may vary instead is the way in which the experimenter has defined the physical dimensions whose integrality is being investigated. Integrality may, thus, be simply the result of an inappropriate specification of stimulation.

This alternative account of integrality begins with the observation that there are any number of potential physical descriptions of a stimulus. Consider, for example, the physical specification of a simple triangle. A particular triangle can unambiguously be specified by the lengths of its three sides. Alternatively, it can be specified by the lengths of two sides and one of its angles; by two of its angles and one side; or, by its area and the length of two sides; etc. These physical descriptions, although equivalent as physical specifications, will not be equivalent perceptually. Suppose, for example, that the salient and compelling attributes of a triangle are its elongation, its size, and its tilt. That is, when an observer perceives a triangle, suppose that the most compelling psychological attributes are how long it is, its area, and its obtuseness (or acuteness). The physical description that would be most relevant perceptually, then, would be that description consisting of physical variables that correlate with these salient features. These physical variables would be "separable" in that changing the value of each would be seen by the observer to change the value of one of the salient attributes.

In contrast, a physical description that would not correspond to these salient attributes would consist of variables that would cut across the perceivable attributes. Consequently, the manipulation of one of the physical variables would be seen by the observer as causing variation in more than one of the perceptual features. Physical variables that would cause variation in the same perceptual attributes would thus be confusable and would be seen to be "integral."

Salience and Emergence

One consequence of this lack of correspondence between the physical and psychological descriptions is the apparent emergent property of the psychological attributes. If an experimenter focuses arbitrarily on a particular physical description that does not correspond to the psychological attributes, the perceivable attributes will vary as a complex function of the physical variables. Because the value of each will covary with several different physical variables, the psychological attributes will be seen by the experimenter as being relatively independent of each of the physical variables. Thus, they will seem to the experimenter to "emerge" from the physical variables.

This emergence will also prove difficult for the subject of an experiment. If the subject is called upon to attend to one of the noncorresponding physical variables, the covariation of the psychological attributes with the irrelevant physical variables will be confusing. In addition, because of the salience of the psychological attributes, the subject will simply be distracted by their variation (see Egeth & Pachella, 1969). In either case, the subject's judgments of the relevant variable will be affected either directly by variation in the irrelevant physical variables, or the effect of these variables on the psychological attributes, or both.

Somers and Pachella (1977) examined these effects of salient, apparently emergent attributes on the perception of simple physical variables in complex stimuli. In this experiment, observers were asked to rate the degree of similarity of pairs of stimuli with regard to particular selected features. Other features of the stimuli were either held constant (control condition) or varied systematically (experimental condition). The use of similarity judgments, without any stress on speed or difficulty in viewing, allowed the measurement of the perceptual distortion of the relevant features due to variation of the irrelevant variables. If the observers could ignore the variation of the irrelevant features, the perceived similarities of the stimuli in the experimental and control conditions would be identical. However, if such selective attention was impossible, if the dimensions were integral, the influence of the irrelevant dimension would be revealed in the pattern of the similarity judgments.

In this experiment, the subject was asked to rate the similarity of schematic faces (see Fig. 7.2) with regard to the shape of the facial outline. In the experimental condition facial expression varied, but the subject was instructed to ignore

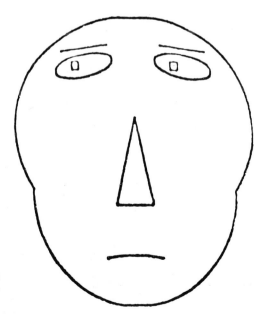

FIG. 7.2. An example of the schematic faces used as stimuli by Somers and Pachella (1977).

it. Figures 7.3 and 7.4 present typical data for one observer. The numbers in Figs. 7.3 and 7.4 are labels for the individual schematic faces that were used in the experiment. The figures summarize the similarity ratings for pairs of faces by representing similarity as interpoint distances. Consequently, faces that were judged to be similar (e.g., faces 12 and 16 in Fig. 7.3) will be close to each other, whereas faces judged to be dissimilar will be far apart (e.g., faces 4 and 9 in Fig. 7.3). Figure 7.3 presents the control condition, in which facial expression was not varied within a block. Figure 7.4 presents the experimental condition. The faces whose numbers are circled were given one facial expression, whereas those represented by uncircled numbers were given a different expression. Note again that the subject was asked simply to judge the similarity of the shapes of the faces in both conditions.

A comparison of Figs. 7.3 and 7.4 shows that varying facial expression had large and systematic effects on the judged similarity of shape for this observer. In Fig. 7.4, faces with common expressions are grouped together. The average similarity for pairs within the groups is far greater than the average similarity of pairs from different groups. The observer was simply unable to ignore the facial expression, and his rated similarity of facial shape was influenced by this irrelevant information. For example, faces 6 and 10 have quite similar shapes, as shown by their proximity in the control condition. In the experimental condition, where they vary in expression, their shapes are perceived to be much less similar. Thus, although there is a degree of identifiability to the separate features for stimuli such as these schematic faces, such attributes can be shown to be integral.

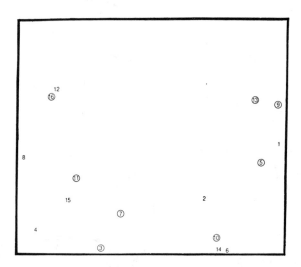

FIG. 7.3. Multidimensional scaling configuration of judged similarity of facial shapes when facial expression was held constant within a block of trials.

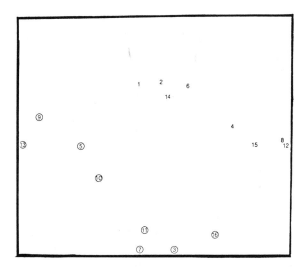

FIG. 7.4. Multidimensional scaling configuration of judged similarity of facial shapes when facial expression varied irrelevantly.

Furthermore, the degree of integrality can be measured directly from Figs. 7.3 and 7.4. This is done by computing the ratio of the average interpoint distance between faces with similar expressions to the average interpoint distance between faces with different expressions in the experimental condition. The ratio of the analogous distances in the control condition serves as a baseline because the outline shapes are identical to those in the experimental condition, but facial expression does not vary. Comparing the ratios for the two conditions yields a continuous quantitative scale of integrality. Thus, facial expression, which is a complex emergent property of the simple features of the face, is a prepotent attribute in determining the appearance of any of the constituent features of the face, such as its outline shape.

Interdimensional Additivity

The theory of integrality that is being suggested here is based on the fact that the dimensions that an experimenter varies independently in a set of stimuli are not necessarily perceived to be independent by an observer. An observer will perceive a stimulus from a given stimulus domain as varying along a set of independent psychological dimensions appropriate for that domain, but these attributes are not necessarily varied independently in the specific subset of stimuli presented. *Perceived attributes* must be independent, or separable, by virtue of their definition as attributes. If perceived differences along an attribute vary with the value of another attribute, they will have little value for the consistent perception of similarity. This concept is formalized in the axioms of the geometric models of similarity underlying multidimensional scaling. These axioms, stated by Tversky and Krantz (1970) and Krantz and Tversky (1975), include interdimensional additivity, which states that the perception of similarity among multidimensional stimuli is an additive combination of their similarity along each of their component dimensions.

To clarify the concept of interdimensional additivity, consider Fig. 7.5a. This is a spatial representation of the physical differences among stimuli varied on two orthogonal dimensions such that the more different two stimuli are, the farther

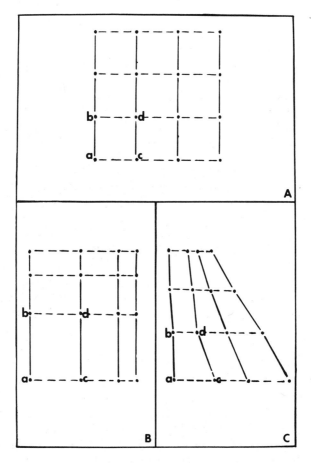

FIG. 7.5.   *A*. Spatial representation of physical differences among stimuli varying on two physically orthogonal dimensions. *B*. Spatial representation of perceived similarity among stimuli of *A* when the physically orthogonal dimensions are perceptually orthogonal. *C*. Spatial representation of perceived similarity among stimuli of *A* when the physically orthogonal dimensions perceptually interact.

apart they lie in the space. The intersections of the lines are the stimuli. Solid lines connect stimuli with equal values on one dimension. Dashed lines connect stimuli with equal values on the second dimension. By definition, the dimensions that are physically orthogonal appear as right angles in the space, and the configuration is rectangular. If a spatial representation of the *similarity judgments* of these stimuli were also rectangular, the two physically orthogonal dimensions would be said to be psychologically additive. Figure 7.5b displays such a spatial representation. In this figure, distance in the space corresponds to psychological dissimilarity, not to physical differences. Again, solid and dashed lines indicate the physically orthogonal stimulus dimensions. They are also psychologically orthogonal. Inasmuch as the physically orthogonal stimulus dimensions correspond to psychologically orthogonal dimensions, the stimulus dimensions would be termed separable. Note that the spacing along each psychological dimension does not correspond to the physical intervals. The values on both of the two dimensions are not equally spaced perceptually, nor are the intervals along one dimension equal to those along the other. This is irrelevant to the question of the interaction between dimensions. The rectangularity of Fig. 7.5b captures the property of interdimensional additivity (Krantz & Tversky, 1975; Tversky & Krantz, 1970) with regard to physically orthogonal dimensions: The dissimilarity between two stimuli is monotonically related to the sum of terms representing the distance between the stimuli on each dimension.

Figure 7.5c displays an alternative spatial representation of dissimilarity judgments of the stimuli of Fig. 7.5a. Solid and dashed lines again represent physically orthogonal dimensions, but here they psychologically interact. There is a systematic departure from rectangularity in this spatial representation of dissimilarity judgments: Equal physical differences along the horizontal dimension are psychologically diminished as the second dimension increases. When physically orthogonal dimensions psychologically interact, as these do, the stimulus dimensions would be termed integral. Another piece of evidence for a violation of interdimensional additivity in this configuration is the consistent inequality of similarities for stimulus pairs that are related diagonally and are therefore physically equal. For example, the physical difference between stimuli labeled b and c in Fig. 7.5 is equivalent to that between a and d, as can be seen in Fig. 7.5a. The effect of the psychological interaction in Fig. 7.5c is to make the pair (b, c) appear more dissimilar than the pair (a, d).

Figure 7.6 presents an even more concrete example of interdimensional additivity. These triangles are constructed from a common base, that is, the length and orientation of the base has been held constant. Therefore, there are only two degrees of freedom of the physical variation among the set of stimuli, so that any particular stimulus can be uniquely specified by a minimum set of two physical parameters. With regard to interdimensional additivity, the goal is to find the physical parameters of the most perceptually salient attributes of the patterns. Let us consider height and length of right side. The four triangles in Fig.

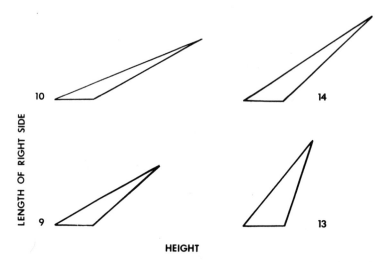

FIG. 7.6.   A set of four triangles constructed from a common base length. The triangles in each row have equal values for the length of their right sides, and the triangles in each column have equal heights.

7.6 were chosen as orthogonal exemplars of these dimensions. That is, the triangles in each row have equal values for the length of their right sides, and the triangles in each column have equal heights. However, as perceptual variables the differences in these variables do not look independent. In fact, we have asked observers to judge the similarity of the pairs on the diagonal—on the one hand the pair 10 and 13, and on the other hand the pair 9 and 14. Invariably, observers state that the pair 9 and 14 looks more similar than pair 10 and 13. Note, however, that in terms of the *physical differences* these two pairs are equally different. It is this lack of correspondence between physical and psychological variables that we have termed integrality because it is clear that the overall similarity of the figures is an interactive function of height and length of right side. Thus, these variables cannot be separated easily by the observer.

   In an effort to discover a set of dimensions corresponding more closely to the psychological attributes for this pattern type, we developed a larger set of triangles. Four values of height and four values of the length of the right side were orthogonally combined to create a set of 16 patterns. Observers were asked to make similarity ratings for each of the possible pairs of triangles within the set. These ratings were then mathematically transformed into a "map" of the psychological distances between the patterns. Figure 7.7 shows the typical data of one subject. The solid lines connect triangles that differ from each other only in terms of height (they are equal in length of side). If there had been a high correspondence between these physical dimensions and the perceivable attributes of the figures, this figure would have been rectangular. This was not the case:

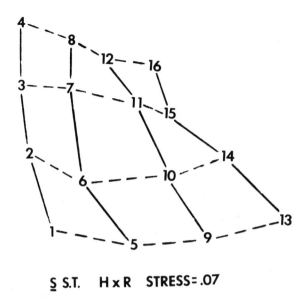

S S.T.   H x R   STRESS= .07

FIG. 7.7.   Multidimensional scaling configuration of perceived similarities between pairs of triangles for observer S.T. The solid lines connect triangles differeing only in height (H). The dashed lines connect triangles differeing only in length
of right side (R).

The pattern of perceived similarities differed markedly from that expected if
judgments were based on the orthogonal dimensions.

This fact can be used to construct sets of displays that will be high in
psychophysical compatibility. For example, we constructed a set of 16 triangles
that differed from each other orthogonally in terms of a topological transformation of height and length of the right side on the one hand, and in terms of interior
obtuse angle (with a slight correction for length of right side) on the other. The
data in Fig. 7.8 show the psychological "map" of the interpoint similarities for
the same observer whose data were shown in Fig. 7.7. Again, the solid lines
connect triangles that differ from each other only in terms of the product of height
and side. The dotted lines connect points that differ only in terms of angle. It is
clear that this manipulation has removed the interaction that was present in Fig.
7.7. That is, the plot is far more rectangular. This plot satisfies a condition of
multidimensional scaling termed interdimensional additivity. In fact, the unsys-
tematic deviations from perfect rectilinearity are not significant for this observer.

To summarize, the method that we have developed for isolating the perceived
attributes of a stimulus is based on the analysis of the perceived similarities
between stimuli varying on two dimensions. Two psychological dimensions are
independent if they satisfy the criterion of interdimensional additivity, that is, if

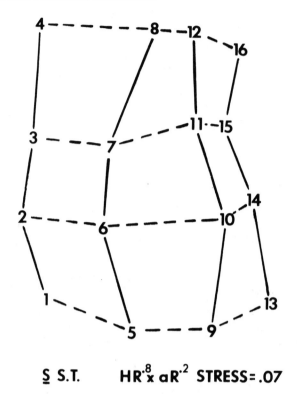

$\underline{S}$ S.T.   HR$^{.8}$x aR$^{.2}$ STRESS=.07

FIG. 7.8.   Multidimensional scaling configuration of perceived similarities between pairs of triangles for observer S.T. The triangles are topological transformations of the stimulus set of Fig. 7.7.

differences along each dimension are independent of the level of the other dimension as in Fig. 7.8. If two display dimensions are varied orthogonally and yield similarity judgments satisfying interdimensional additivity, then the physical dimensions correspond to the psychological dimensions; the dimensions are separable. If the orthogonal physical dimensions do not yield similarity judgments satisfying interdimensional additivity, the form of the interaction can be used to derive a new set of stimulus dimensions that will correspond more closely to perceived attributes.

Psychophysical Compatibility and Performance Measures

The present theory has defined dimensional integrality as a property of the mapping of the multidimensional physical specification of a stimulus set into the perceivable psychological attributes of the stimuli. This property of the multidimensional psychophysical mapping, which involves the correspondence between the physical dimensions and psychological attributes, is an important enough theoretical concept to require a label—*psychophysical compatibility*. When the correspondence is high, the mapping will be psychophysically compatible, and the dimensions will be separable. When the correspondence is low, the mapping will be incompatible, and the dimensions will be integral. The use of the term "compatibility" has been chosen specifically because of its linkage to the classic information-processing and reaction-time literature (see Fitts & Posner, 1967). Psychophysical compatibility provides a straightforward account of the interference and facilitation obtainable in reaction-time experiments as a result of the integrality of the dimension types. It should be noted, however, that the present approach, in contrast to Garner's operational approach described earlier, makes these patterns of results from speeded information-reduction tasks a prediction rather than a definition. That is, the present approach explains *how* integrality *leads to* filtering decrements and redundancy gains in performance instead of taking these results as part of the definition of integrality.

Information-reduction tasks (see Posner, 1964) have classically been defined relative to the arbitrary physical dimensions that an experimenter has chosen to vary in an experiment. However, the type of information required of an observer—filtering or condensing—should be defined with regard to the *perceived* attributes of a set of stimuli. Filtering one perceived attribute from another will be easy because perceived attributes are by definition independent. If dimensions are psychophysically incompatible, however, filtering on the basis of the physical dimensions requires condensing perceived attributes because the value of a stimulus on a physical dimension is perceived as a combination of values of those attributes. Thus, only with perfect psychophysical compatibility will the instruction to filter display dimensions be equivalent to filtering the perceived attributes of the stimulus. Redefining integrality as psychophysical incompatibility, then, indicates the basis for finding that integral dimensions are difficult to filter but easy to condense. Similarly, the theory also predicts that the ease of condensing will depend on the degree to which the condensing rule matches the function relating physical to psychological dimensions.

To test these notions, the triangles that were scaled for the observer whose data were shown in Fig. 7.7 and 7.8 were used in a series of information-processing experiments where his reaction time for various tasks was measured. He was asked to classify these stimuli, from either the compatible set (i.e., those of Fig. 7.8) or from the incompatible set (i.e., those of Fig. 7.7) in various ways. In the unidimensional condition, he was presented with subsets of the stimuli to classify, which only varied with regard to one of the dimensions. In the orthogonal condition, he was asked to classify subsets of the stimuli that varied on both of the dimensions, but his judgments were to be based on only one of the dimensions. In other words, he was asked to filter the relevant dimension from the irrelevant dimension. In the third condition, he was presented with subsets of the stimuli in which the two dimensions of the stimuli were correlated (either negatively or positively) with each other. In these conditions the dimensions are redundant with each other, and the extent to which the observer can utilize this redundancy can be taken as an index of how well the dimensions can be condensed. Again, note that the subject of this experiment is the same as the one for whom the psychophysical compatibility was determined in Fig. 7.7 and 7.8.

The basic result of the experiment is shown in Fig. 7.9. On the left are the data for the psychophysically compatible dimensions (i.e., the noninteracting set). On the right are the data from the psychophysically incompatible dimensions (i.e., the interacting set). The control condition is the unidimensional condition, where there was only one aspect of the stimuli to classify. In each graph the reaction time for this control condition is indicated by the dashed line. Reaction times longer than this value represent decrements in performance; reaction times shorter than this value demonstrate improved performance. For the compatible set of stimuli, neither the orthogonal nor the correlated (i.e., the redundant) conditions differed significantly from the control. However, for the psychophysically incompatible set of stimuli, there was a large decrement in performance for the orthogonal condition and a large gain in performance for the correlated conditions. In other words, the subject found it difficult to filter the relevant from the irrelevant information but was able to make use of the redundancy of the two dimensions in order to increase his reaction time when the dimensions were

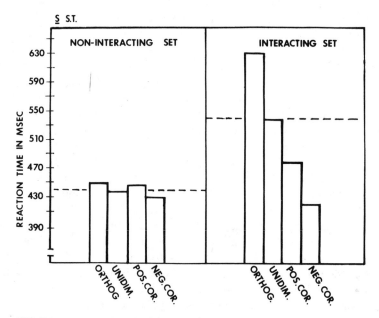

FIG. 7.9. Mean reaction time for speeded sorting of the two sets of triangles for four classification conditions. The data are for observer S.T.

correlated. As indicated earlier, this pattern of results is exactly that which Garner has used in order to define integrality. However, here the pattern is the consequence of an independently determined psychophysical mapping.

Limitations of the Psychophysical Approach

As noted earlier, there are at least two limitations to the psychophysical approach to integrality suggested in the present paper. These can be briefly presented in this concluding section.

First, the definition of integrality presented here is intimately related to the notion of interdimensional additivity. Before the present theory can be considered complete, however, it must be shown whether interdimensional additivity alone is sufficient to account for the results described in the last subsection. It should be noted that the transformation of the physical variables that removed the interaction found in Fig. 7.7 is just one of a potentially infinite number of transformations that could lead to the kind of rectangularity found in Fig. 7.8. For example, one might think of the possibility of producing rigid rotations of the configuration of Fig. 7.8 in some similarity space. The critical question is: Will each of these transformations, given the rectangularity of the configurations, lead to results such as those found in Fig. 7.9? Alternatively, will one of these rotations be a preferred set of axes? Affirmation of the first question (i.e., the demonstration that interdimensional additivity is a sufficient condition for obtaining the results of Fig. 7.9) will lead to the notion that the salient perceptual attributes of a set of stimuli are a consequence of the context of the set of stimuli themselves. However, affirmation of the second question will argue that the salient attributes are a consequence of the particular stimulus domain that is exemplified by the particular set of stimuli used in the experiment. Of course, the question of context dependency is one of the most fundamental questions that can be asked about perceptual processing, and the extension of the present approach in examining this question should be equally fundamental.

Second, data obtained by Somers (1978), in addition to those presented here, indicate clearly the existence of phenomena that a simple psychophysical approach cannot handle easily. In particular, her experiments manipulated the relative discriminability of the dimensions used to define the stimuli as well as their psychophysical compatibility. Her data demonstrate effects on performance of relative discriminability that seem to be quite different from, and independent of, psychophysical compatibility. Highly discriminable dimensions seem to acquire a salience that can dominate performance regardless of their interaction with other stimulus dimensions. This dominance of performance seems to indicate that some form of attentional mechanism will be needed to account for the ability of the subject to switch from one dimension to another, when their discriminability varies greatly. Thus, it seems clear that some process account, in addition to psychophysical factors, will be needed to bring any form a completeness to the definition of integrality.

ACKNOWLEDGMENTS

This work was supported by ONR Contract N00014-76-C-0648.

REFERENCES

Egeth, H., & Pachella, R. G. Multidimensional stimulus identification. *Perception & Psychophysics, 5,* 1969, 341–346.

Fitts, P.M., & Posner, M. I. *Human performance.* Monterey, Cal.: Brooks/Cole, 1967.

Garner, W. R. *The processing of information and structure.* Hillsdale, N.J.: Lawrence Erlbaum Associates, 1974.

Garner, W. R., & Felfoldy, G. L. Integrality of stimulus dimensions in various types of information processing. *Cognitive Psychology,* 1970, *1,* 225–241.

Gibson, J. J. The concept of the stimulus in psychology. *American Psychologist,* 1960, *15,* 233–259.

Gibson, J. J. *The senses considered as perceptual systems.* Boston: Houghton Mifflin, 1966.

Guttman, L. A general non-metric technique for finding the smallest coordinate spaces for a configuration of points. *Psychometrika,* 1968, *33,* 469–506.

Hardzinski, M., & Pachella, R. G. *A psychophysical analysis of complex integrated displays* (Human Performance Center Technical Report No. 59). University of Michigan, February 1977.

Krantz, D. H., & Tversky, A. Similarity of rectangles: An analysis of subjective dimensions. *Journal of Mathematical Psychology,* 1975, *12,* 4–34.

Pomerantz, J. R., & Garner, W. R. Stimulus configuration in selective attention tasks. *Perception & Psychophysics,* 1973, *14,* 565–569.

Pomerantz, J. R., & Sager, L. C. Asymmetric integrality with dimensions of visual pattern. *Perception & Psychophysics,* 1975, *18,* 460–466.

Posner, M. I. Information reduction in the analysis of sequential tasks. *Psychological Review,* 1964, *71,* 491–504.

Roskam, R., & Lingoes, J. C. MINISSA-I: A Fortran-IV (G) program for the smallest space analysis of square symmetric matrices. *Behavioral Science,* 1970, *15,* 204–205.

Shepard, R. N., & Chipman, S. Second-order isomorphism of internal representations: Shapes of states. *Cognitive Psychology,* 1970, *1,* 1–17.

Somers, P. *Perceptual interaction between stimulus dimensions as the basis of dimensional integrality* (Human Performance Center Technical Report No. 61). University of Michigan, October 1978.

Somers, P., & Pachella, R. G. *Interference among sources of information in complex integrated displays* (Human Performance Center Technical Report No. 58). University of Michigan, February 1977.

Torgerson, W. S. *Theory and methods of scaling.* New York: Wiley, 1958.

Tversky, A., & Krantz, D. H. The dimensional representation and the metric structure of similarity data. *Journal of Mathematical Psychology,* 1970, *7,* 572–596.

III
THEORETICAL APPROACHES TO PATTERN RECOGNITION

8 A Feature-Extraction Approach to Auditory Pattern Recognition

Julius T. Tou

INTRODUCTION

Recognition is often regarded as a basic attribute of human beings and other living organisms. A pattern is the description of an object or a phenomenon, and this description can be numerical, physical, statistical, geometrical, structural, or literal. Recognition of visual or aural patterns by human beings may be considered as psychophysical problem involving a relationship between a person and a physical stimulus. When people perceive patterns, they associate the perceived information with some general concepts or clues, which they have acquired from past experience. Human recognition may be characterized as estimating the relative odds of associating the input data with one of a set of statistical populations, which depend on our past experience and which form the clues and the a priori information for recognition. The problem of pattern recognition may be treated as one of discriminating the input data, not among individual patterns but among pattern classes, via the search for features or attributes among members of a class.

The subject of pattern recognition spans a number of scientific disciplines, uniting them in the search for a solution to the common problem of identifying members of a given class in a set containing fuzzy elements from many pattern classes. A pattern class is a category defined and characterized by certain common attributes. A pattern provides the description of any member of a category representing a pattern class. When a set of patterns falling into disjoint classes is given, we wish to categorize these patterns into their respective classes by the use of some automatic device. The reading and processing of canceled checks exemplifies a visual pattern-recognition problem. Such tasks can be readily performed by human workers. However, a machine can achieve much greater speed. On the other hand, some recognition tasks are of such a nature that they can hardly be performed by human beings alone. An example of such a recognition problem is the identification of the sound of a submarine in the midst of other marine signals and noise through the analysis of subaquatic sound.

This chapter is concerned with an approach to the recognition of auditory signals via feature extraction. Figure 8.1 illustrates a typical auditory signal. Auditory, nonspeech signals are generally characterized by loudness, pitch, duration, and timbre as primary perceptual attributes (Plomp, 1970). Loudness of sound is the apparent strength of the sensation received by the human auditory system. The primary physical correlate of loudness is called the intensity, which refers to the amount of energy flowing in the sound wave. Pitch is determined by the frequency of sound waves produced by a vibrating object. Change in duration is a measure of temporal resolution. "Timbre is that attribute of auditory sensation in terms of which a listener can judge that two sounds similarly presented and having the same loudness and pitch are dissimilar." Schouten (1968) proposed five major physical parameters of timbre: tonal vs. noiselike character, spectral envelope, time envelope, change, and acoustic prefix. These parameters together with frequency and duration may be considered as the features of auditory signals.

PATTERN RECOGNITION

The pattern-recognition process may be modeled as a mapping process that consists of three spaces: measurement space, feature space, and category space. Pattern recognition involves the mapping from the measurement space to the

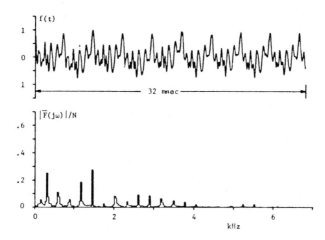

FIG. 8.1.   Sample auditory signal.

feature space and then to the category space (Fig. 8.2). Upon presentation of a set of measurements taken from an object (or a stimulus) to be recognized, the recognition system determines the set of features that characterizes the pattern class to which the object belongs. We may consider this process as mapping from the measurement space to the feature space. From the set of discriminating features, the system identifies the appropriate category for the object under consideration. This process may be regarded as mapping from the feature space to the category space.

The design concepts for automatic pattern classification are motivated by the ways in which pattern classes are characterized and defined. When a pattern class is characterized by a roster of its members, a pattern-classification system may be designed by the template matching concept. When a pattern class is characterized by common properties shared by all its members, the design may make use of the feature matching concept. When pattern classes exhibit clustering properties in the pattern space, the concept of decision boundaries and cluster analysis may be used in the design.

Classification Via Cluster Seeking

Auditory pattern classification may be considered as a problem in unsupervised pattern recognition. Suppose that we are given a set of auditory patterns without any information whatsoever as to the number of classes present in the group. The unsupervised learning problem may be stated as that of identifying the classes in a given set of patterns. If we accept cluster centers as a method of representing classes, one obvious way of characterizing a given set of data is by cluster identification.

A number of cluster-seeking methods have been proposed in the literature (Anderberg, 1973; Diday, 1973; Tou & Gonzalez, 1974). These cluster-seeking algorithms are derived on the basis of a simple thresholding concept, maximin distance concept, K-means approach, Isodata approach, or graph-theoretic approach. In this subsection, we introduce a min/max distance approach. From our experience, this method yields satisfactory results on auditory patterns.

In automatic classification by cluster seeking, we usually encounter two basic problems. The first is the determination of an optimal number of cluster centers; the second is the assignment of patterns into identified clusters. Thus, a cluster-

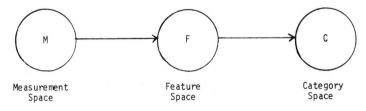

FIG. 8.2. Pattern-recognition model.

seeking procedure should yield clusters with small intraset distances and large interset distances. In the proposed min/max distance approach, the method determines an optimal number of clusters and makes optimal assignment of patterns by maximizing the minimum interset distance and minimizing the maximum intraset distance. At each iteration, we compute the ratio of minimum interset distance to the maximum intraset distance as a measure of the quality of the cluster distribution. Best quality is achieved when this ratio reaches a maximum. The proposed min/max distance algorithm is summarized as follows:

1. Determine the extreme pattern points that are close to the circumscribing hypersphere or several extreme pattern points that are far apart.
2. Form minimal clusters by grouping patterns in the vicinity of the extreme pattern points.
3. Compute the centroid for each of the clusters.
4. Compute the intraset distance for each cluster and the interset distances between two clusters.
5. Select the minimum interset distance and the maximum intraset distance and compute the ratio.
6. Create more clusters by changing the thresholds for clusters with large intraset distances.
7. Merge small clusters into neighboring large clusters if the interset distances are small.
8. Repeat steps 3–5 and check the value of the min/max ratio.
9. If the min/max ratio decreases and has reached a global maximum value, stop the procedure and take the number of clusters corresponding to the maximum ratio.
10. If there are alternative groupings with equal number of clusters, choose one with the largest min/max ratio.

An alternative approach based on the min/max distance concept is to convert pattern points into a pattern matrix by correlation analysis. By specifying a threshold, the pattern matrix can be converted to a pattern graph. We may then form initial clusters with connected pattern points. Once the initial clusters are established, we may proceed with steps 3 through 10 of the aforementioned algorithm until an optimal result is obtained. A new powerful approach known as DYNOC has been developed by the author (Tou, 1979).

Functional Organization of the Pattern-Recognition Process

Pattern recognition by machine bears some resemblance to pattern recognition by humans. In this subsection, we make a comparative study of similarities and differences. We have observed several important aspects in the process of pattern recognition by humans. These are adaptation, learning, memory, past experience, feature extraction, pattern matching, contextual understanding, decision making, and deciphering. Humans can learn new methods and techniques and adapt to new environments. They possess sophisticated memory, but it is always fading. Human individuals acquire past experience and can extract physical, structural, and perceptual features from sample patterns. They perform pattern matching, make use of contextual information, and make decisions.

By analogy, a pattern-recognition machine involves similar aspects and functions. These are: training, storage, a priori information, feature extraction, feature matching, contextual analysis, decision function generation, and decoding. The pattern-recognition machine is often designed through a training procedure. It is equipped with a storage device that memorizes a priori information permanently. The pattern-recognition machine generally possesses the capability of extracting structural and mathematical features from input data. It can perform feature matching and conduct contextual analysis. It generates decision functions for classification. The functional organization of the pattern-recognition process is depicted in Fig. 8.3.

Features represent the invariant attributes of a given pattern, which may be divided into two types: local features and global features. In a pattern-recognition machine, both types of features should be considered in order to achieve high performance of recognition. In conducting machine design, we further divide features into intraset features and interset features. The former characterizes the attributes within a category, and the latter represents the attributes between two categories. Both human pattern recognition and machine pattern recognition involve feature extraction. In the case of human recognition, both physical, structural, and perceptual attributes are extracted. These attributes are often descriptive in nature and characterize the object under consideration. Humans have a tendency to forget infrequently used attributes, and always make use of contextual information. When we talk to someone over the telephone and say "my name is TOU," what he has heard may be Tou, Pou, or Kou. To avoid auditory confusion, we try to say Tou—T as in Tom, because from a contextual point of view Tom is well understood, Pom is rare, and Kom is unheard of. The

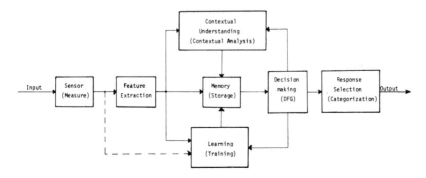

FIG. 8.3.   A pattern-recognition scheme.

contextual information will eliminate both Pou and Kou, thus enhancing recognition efficiency. In the case of machine recognition, discriminating attributes are extracted to form a feature vector or a feature string. These features represent physical, structural, and mathematical attributes. One of the major functions of feature extraction is to reduce the dimensionality of measurement vectors. This process is analogous to forgetting or ignoring infrequently used attributes in human recognition. Contextual statistics provide useful information in the design of pattern-recognition machines.

In pattern recognition by humans, contextual information is often used to resolve ambiguities and to improve recognition performance. Among the commonly used types of contextual information are semantic information, past experience, word structure, relational data, and conventional rules. In the case of machine recognition, contextual information may be expressed in terms of feature sequence, feature probability, syntactic information, connectivity, and optimal policy. To perform contextual analysis by machine, we make use of rank order of patterns, conditional probabilities, parsing rules, and dynamic programming. In auditory pattern recognition, humans often extract such auditory features as loudness, pitch, duration, and timbre. When a machine is designed to recognize auditory patterns, such features as intensity, fundamental frequency, wave-form propagation, harmonic contents, correlation coefficients, eigenfunctions, and eigenvalues may be exploited. Major approaches to pattern recognition by machine include feature extraction, statistical decision, and syntactical analysis. This chapter is concerned with a feature-extraction approach to auditory pattern recognition.

FEATURE EXTRACTION

It has been pointed out that feature selection and extraction play a central role in pattern recognition (Tou & Gonzales, 1974; Tou & Heydorn, 1967). Any object or pattern that can be recognized and classified possesses a number of discriminatory properties or features. A recognition process, performed either by a machine or by a human being, often starts with consideration of the problem of what discriminatory features to select and how to extract or measure these features. The number of features needed to perform a given recognition task successfully depend on the discriminatory quality of the chosen features. However, the problem of feature selection is usually complicated by the fact that the most important features are not necessarily easily measurable, or in many cases their measurement is inhibited by economic considerations. The selection of an appropriate set of features from sample patterns in one of the most difficult tasks in the design of pattern-recognition systems. To facilitate the analysis of this problem, we can classify features into three types: (1) physical features; (2) structural features; and (3) mathematical features (Tou & Gonzalez, 1974).

Inasmuch as the human perceptual system is organized to recognize physical and structural properties, it is natural for people to use these features as the basis for classification and recognition. However, when machines are designed to recognize patterns, the effectiveness of these features in the recognition process may be sharply reduced because the functions and capabilities of human sensory organs are generally difficult to imitate and implement in most practical situations. On the other hand, machines can be designed to extract mathematical features of patterns, which a human being may have some difficulty in determining without mechanical aid. Examples of these kinds of features are statistical means, correlation coefficients, eigenvalues, eigenvectors of covariance matrices, Fourier coefficients, and other invariant properties. The extraction of features from auditory patterns by computer may be accomplished by several methods. We discuss the Fourier series expansion approach and the Karhunen-Loéve expansion technique.

Fourier Series Expansion

When an auditory pattern is represented by a stationary periodic random process, its features may be extracted by Fourier series expansion. The Fourier coefficients may be chosen as the features characterizing the pattern class. Let $f(t)$ be such an auditory pattern. Then, the Fourier series expansion is given by:

$$f(t) = \sum_{n=0}^{\infty} a_n \exp(jn\omega_0 t) \tag{8.1}$$

where $\omega_0 = 2\pi/T$ is the angular frequency, T is the period of the pattern wave form, and

$$a_n = \frac{1}{T} \int_0^T f(t) \exp(-jn\omega_0 t)\, dt \tag{8.2}$$

are the Fourier coefficients, which are random variables. For different sample auditory patterns in the same class, Eq. 8.2 yields, in general, different values for a_n. If the whole ensemble of sample patterns is considered, Eq. 8.2 defines a_n as a random variable.

In view of the periodicity of the auditory pattern, it has been shown that the Fourier coefficients a_n and a_m are uncorrelated for $n \neq m$. Let the correlation function for the sample patterns be denoted by $r(\tau)$, then:

$$r(\tau) = E\{f(t)\, f(t - \tau)\}. \tag{8.3}$$

$r(\tau)$ is periodic and can be expressed as:

$$r(\tau) = \sum_{k=-\infty}^{\infty} b_k \exp(jk\omega_0 \tau) \tag{8.4}$$

It can readily be shown that the coefficients b_k of the correlation function is given by the variance of the kth Fourier coefficient of $f(t)$. Thus, the coefficients of the correlation function may be chosen as the features characterizing the auditory pattern class.

Karhunen-Loéve expansion

When an auditory pattern is a nonperiodic random process, it cannot be expressed as a Fourier series with uncorrelated random coefficients. But it can be expanded in a series of orthogonal functions $\phi_n(t)$ with uncorrelated coefficients. Let $f(t)$ be such an auditory pattern. We expand $f(t)$ in an interval $[a, b]$ into:

$$f(t) = \sum_{n=1}^{\infty} \gamma_n \alpha_n \phi_n(t), \qquad a \leqslant t \leqslant b \tag{8.5}$$

where γ_n are real or complex numbers,

$$E\{\alpha_n \tilde{\alpha}_m\} = \begin{cases} 1 & \text{if } m = n \\ 0 & \text{if } m \neq n \end{cases} \tag{8.6}$$

$$\int_a^b \phi_n(t) \tilde{\phi}_m(t)dt = \begin{cases} 1 & \text{if } m = n \\ 0 & \text{if } m \neq n \end{cases} \tag{8.7}$$

The orthogonal functions $\phi_n(t)$ and the coefficients γ_n can be obtained from correlation analysis. The correlation function $r(t, s)$ for the auditory pattern $f(t)$ is given by:

$$\begin{aligned} r(t, s) &= E\{x(t)\ \tilde{x}(s)\} \\ &= \sum_n b_n \phi_n(t)\ \tilde{\phi}_n(s) \end{aligned} \tag{8.8}$$

where

$$b_n = |\gamma_n|^2$$

and

$$a \leqslant t \leqslant b,\ a \leqslant s \leqslant b. \tag{8.9}$$

From Eq. 8.7 we have:

$$\int_a^b r(t, s)\ \phi_k(s)\ ds = |\gamma_k|^2\ \phi_k(t). \tag{8.10}$$

Thus, the coefficients $|\gamma|^2$ are the eigenvalues, and the functions $\phi_k(t)$ are the eigenfunctions of the familiar integral equation whose general form is:

$$\int_a^b r(t, s)\ \phi(s)\ ds = \lambda\ \phi(t) \tag{8.11}$$

where $a \leq t \leq b$. The solution of this integral equation yields γ_n and $\phi_n(t)$. It can be shown that b_n and $\phi_n(t)$ are the eigenvalues and eigenfunctions of Eq. 8.11, respectively. The correlation function $r(t, s)$ may be used to characterize the auditory pattern class, and the coefficients b_n may be chosen as the features for the class.

EXTRACTION OF PHYSICAL FEATURES

It has been pointed out that human abilities to detect, discriminate, and identify sounds are largely determined by the sensitivity and resolving power of their auditory systems (Howard, 1977; Watson, 1976). Human ears are capable of extracting physical features such as loudness, pitch, duration, and tonal quality. To study human extraction of physical features in auditory patterns, we may consider the model shown in Fig. 8.4.

Some vibrating object generates an auditory pattern $f_a(t)$, which is transmitted through a channel to the auditory system. The transmitted auditory pattern forms the sound wave, which is characterized by $f_b(t)$. It is the sound wave that is received by the auditory system, which converts it into an auditory pattern, $f_c(t)$. The auditory system extracts features from the received auditory pattern. It is noted that $f_c(t)$ is not a replica of $f_a(t)$, although it is an approximation of $f_a(t)$. The received auditory pattern $f_c(t)$ is different for different listeners. Even for the same listener, $f_c(t)$ may be different on different occasions because the conversion process involves the mechanisms of learning, memory, and selective attention. Even though the received auditory patterns from the same source differ, they belong to the same pattern class.

The conversion process will retain the discriminatory features of the source auditory pattern. When musical note middle C is played, all trained listeners will recognize it as middle C by identifying its discriminatory feature—pitch (Wightman, 1973). When we want listeners to discriminate a musical note from violin and oboe, pitch is no longer a discriminatory feature. Their ears must extract complex tones. The quality of sound is determined by the number and relative strength of the overtones.

Using this model, we may be able to design experiments to determine the conversion function of the auditory system. With the source auditory pattern specified and the characteristics of the transmission channel known, we may train

FIG. 8.4.   A test model.

the subjects to paint the received auditory pattern $f_c(t)$ and to identify such features as pitch, change in frequency, and change in duration. This type of experimentation may yield quantitative characterization of the conversion function of the auditory system. Such information is needed in the understanding of the human auditory system and may be useful for the correction of human auditory defects.

MATHEMATICAL CHARACTERIZATION OF RECEIVED AUDITORY PATTERNS

Referring to Fig. 8.4, we assume that the combined transfer function of the transmission channel and the auditory system be $G(j\omega)$. Let the autocorrelation and spectral density of $f_a(t)$ and $f_c(t)$ be $r_{aa}(\tau)$, $R_{aa}(\omega)$ and $r_{cc}(\tau)$, $R_{cc}(\omega)$, respectively. It has been shown (Tou, 1959) that:

$$R_{aa}(-\omega) = R_{aa}(\omega) \tag{8.12}$$

$$R_{ac}(\omega) = R_{ca}(-\omega) \tag{8.13}$$

$$R_{ac}(\omega) = G(j\omega) R_{aa}(\omega) \tag{8.14}$$

$$R_{cc}(\omega) = G(j\omega) R_{ca}(\omega). \tag{8.15}$$

Making use of these equations, we obtain:

$$R_{cc}(\omega) = G(j\omega) G(-j\omega) R_{aa}(\omega) \tag{8.16}$$

from which we may determine the spectral density of the received auditory pattern.

The autocorrelation function of the generated auditory signal $f_a(t)$ is given by:

$$r_{aa}(\tau) = \lim_{T_0 \to \infty} \frac{1}{2T_0} \int_{-T_0}^{T_0} f_a(t) f_a(t + \tau) \, dt \tag{8.17}$$

The spectral density $R_{aa}(\omega)$ of $f_a(t)$ is given by the Fourier transform of its autocorrelation function. Thus,

$$R_{aa}(\omega) = \int_{-\infty}^{\infty} r_{aa}(\tau) e^{-j\omega\tau} d\tau \tag{8.18}$$

The autocorrelation function of the received auditory pattern $f_c(t)$ is given the inverse Fourier transform of Eq. 8.16:

$$r_{cc}(\tau) = \frac{1}{2\pi} \int_{-\infty}^{\infty} R_{cc}(\omega) e^{j\tau\omega} d\omega. \tag{8.19}$$

When $\tau = 0$, we have:

$$r_{cc}(0) = \frac{1}{2\pi}\int_{-\infty}^{\infty} R_{cc}(\omega)\, d\omega \qquad (8.20)$$

which equals the mean-square value of the received auditory pattern $f_c(t)$. The mean-square value $\overline{f_c^2(t)}$, which is related to frequency resolution and temporal resolution, may be chosen as a feature for auditory patterns.

DIGITAL FEATURE EXTRACTION OF AUDITORY PATTERNS

When we use a digital computer to recognize auditory patterns, we consider sampled values of the pattern wave forms. Let $f_k = f(t_k)$ be the sampled value of $f(t)$ at $t = t_k$. We take n sampled values of $f(t)$—$f_1, f_2, f_3, \ldots, f_n$—and form a vector, F, which we refer to as the pattern vector for $f(t)$ Fig. 8.5. Because $f(t)$ is a random process, the pattern vector F is a random process. Vector F may be expanded in a linear combination of orthogonal basis

$$F = \sum_{k=1}^{N} c_k \boldsymbol{\phi}_k \qquad (8.21)$$

where the coefficients c_k are statistically independent, and $\boldsymbol{\phi}_k$ are orthogonal basis vectors,

$$\boldsymbol{\phi}_k = \begin{bmatrix} \varphi_k(t_1) \\ \varphi_k(t_2) \\ \cdot \\ \cdot \\ \cdot \\ \varphi_k(t_n) \end{bmatrix} \qquad (8.22)$$

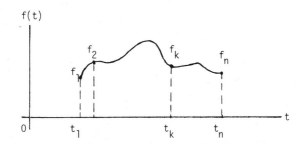

FIG. 8.5.   A digitized auditory pattern.

If we let:

$$C = \begin{bmatrix} c_1 \\ c_2 \\ \cdot \\ \cdot \\ \cdot \\ c_N \end{bmatrix} \quad \text{and} \quad \Phi = (\phi_1 \phi_2 \ldots \phi_N) \tag{8.23}$$

the pattern vector in Eq. 8.21 may be written as:

$$F = \Phi \, C. \tag{8.24}$$

The correlation matrix for pattern vector F is given by:

$$R = \text{E} \{F \, F'\}. \tag{8.25}$$

Combining Eqs. 8.24 and 8.25, we have:

$$R = \Phi \, \Lambda \, \Phi' \tag{8.26}$$

where:

$$\Lambda = \begin{bmatrix} \lambda_1 & & & 0 \\ & \lambda_2 & & \\ & & \cdot & \\ & & & \cdot \\ 0 & & & \lambda_N \end{bmatrix} \tag{8.27}$$

and

$$\lambda_k = \text{E} \{c_k{}^2\}.$$

Making use of Eq. 8.21, we obtain

$$R = \sum_{k=1}^{N} \text{E} \{c_k^2\} \, \phi_k \phi_k' = \sum_{k=1}^{N} \lambda_k \phi_k \phi_k' \tag{8.28}$$

Postmultiplying both sides by ϕ_j and simplifying yields:

$$R \, \phi_k = \lambda_k \, \phi_k. \tag{8.29}$$

Thus, the basis vectors ϕ_k are the eigenvectors of correlation matrix R, and λ_k are the corresponding eigenvalues. The eigenvalues λ_k may be chosen as features for auditory pattern recognition by computer. The value of λ_k is equal to the variance of the kth random "Fourier" coefficient c_k of the pattern vector F.

The foregoing analysis suggest that an auditory pattern may be characterized by N eigenvalues of the correlation matrix R. However, the value of N may be quite large. We want to choose the most important eigenvalues from the N eigenvalues. This feature-selection process may be accomplished by minimizing a mean-square error criterion.

When all N basis vectors are used, the random vector F is expanded in terms of orthogonal vectors without error. If we select fewer basis vectors, the expansion becomes an approximation of F. The features may be selected by minimizing the mean-square error defined by:

$$\varepsilon^2 = E\left\{ \left(F - \sum_{k=1}^{N_1} c_k \phi_k\right)' \left(F - \sum_{k=1}^{N_1} c_k \phi_k\right) \right\} \tag{8.30}$$

where $N_1 < N$. Equation 8.30 may be reduced to:

$$\varepsilon^2 = E\left\{ \left(\sum_{k=N_1+1}^{N} c_k \phi_k\right)' \left(\sum_{k=N_1+1}^{N} c_k \phi_k\right) \right\} \tag{8.31}$$

Because

$$\phi_k' \phi_j = \begin{cases} 1 & \text{if } k = j \\ 0 & \text{if } k \neq j \end{cases}$$

the mean-square error reduces to:

$$\varepsilon^2 = \sum_{k=N_1+1}^{N} E\left\{ c_k^2 \right\}$$

$$= \sum_{k=N_1+1}^{N} \lambda_k \tag{8.32}$$

Thus, the mean-square error is given by the sum of the eigenvalues corresponding to those eigenvectors that are not selected in the approximation of F. It is apparent that to obtain a minimum of the mean-square error, the eigenvalues in Eq. 8.32 are chosen as the smallest ones. In other words, the features of the pattern are represented by the N_1 larger eigenvalues.

Hence, to insure minimum mean-square error, the orthogonal expansion of Eq. 8.21 will rank the eigenvectors ϕ_k in the order of decreasing eigenvalues. The basis vectors are selected in the order of the eigenvalues λ_k, until ε^2 becomes smaller than some specified value. Assume the selected eigenvectors are ϕ_1, $\phi_2, \ldots, \phi_{N_1}$. Then the corresponding eigenvalues are $\lambda_1, \lambda_2, \ldots, \lambda_{N_1}$. These eigenvalues are ordered according to the relationship:

$$\lambda_1 > \lambda_2 > \lambda_3 > \ldots > \lambda_{N_1} \tag{8.33}$$

CONCLUSIONS

This chapter makes a comparative study of pattern recognition by humans and pattern recognition by machine. Cluster-seeking and feature-extraction approaches are proposed for automatic recognition of auditory patterns. A model for the extraction of physical features in auditory patterns is presented. Mathematical characterization of received auditory patterns is discussed. The use of eigenvalues to characterize auditory patterns is introduced. It has been shown that larger eigenvalues of the correlation matrix for the auditory pattern vector carry more discriminatory information of the auditory pattern. This provides a method to select more important features. A sophisticated auditory pattern-recognition system may be designed by transferring the experience of experts to the system via man–machine interaction. The design of such a system can be accomplished by making use of the MEDIKS concept (Tou, 1978).

REFERENCES

Anderberg, M. R. *Cluster analysis for applications*. New York: Academic Press, 1973.

Diday, E. The dynamic clusters method in nonhierarchical clustering. *International Journal of Computer and Information Sciences*, 1973, *2*, 61–88.

Howard, J. H., Jr. Psychophysical structure of eight complex underwater sounds. *Journal of the Acoustical Society of America*, 1977, *62*.

Plomp, R. Timbre as a multidimensional attribute of complex tones. In R. Plomp & G. F. Smoorenburg (Eds.), *Frequency analysis and periodicity detection in hearing*. 1970, A. W. Sijthoff Leiden.

Schouten, J. F. The perception of timbre. *Reports of the 6th International Congress on Acoustics*. Tokyo: 1968.

Tou, J. T. *Digital and sampled-data control systems*. New York: McGraw-Hill, 1959.

Tou, J. T. MEDIKS—A medical knowledge system. *Proceedings of the 31st Annual Conference on Engineering in Medicine and Biology*, 1978.

Tou, J. T. Design of a medical knowledge system for diagnostic consultation and clinical decision-making. *Proceedings of the 1978 International Computer Symposium*, 1978, *1*, 80–99.

Tou, J. T. "DYNOC - A Dynamic Optimal Cluster-seeking Technique." *International Journal of Computer and Information Sciences*, 1979, *8*, 541–547.

Tou, J. T. & Gonzalez, R. C. *Pattern recognition principles*. Reading, Mass.: Addison-Wesley, 1974.

Tou, J. T. & Heydorn, R. P. Some approaches to optimum feature extraction. In J. T. Tou (Ed.), *Computer and information sciences—II*. New York: Academic Press, 1967.

Watson, C. S. Factors in the discrimination of word-length auditory patterns. In Hirsh, S. K. *et al.* (Eds.), *Hearing and Davis: Essays honoring Hallowell Davis*. St. Louis, Mo.: Washington University Press, 1976.

Wightman, F. L. The pattern-transformation model of pitch. *Journal of the Acoustical Society of America*, 1973, *54*.

9 Pattern Recognition in Ocean Acoustics

Arthur E. Bisson

INTRODUCTION

From childhood we are trained to recognize and identify out-of-sight events and occurrences by means of only the acoustic noise produced. The slam of a car door, footsteps in the hall, and rain outside a window all can be identified by distinguishing characteristics or patterns that differentiate one sound or group of sounds from the other. These are examples of the "passive" emissions that are generated as unwanted byproducts that accompany the transfers of energy from one form to another, i.e., kinetic to heat, electrical to mechanical, etc.

We are also surrounded by a variety of "active" acoustic emissions created to inform, alert, or warn. Air-raid sirens, fire alarms, automobile horns, and speech are examples of the active sound emissions that accompany daily life. These sound characteristics are chosen to be distinct so that there will be a minimum of confusion with other sounds. The human ability to understand and recognize the abstract thoughts and ideas conveyed by speech show people to be a highly developed and skilled pattern-recognition "machines."

How do people recognize or discriminate one sound from another? What are the basic features or characteristics of sounds that they use to discriminate? Can these features or characteristics be understood in a mathematical sense, or does the human individual's gestalt nature come into play in the recognition process? As of now, there are no obvious or general answers to these questions.

Although questions regarding the human learning and recognition process are not easily answered, we do have at our disposal a formalism that aids in identifying and utilizing distinct features of sounds for classification. This formalism is called pattern recognition. The rest of this chapter is devoted to an overview of pattern recognition as it applies to the classifications of acoustic sounds in the ocean. This material on pattern recognition is not original but merely represents a collection from the various relevant sources listed as references.

ACOUSTIC CHARACTERISTICS OF SOUNDS IN THE OCEAN

Acoustic Recognition by Humans

Many of the acoustic sounds familiar to us on land are also found underwater. Along with the familiar machinery-associated sounds are those obviously indigenous to the ocean environment—the sound of fishes, crustaceans, and sea mammals to name a few. Figure 9.1 is a schematic representation of various sounds in the ocean. What may not be obvious at first glance is that the sounds have been "tagged" with descriptive featurelike words that immediately convey information relative to both sound source and type. Many of the word tags used in Fig. 9.1 have been used for years by sonar operators as descriptions for events and occurrences that they can merely hear but not see. In fact, pattern recognition in the ocean environment is important today because of the high degree of accuracy in sound identification shown by well-trained and dedicated sonar operators (for a general treatment of recognition by human observers see Flanagan, 1972 and Swets, 1964).

If people can identify acoustic events accurately, can machines be designed to do it better? Can we propose ways to aid individuals in identifying acoustic events better than they do presently? In answer to the first question: Machines can probably be expected to do better than people. They can certainly do better in some restricted problems that require speed or an extremely large accurate memory. In answer to the second question: We can definitely propose ways to aid individuals in identifying acoustics events. Machines can provide measurement accuracy, memory, various displays, etc. At this point, let's concern ourselves with how we would go about building a machine to recognize or classify underwater acoustic sounds. To do this, we first describe the general nature of the underwater sound itself in terms of the generating source, the structure through which it might pass, the propagation medium, and finally the pressure wave presented to a listening hydrophone. Next, we describe how existing pattern-recognition techniques can be used to build a possible automatic recognition-processing system.

Nature of the Acoustic Pressure Wave

Underwater sounds, like those in air, can be grouped into two main classes: passive and active. Passive sounds are the minimized, but generally unavoidable, noises that accompany human activities on, above, and under the sea. Noises that occur above the sea surface are included wherever a suitable path—such as a structure of air column—exists that guarantees the existence of a measurable

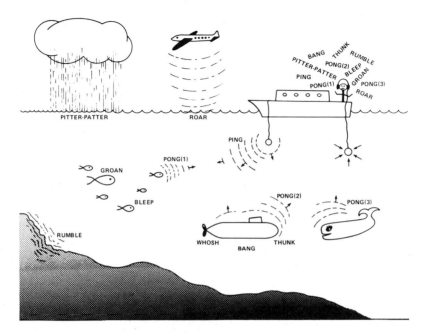

FIG. 9.1.   Schematic representation of various sounds in the ocean.

pressure wave in the water. All ambient noise as well as noise generated by biologics and the like are also categorized as passive for convenience sake. Active sounds include those produced by people to communicate, explore, detect, localize, experiment, and map. The "echoes" of active sounds reflected by objects and the ocean's sea surface or bottom are also classified as active sounds.

Based on the approach of established aural classification clues, the major underwater-noise source classes are identified and listed in Table 9.1. It should be noted that this list differs from the usual listing of underwater sources in terms of the specific source due to propulsion machinery, auxiliary machinery, propulsor, hydrodynamic flow, and others.

Because some major aspects of the effort in the application of pattern recognition to underwater sounds are in their infancy, this list might change in the future. In addition, under certain circumstances and for certain noise types within these classes, misclassification does occur based on aural clues alone.

TABLE 9.1
Major Underwater Sound Source Classes

Machinery	Steam flow	Ambient noise
Impacts	Cavitation	Active emissions
Air flow	Biologics	Others
Water flow		

Classification information of acoustic sources is buried in the detailed, time-dependent source function $i(t)$, which is expressed as:

$$\text{Acoustic source information in the time domain} = i(t) \qquad (9.1)$$

with an equivalent frequency domain expression based on its Fourier transform $I(\omega)$ given by:

$$I(\omega) = \int_{-\infty}^{+\infty} i(t)e^{-j\omega t}\, dt \qquad (9.2)$$

How are the source characteristics affected by passage through or reflection by a structure? Assuming a linear system that contains a single source whose amplitude is denoted by the function $i(t)$, then the time-dependent response denoted by $\psi(t)$ is related to the source function by the following integrodifferential equation:

$$\psi(t) = \equiv H(L)i(t) \qquad (9.3)$$

where $H(L)$ is the transfer operator that relates the response $\psi(t)$ to the input $i(t)$.

By taking the Fourier transform of Eq. 9.3, we obtain the equivalent frequency domain equation:

$$\Psi(\omega) = H(\omega)I(\omega). \qquad (9.4)$$

Furthermore:

$$\psi(t) = \frac{1}{2\pi}\int_{-\infty}^{+\infty} H(\omega)I(\omega)e^{j\omega t}\, d\omega. \qquad (9.5)$$

The importance of Eqs. 9.4 and 9.5 is threefold. First, they demonstrate simple relationships between source function and response function. Second, in both passage through and reflection from a structure, the system transfer function $H(\omega)$ leaves a characteristic "imprint" that conveys information about the structure itself. Third, and most important, both the transfer function and its characteristics are independent of source type, i.e., it remains the same regardless of the source acting on it. As we have just mentioned, properly applied Eq. 9.4 generally holds for both passive acoustic emission as well as for the active target-return case where manufactured signals are used as a probe for structural characteristics.

Based on existing established aural classification clues, the major underwater noise structure classes are given in Table 9.2.

The attributes of the sound that allow distinguishing between structural classes are not as obvious as those that allow discrimination between the various source classes. The structural classes are distinguished by the value of specific attributes, the more important of which are listed in Table 9.3.

As an example, flow into a container may excite container resonances, whereas flow out may not. Flow through a lightly damped piping system may show complex piping resonances, whereas flow through a highly damped

TABLE 9.2
Major Underwater Sound Structure Classes

Flow into containers	Flow through piping	No structure
Flow out of containers	Within a structure	Others
Flow through an orifice		

piping system will not, etc. A few words are probably in order regarding the structural spatial filtering attribute: The structural transfer function is in general dependent on the orientation of the structure relative to the measurement hydrophone. This occurs because acoustic radiation from a structure is generally complex and directional in nature.

Figure 9.2 schematically shows the relationship between the source characteristics and the pressure wave characteristics for the case where the source is modified by a structure and the propagation medium. In this case, the final pressure time wave form p(t) is given by:

$$p(t) = m(g)\ s(v)\ i(t) \tag{9.6}$$

where m(g) and s(v) are the time domain transfer operators of the ocean medium and structure, respectively, and $i(t)$ is the source time function. In the frequency domain, the pressure wave is given by the following integrodifferential equation:

$$P(\omega) = M(\omega)\ S(\omega)\ I(\omega) \tag{9.7}$$

where $M(\omega)$ and $S(\omega)$ are the frequency domain transfer operators of the ocean medium and structure, respectively, and $I(\omega)$ is the source frequency function. For the case of an active echo probe, Fig. 9.2 would have to be modified to include the propagation medium both before and after the structure term. The major effect of the propagation medium is in corrupting and otherwise diminishing the ''features'' used in classification of sounds.

PATTERN-RECOGNITION OVERVIEW

General Formalism

Pattern recognition or pattern classification is a field of study with a rich variety of detailed procedures that cannot possibly be covered here (for excellent texts on the subject see Andrews, 1972; Fu, 1974; Fukunaga, 1972; Meisel, 1972). All we can hope to accomplish here is to give the flavor of the general approach.

TABLE 9.3
Distinguishing Attributes for Delineation of Structural Classes

Laminar or turbulent nature of flow	Structural frequency filtering
Structural resonance(s)	Structural spatial filtering
Structural damping	Others

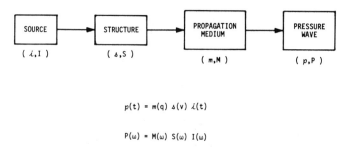

$$p(t) = m(q)\ s(v)\ i(t)$$

$$P(\omega) = M(\omega)\ S(\omega)\ I(\omega)$$

FIG. 9.2.   Time and frequency domain transfer characteristics.

Figure 9.3 is a schematic representation of the major stages in the pattern-recognition process. First, the physical system produces an output that is measured. These measurements of "events" generally occupy an infinite dimensional *measurement space*. Signal processing is performed on the measurement space data to transform, filter or enhance with the result that the data are placed in a finite-dimensional *pattern space*. The pattern-space dimension need only be large enough to carry out the classification satisfactorily. Next, the pattern-space dimensions are changed to new dimensions, which may or may not be recognizable combinations of the pattern-space dimensions. This redimensioning into *feature space* occurs for two reasons: (1) redimensioning can enhance the classification; (2) it can reduce the number of dimensions needed for the same degree of correct classification. Finally, decision rules are adopted that divide the feature space into separate regions for each class of events.

Before a measurement can be processed by a machine, it is necessary to convert it to a description acceptable by a processor. Figure 9.4 illustrates a variety of measurement-space vectors defined as:

$$\bar{X} = \begin{matrix} X_1 \\ X_2 \\ X_3 \\ \cdot \\ \cdot \\ \cdot \\ X_N \end{matrix} \tag{9.7}$$

In Fig. 9.4a, X_i is the radial length for character recognition. In Fig. 9.4b, X_i is the x and y coordinate projection density for the number of grids occupied by the handwritten character, where 1 symbolizes that the grid is occupied by the character stroke and 0 that the grid is empty. The rows and columns are then summed to produce the x and y density. In Fig. 9.4c, individual grids are recorded as being occupied (1) or not (0) by the stroke of the character. In Fig. 9.4d, we see an example of a digitized amplitude wave-form presentation.

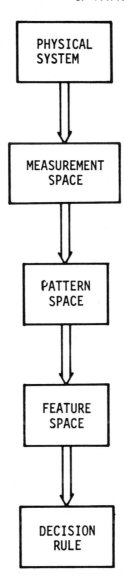

FIG. 9.3. Stages in the pattern-recognition process.

In dealing with the classification information in the underwater pressure wave, it is useful to note the existence of the sampling theorem (Black, 1953) that specifies the least number of discrete samples of an unknown wave form necessary for its complete and unambiguous definition. The theorem states: If a signal f(t) is sampled at regular intervals and at a rate slightly higher than twice the highest significant signal frequency, then the digitized samples contain all the information of the original signal. Therefore, if the signal has a highest frequency

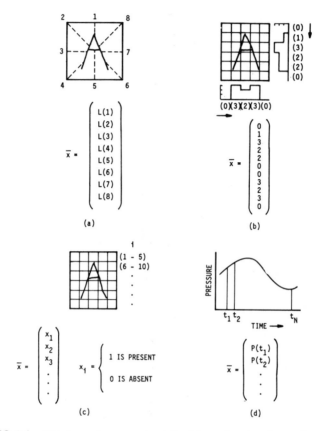

FIG. 9.4. Measurement space vector defined for various transforms: *A*. radial length for character recognition; *B*. x and y projection density for character recognition; *C*. matrix density for character recognition; *D*. digitized pressure amplitude time wave form.

of 20 kHz, then we need to digitize the amplitude at a rate of 40×10^3 times per second. If we are dealing with a signal of 1-minute duration, then we must have 2.4×10^6 amplitude terms in order to have no loss of information! Fortunately, much of the information in any signal is highly redundant. With this example, we have gone from an infinite dimensional *measurement space* to a 2.4×10^6 dimensional *pattern space*. Feature selection provides a formalism to reduce this high-dimensional space to a more tractable low-dimensional space by the elimination of redundant information and certain types of noise. We return to this later, but now let us consider what is called the curse of dimensionality.

If it takes only two samples to make a meaningful measurement in one dimension (e.g., noise corruption might make it necessary to obtain a mean value), then it takes four samples in two dimensions and eight samples in three dimensions. In 10 dimensions, it would take 2^{10} sample points to obtain a meaningful result. As we must rely on clustering of points in pattern and feature space in order for a simple decision boundary to delineate between classes, then if we blindly choose the dimensions, we need an inordinately high number of sample data to obtain a reasonably accurate measure of class variability in feature space. In most practical problems, the number of class data samples is limited. Therefore, we must use methods that will extract as much information as possible from what is most often, relative to the size of the space, a relatively small data sample.

In general, a heuristic approach is taken in obtaining the initial specific dimension that allows for maximum class separation. This is where experience in the field of the general classification problem pays off. The specific dimension can be initially chosen on the basis of experience along with well-considered engineering guesses. The suitability of the initial dimensions can be assessed on the basis of chosen measurement criteria covering a range of conditions, so that there are sufficient statistical data to insure the ability to classify. If an unacceptable error in the correct classification exists, then other characteristics and dimensions can be tried out.

Decision Boundaries

We can define a decision boundary as the boundary surface encompassing all members of class and excluding all members not of that class. In general, for N classes, there would be $N(N-1)/2$ boundaries. Ten classes would require 45 decision boundaries.

There exists an alternate approach based on measured or hypothesized probability distributions for members of the class within the feature space. In this case, the number of decision rules is one per class or N for N classes. Decision for classification is based on belonging to that class for which greatest probability exists based on the probability distribution.

A third alternative for generation of decision boundaries is called successive dichotomies. In this case, only $N-1$ functions need to be obtained to classify an N-class problem. In practice, successive dichotomies is less successful than the probability distribution in ability to classify correctly.

A fourth method of obtaining decision boundaries is called the nearest neighbor rule. In this method, the membership in a particular class is decided by a majority vote of the nearest neighbors. This method assumes that the distance between points is a legitimate measure of the similarity of the patterns they represent. For details on these methods of obtaining decision boundaries see Meisel (1972), Fukunaga (1972), and Fu, (1974).

Syntactic Recognition

In general, underwater acoustic events are often composed of a string of various and distinct acoustic sounds. In many cases, it is this string of sounds that holds the key to correct identification of what has taken place. In this case, it is useful to consider the sound itself as the basic building blocks or "primitives." The concatenation of the string of primitives itself can turn out to be of great importance to a final event classification. This concatenation approach is important because it often encompasses redundant information, thus minimizing the presence of noise in the system. Also, the concatenation may remove ambiguities in final classification by making the total string ineligible for assignment to certain classes.

For concreteness look at Fig. 9.5. First, the input measurements are transformed into a primitive pattern space, which is nothing more than the feature space we discussed previously. The exception is that by now our pattern recognition capability has advanced far enough so that we obtain a high degree of correct classification for the individual primitives.

In Fig. 9.5, we see that after the decision rule is used to classify primitives themselves, we are left with an ordered string of concatenated primitives. The syntax analyzer, or parser, can then match this string in terms of strings of primitives representing each prototype or reference pattern. Based either on a matching or selection criterion, the input string can then be classified. We discuss this in more detail in the following subsection. For a complete treatment of syntactic recognition, see Fu (1974).

Pattern-Recognition Approach to Underwater Sounds

For classification of underwater sounds, the measurement space consists of the analog voltage time wave form generated by various acoustic events as an output from the hydrophone(s). Because of the sampling theorem, an immediate reduction to a finite-dimensioned pattern space is possible. If we are interested in understanding or aiding aural classification only, then the highest frequency of interest is about 20 kHz (Swets, 1964) or a digitized sampling rate of 40×10^3 data points/sec. Even if we are solving the general problem, frequency attenuation by the ocean medium and ambient noise makes the information content from high frequencies unusable at moderate ranges from the sound source. The highest possible frequencies of any use would therefore be in the range of 50 kHz to 80 kHz. Hence, the general problem has a maximum digitizing rate of between 1×10^5 and 1.6×10^5 data points/sec.

Figure 9.6 is a schematic representation of the pattern-space representation for two different class events that each contain two sounds. Notice that the time wave-form information is contained in the ordered sequence of digitized pressure amplitudes I_A and I_B. The number of dimensions for each event is equal to the digitizing rate multiplied by the event duration.

A rich variety of complex sounds occur in the ocean that are due only to changes in the manner or speed with which the same events are performed. For statistical purposes, these variations and the variety of events that occur need a large data base. The curse of dimensionality dictates that a blind statistical

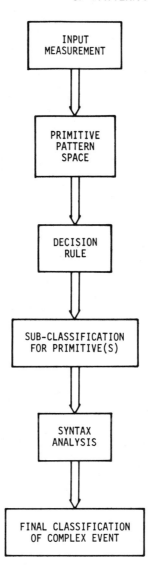

FIG. 9.5. Stages in syntactic pattern recognition.

approach to the choosing of dimensions for a feature space and the resulting decision boundaries for classification would probably not work well. Therefore, instead of a blind statistical approach with a fixed decision rule, it is useful to guess at discriminatory dimensions for the feature space and allow the decision rule to adapt iteratively until a sufficient degree of correct classification is achieved.

Figure 9.7 is a schematic representation of a possible dimensioning of the feature space in terms of guessed-at features that are judged to be important due

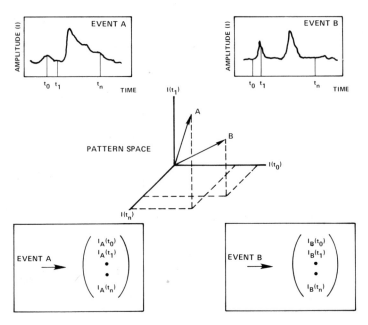

FIG. 9.6. Schematic representation of the pattern space for two different events.

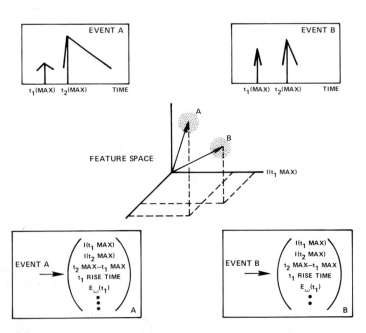

FIG. 9.7. Schematic representation of feature space for two different events.

154

to engineering familiarity with the signals and the signal classes to be separated. In this example, it is judged that there exists discrimination potential in the maximum amplitudes for each sound, the times between the occurrence of the maximum amplitude for each sound, the rise time of the first sound, the frequency spectrum of the first sound, etc. The smear in feature space seen in the figure represents the loss of nonredundant information and the effects of noise. Figure 9.8 shows the schematic decision boundary that divides the classification space separating the two classes.

Figure 9.9 shows how a syntactic representation in terms of sound primitives can be used for classification of acoustic events. The figure portion 9.9a shows a time wave form where individual sounds have been segmented, classified, and tagged. For purposes of concreteness, the wave form is the result of the following series of fictitious events: First, a valve is opened producing a metallic "bang" (BA). This is followed a short time later by a "bleep" (BL) as water begins to flow through the partially opened valve. Next, the "whoosh" (W) is heard as water flows through the piping system into a tank. When the valve is closed another "bang" (BA) is heard. Finally, a "tinkle" (T) is produced by the water left in the piping as it drips into the tank. In Fig. 9.9b, various possible combinations of these sounds are presented that relate to the operation of various systems and possible operation of the same system. In Fig. 9.9c, a parsing tree is set up in

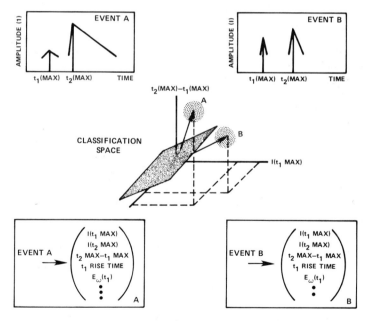

FIG. 9.8. Schematic representation of the decision boundary separating two different events.

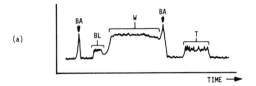

(a)

TIME →

(b)

(1) BA + T
(2) BA + BA
(3) BA + BL + BA
(4) BA + BL + W + T
(5) BA + BL + W + BA + T (WAVEFORM SHOWN)
(6) BA + W + BA + T
(7) BA + W + BA + BL + T
(8) BA + W + T

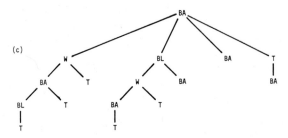

(c)

FIG. 9.9. Hierarchical parsing in syntactic recognition: *A*. possible system operation time wave form; *B*. allowable concatenations for system operation primitives; *C*. parsing tree.

order to provide the logic that can be used in arriving at an unambiguous classification for this specific operation.

Figure 9.10 shows the iterative approach to the classification of underwater sounds, necessary because of the corruptive effects on classification from the ocean medium and the simultaneous occurrence of events from a variety of sources. Speech recognition is just now moving out of the acoustically sound isolated booth into the real world. Similarly, for underwater sound, it is neces-

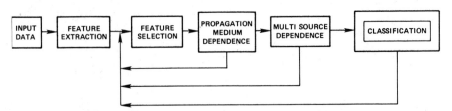

FIG. 9.10. Schematic of iterative feature selection for underwater sounds.

sary to show how accurately the general classification problem can be accomplished under ideal conditions in which the medium and the multisource dependence is neglected. Next, both can be sequentially introduced to quantify their influence on classification.

REFERENCES

Andrews, H. A. *Introduction to mathematical techniques in pattern recognition.* New York: Wiley, 1972.

Black, H. S. *Modulation theory.* Princeton, N.J.: Van Nostrand, 1953.

Flanagan, J. L. *Speech analysis synthesis and perception.* New York: Springer-Verlag, 1972.

Fu, K. S. *Syntactic methods in pattern recognition.* New York: Academic Press, 1974.

Fukunaga, K. *Introduction to statistical pattern recognition.* New York: Academic Press, 1972.

Meisel, W. S. *Computer-oriented approaches to pattern recognition.* New York: Academic Press, 1972.

Swets, J. A. *Signal detection and recognition by human observers.* New York: Wiley, 1964.

IV MULTIDIMENSIONAL PERCEPTUAL SPACES

10 Multidimensional Perceptual Spaces: Similarity Judgment and Identification

David J. Getty
John A. Swets
Joel B. Swets

We tend to make confusion errors when identifying complex stimuli that are highly similar. The greater the judged similarity of a pair of stimuli, the greater the probability of misidentifying one for the other. In this chapter, we explore the relationship between the perceptual representation of complex stimuli and decision processes. We present a view of similarity-judgment and identification processes that assumes: (1) that complex visual or auditory stimuli are represented perceptually as points in a multidimensional, geometric space; (2) that similarity judgments are (inversely) related to interstimulus distance in the perceptual space; and (3) that identification judgments are described by a probabilistic decision rule based on the pattern of interpoint distances in the perceptual space.

The concept of a perceptual space permits a logical distinction between perceptual processes that locate stimuli at positions in the space and subsequent decision processes that make use of the information contained in the representation. For example, similarity-judgment and identification tasks require different decision processes of the observer. However, when the tasks utilize a common set of stimuli, each decision process is applied to the same perceptual space. It is the common structure of the perceptual space that forms the basis for related performance in the two tasks. We suggest, at least as a reasonable approximation, that the perceptual representation of a particular set of stimuli is invariant with regard to the nature of the task required of the observer. On the other hand, we later present data showing that the way in which observers make use of the invariant information in the space is very much dependent on the requirements of the task.

A difficulty with the concept of a perceptual space is that the space is not directly observable and, therefore, must be inferred by indirect methods. Presumably, if we are able to understand and model the decision process of the observer in a particular task sufficiently well, then we should be able to work backwards from the observer's judgments to the structure of the space underlying them. We might do this in the context of various tasks: identification, classification, similarity judgment, dissimilarity judgment, etc. Considerable effort has been expended in recent years in modeling the similarity-judgment process. One product of these efforts is a collection of multidimensional scaling (MDS) procedures, each of which is designed to abstract the dimensions of the underlying perceptual space, and the loci of the stimuli within that space, from judgments of stimulus similarity or other measures of proximity.

In the next section of the paper, we discuss the specific assumptions made in MDS procedures regarding the perceptual space and the similarity-judgment process. We then present a model of the identification process that permits the cell-by-cell prediction of an observer's confusion matrix, based on the same model of the perceptual space. Finally, we illustrate the application of these models to similarity-judgment and identification-confusion data from several studies in which the stimuli were a set of visual transforms of underwater sounds.

THE PERCEPTUAL SPACE

We make two major assumptions regarding the nature of the perceptual representation of a set of complex stimuli. First, we assume that the perceptual representation is a multidimensional space consisting of a number of continuous orthogonal dimensions and that each stimulus is represented as a point in the space. Second, we assume that we may measure interstimulus distance between any pair of stimuli in the space and that this distance is given by a power metric. We examine the significance of these assumptions in the following subsections.

Orthogonal Dimensions

A set of complex auditory or visual stimuli may be *physically* represented in a multidimensional space consisting of some number, perhaps very large, of orthogonal physical dimensions. Each stimulus is defined as a point in this physical space. A central assumption, implicit in much of the research on the perception of complex stimuli, is that the perceptual space is, similarly, a multidimensional space composed of a number of orthogonal *perceptual* dimensions. The perception corresponding to a stimulus is represented as a point in this space. What can we say about the relationship between the perceptual and physical spaces? Although we may generally expect a high degree of correspondence between the two, there are several ways in which perceptual and physical spaces may be significantly different.

First, the dimensionality of the perceptual space may differ from that of the physical space. For example, the physical dimensionality of a stationary complex sound, as determined by spectral analysis, may be extremely large. By contrast, the dimensionality of the corresponding perceptual space may be relatively small. Plomp (1970, 1976) has reported that the perceptual space related to the timbre of complex tones has on the order of 18 dimensions, corresponding essentially to the output of a set of $\frac{1}{3}$-octave filters spanning the frequency domain.

Second, there often exist different sets of orthogonal physical dimensions that provide equivalent specification of the stimulus set. For example, each of a set of rectangles is determined by two independent measures—by its length and height, or, equivalently, by its longer side and area, or by the average of its sides and their ratio, etc. There is no sense in which one of these descriptions is logically more fundamental than another, although there may be other reasons for preferring one to another. On the other hand, it seems likely that the structure of our sensory and perceptual systems determine a psychological space in which: (1) only certain perceptual dimensions are represented; and (2) in which the represented dimensions are not of equal salience. Consequently, there may be a unique perceptual representation for rectangles, or perhaps a preferred representation among several possibilities.

Third, a perceptual dimension may correspond to some function of several physical dimensions, rather than to any single physical dimension. This issue bears directly on the concept of integrality and separability of physical stimulus dimensions (Garner, 1974). In Chapter 7 of this volume, Pachella, Somers, and Hardzinski suggest that integrality of several physical dimensions—the phenomenal coherence of dimensions—is observed when those physical dimensions combine in a single perceptual dimension. Thus, independent experimental variation in each of the physical dimensions is mapped into common variation in a single perceptual dimension. Separable physical dimensions—dimensions, phenomenally, that are separable—arise when each physical dimension is mapped into a different, independent perceptual dimension. In this case, independent variation of each physical dimension results in independent variation in the different perceptual dimensions. Thus, Pachella et al. propose that the experience of integrality or separability is determined by the mapping of the physical space of a stimulus set into the corresponding perceptual space and that the dimensions of the perceptual space are independent by definition.

Interstimulus Distance

We assume that the distance $d(x, y)$ in the perceptual space between two stimuli $x = (x_1, \ldots, x_n)$ and $y = (y_1, \ldots, y_n)$ is given by the Minkowski power metric:

$$d(x, y) = \left[\sum_{i=1}^{n} | x_i - y_i |^r \right]^{1/r}, r \geq 1. \tag{10.1}$$

This family of distance measures, which includes the Euclidean ($r = 2$) and city-block ($r = 1$) metrics, has three important properties: (1) decomposability;

(2) intradimensional subtractivity; and (3) interdimensional additivity (Tversky & Krantz, 1970).

Decomposability means that the distance between any two points in the space is a function of dimensionwise contributions. This property further implies that the scales on which the dimensions are represented are *commensurable,* one with another. In order to make clear the significance of commensurability, consider the problem encountered in defining a physical distance measure on a set of gray circular disks. The two dimensions of the physical space are diameter and grayness of the disk. For a pair of disks, how should one combine a measure of the difference in grayness with a measure of the difference in diameter to obtain interstimulus distance? Any particular choice of a function combining the contribution from each dimension is arbitrary. On the other hand, observers are able to make judgments of the similarity of pairs of such stimuli, indicating that they are able to measure the psychological distance within the perceptual space that corresponds to the gray circles. The implication is that the scales on which the perceptual dimensions are represented are commensurable. That is, they share a common measurement unit. If this is so, then it is the set of psychophysical functions relating physical to perceptual dimensions that determines the otherwise arbitrary combination rule. Thus, the relative salience of the perceptual dimensions is determined by the mappings of physical dimensions into the common perceptual scale.

The property referred to as intradimensional subtractivity asserts that the contribution to distance from a given dimension is the absolute difference between the loci of the two points on that dimension. Lastly, interdimensional additivity specifies that interstimulus distance is a function of the sum of the dimensionwise contributions.

SIMILARITY JUDGMENT

Multidimensional Scaling

Multidimensional scaling has emerged in recent years as the primary methodology for deriving the perceptual space based on similarity judgments of other forms of proximity measures such as dissimilarity judgments, association measures, or identification-confusion matrices (Carroll & Wish, 1974b; Romney, Shepard, & Nerlove, 1972; Shepard, Romney & Nerlove, 1972). It is important to keep in mind that use of these procedures entails the assertion of a specific formal model of the similarity-judgment process. The fundamental assumption made in the model underlying many MDS procedures—in addition to the assumptions we have already made regarding orthogonal perceptual dimensions and distance defined by a power metric—is that judged similarity is some particular, but generally unspecified, monotonic function of interstimulus distance. The smaller the distance between two stimuli in the perceptual space, the greater will be their judged similarity. For a set of pairwise similarity judgments and a space of experimenter-specified dimensionality, the MDS procedure iteratively determines the optimal geometric configuration of the stimuli in the space that minimizes a measure of the departure between derived interstimulus distances and those required to satisfy ordinality with the judged similarities. The process is repeated for a number of different dimensionalities, and a plot of goodness of fit vs. dimensionality is used to determine the appropriate dimensionality for the data. This can be a troublesome step in that goodness of fit will necessarily improve with increasing dimensionality; the usual decision criterion is the presence of an elbow in the function or attainment of a sufficiently high level of variance-accounted-for. The final stage in the use of MDS procedures concerns the identification of each of the derived perceptual dimensions with physical dimensions of the stimuli. This is particularly difficult when using a standard Euclidean metric with most MDS procedures, because the set of derived axes are often an arbitrary rotation of the true perceptual axes. This can occur because the derived Euclidean interstimulus distances are invariant under rigid rotation of the axes, and, therefore, all possible rotations of the axes are equivalent. This means that the axes may be interpretable only after submitting them to a suitable rotation (Shepard, 1972b).

One MDS procedure, INDSCAL, is not subject to the rotation-of-axes problem just discussed. INDSCAL differs from other MDS methods in assuming that different individuals perceive a given set of stimuli in terms of the same set of perceptual dimensions but with different weights (or saliencies) applied to these shared dimensions (Carroll, 1972; Carroll & Chang, 1970; Carroll & Wish, 1974a,b; Wish & Carroll, 1974). According to this model, interstimulus distance is determined by a weighted generalization of the Euclidean metric in which the contribution of each dimension to distance is modified by an individual's salience weight for that dimension. An important property of this method is that the axes of the derived space are not subject to rotation and, consequently, may be interpreted as corresponding directly to the observers' perceptual dimensions.

Recently, Tversky (1977) has questioned both the assumption that judged similarity can be described as a monotonic function of the metric interstimulus distance and, more fundamentally, the assumption that the perceptual space is dimensionally organized. He cites empirical evidence that, in some instances, similarity judgments are asymmetric and self-similarity is not equal across stimuli—both violations of metric axioms. He suggests that although the dimensional assumption may be appropriate for certain types of stimuli, it appears inappropriate for others that may be better described as a collection of features. He proposes a feature-matching model in which pairwise similarity is a function of both shared and distinctive feature sets. This model is able to accommodate the empirical similarity data that violate the metric axioms. On the other hand, Krumhansl (1978) has pointed out that multidimensional geometric models of perceptual space are able to account for the apparent metric violations if similarity is regarded as a function of both the metric interstimulus distance and the local spatial density of stimulus points. The major assumption of her model (Krumhansl, (1978) is that: "two points in a relatively dense region of a stimulus space would have a smaller similarity measure than two points of equal interpoint distance but located in a less dense region of the space [p. 446]." In anticipation of our later discussion of the identification model, we note here that the dependence of similarity judgments on the local stimulus density that characterizes Krumhansl's model of the similarity-judgment process is also a property of our model of the identification process. In identification, two stimuli in a relatively dense region of the space would have a lower probability of confusion than two equally separated stimuli located in a less dense region of the space.

The issues raised by Tversky and Krumhansl make clear that the assumptions underlying current MDS procedures, which do not accommodate metric violations, cannot be entirely correct or complete. However, departures from the assumptions are minor in many applications, and the consequences of these departures for the derived space are probably small.

Applications of MDS Procedures

Over the past 10 years, MDS procedures have been applied with increasing frequency in studies of complex auditory and visual stimuli. In general, the goals of these applications have been: (1) to derive a multidimensional representation of the psychological space for a particular stimulus domain; and (2) to identify each perceptual dimension as a function of physical dimensions. We review here some of the major findings in the areas of: (1) speech sounds; (2) nonspeech sounds; and (3) visual transforms of nonspeech sounds.

Speech Sounds. In a pair of related experiments, Pols, van der Kamp, & Plomp (1969) and Klein, Plomp, & Pols (1970) submitted identification-confusion matrices obtained for a set of vowel sounds to MDS analysis. In the latter study, they derived a four-dimensional perceptual space in which the first two dimensions were identified as the first and second formant frequencies. They also performed a physical analysis of the sounds, passing them through a set of $\frac{1}{3}$-octave filters. The resulting frequency spectra were then submitted to a principal components analysis; four factors were found to account for 98% of the variance. The first two factors of this physical analysis were identified as the first and second formants, as in the perceptual analysis, accounting between them for 83% of the variance. Finally, each of the four perceptual dimensions correlated highly with one of the four physical factors (coefficients of .997, .995, .907, and .794, respectively). These results support the view that the auditory system performs a fairly coarse spectral analysis on acoustic signals corresponding to about 18 frequency bands. In addition, the final perceptual representation for vowels is further reduced to approximately four dimensions.

The perceptual space for spoken consonants has also been investigated. Shepard (1972a) applied an MDS procedure to a confusion matrix formed by pooling several matrices obtained previously by Miller and Nicely (1955) for 16 English consonants under 17 different conditions of S/N ratio and bandwidth. It was found that 99.4% of the variance could be accounted for by a two-dimensional perceptual space. These two dimensions were identified, after rotation, as the linguistic distinctive features "voicing" and "nasality." Shephard notes that the data suggest the existence of additional dimensions; their importance in this context must be small, however, because they could account for, at most, the remaining .6% residual variance. Recently, Wish and Carroll (1974) reanalyzed the Miller and Nicely data using the INDSCAL individual differences MDS procedure. All 17 matrices, each corresponding to a different signal degradation condition, were submitted to a single analysis. The results were: (1) the loci of the consonants in a six-dimensional space; and (2) a set of salience weights on the dimensions for each of the 17 conditions. Each of the six derived dimensions was identified as a particular linguistic distinctive feature. As in Shepard's analysis, the two major perceptual dimensions were identified as voicing and nasality. However, they were determined to account for only 34% of the variance, averaged over all 17 conditions, with the other four dimensions accounting for an additional 44% of the variance. Of particular significance was their finding that the dimension salience weights changed across the 17 conditions in ways that were interpretable on acoustic grounds. These weight patterns provide important information about how an observer's use of available perceptual information changes as a function of different types of stimulus degradation.

Nonspeech Sounds. In parallel with the work on speech sounds, other research has sought to understand the psychological space underlying the perception of similarly complex nonspeech sounds. One group of studies may be identified by their use of complex synthesized sounds that varied in controlled ways along specific physical dimensions. For example, Plomp and Steeneken (1969) applied an MDS procedure to judgments of the similarity of complex steady-state tones differing only in the phase pattern of their harmonics. The stimuli were found to cluster in two regions in a two-dimensional space, the dimensions of which they did not attempt to identify. The two clusters revealed that a phase difference of a particular type does, in fact, affect the perception of timbre. The success of this study led Morgan, Woodhead, and Webster (1976) to apply an MDS procedure to the identification of confusion data collected in an earlier study (Webster, Woodhead, & Carpenter, 1973). The stimuli were a set of 16 synthesized sounds that varied binarily on four acoustic dimensions: fundamental frequency, harmonic structure, number of formants, and formant position. The MDS analysis revealed a three-dimensional space with one of the perceptual dimensions corresponding to each of the physical dimensions except for the number of formants. Recently, Howard and Silverman (1976) reported a study in which they used Webster's stimulus set but with the observers making pairwise similarity judgments rather than identification judgments. Using the INDSCAL procedure, they also derived a three-dimensional perceptual space, the dimensions of which were identified as fundamental frequency, harmonic structure, and a combination of the number of formants and their locations.

These studies have demonstrated that judgments of stimulus proximity reflect aspects of the known physical structure of the synthesized stimuli and that MDS procedures are able to recover this structure from the judgments. In contrast, other studies have sought to identify dimensions in the perceptual space corresponding to sets of real-world, nonsynthesized sounds. In one such study, Cermak and Cornillon (1976) had observers rate the similarity of samples of traffic noise. Using INDSCAL, they found that the primary perception dimension corresponded to subjective noise intensity; they were unable to identify firmly a second derived perceptual dimension. In another study, Howard (1977) had observers rate the similarity of a set of eight passive sonar sounds representing natural and mechanically produced underwater sounds. He derived a two-dimensional perceptual space in which the first dimension reflected spectral shape and the second the prominance of a low-frequency periodicity component.

The development of INDSCAL, and other similar MDS procedures, has made possible the examination of differences among individuals (or groups of individuals) with regard to the relative salience of different perceptual dimensions. For example, Miller and Carterette (1975) had observers judge the similarity of pairs of complex synthetic tones that varied in fundamental frequency, envelope, and relative harmonic amplitude. The tones were chosen to represent timbres associated with different musical instruments. Separate INDSCAL analyses of two sets of data each revealed an interpretable three-dimensional space. Large differences in dimension salience weights were observed between musically experienced and musically nonexperienced subjects. Similar differences related to musical experience were obtained in the studies by Howard and Silverman (1976) and Howard (1977), described earlier, in which nonmusical sounds were used. These findings make clear that prior experience, in this case with music, can alter the relative importance of perceptual dimensions.

Visual Transforms of Nonspeech Sounds.   Several studies have enabled a comparison to be made of the perceptual space associated with auditory vs. visual presentations of related complex stimuli. The visual signals have typically consisted of sonograms of the auditory signals, that is, frequency vs. time displays in which trace darkness represents energy. In a study mentioned earlier, Morgan et al. (1976) scaled confusion data for a set of 16 synthetic sounds and for visual transforms of the same sounds. The MDS solutions revealed a three-dimensional perceptual space for both auditory and visual stimuli. In both cases, the first two dimensions were fundamental frequency and source wave form. However, the third acoustic dimension was formant location, whereas the third visual dimension was number of formants.

In another comparison of visual and auditory spaces, Swets, Green Getty, and Swets (1978) applied INDSCAL to similarity judgments of visual transforms of eight underwater sounds highly similar to those analyzed by Howard (1977) with auditory presentation. Two of the four dimensions revealed in our analysis of the visual data (contrast and low-frequency periodicity) corresponded to the two dimensions (spectral shape and low-frequency periodicity) reported by Howard. These comparisons indicate that the structure of the visual and auditory perceptual spaces may be similar when the stimuli in the two modalities are related by the types of transformations previously described. On the other hand, the relative saliencies of corresponding dimensions may be quite different for the two modalities.

IDENTIFICATION

The starting point for the identification model is the set of spatial coordinates, $\psi_{i,k}$ for each of m stimuli $(1 \leq i \leq m)$ on each of n dimensions $(1 \leq k \leq n)$, in the perceptual space. We define the interstimulus distance $D_{i,j}$ between stimulus i and j to be the weighted Euclidean metric given by:

$$D_{i,j} = \left[\sum_k w_k (\psi_{i,k} - \psi_{j,k})^2 \right]^{1/2}. \qquad (10.2)$$

The set of weights, w_k, in Eq. 10.2 describe the relative salience, or importance, of each dimension in determining interstimulus distance. These are treated as parameters to be estimated from the confusion data, subject to the normalizing convention that $\sum_k w_k = 1$.

We define the confusability of stimulus i with stimulus j as:

$$C_{i,j} = \exp(-a\, D_{i,j}), \qquad (10.3)$$

where a is an observer-sensitivity parameter $(a > 0)$. Thus, the confusability of two stimuli is assumed to be a monotone decreasing, symmetric function of their separation in the perceptual space. Shepard (1957, 1958a, and 1958b) found empirical support for this exponential relationship in his related work on stimulus and response generalization.

Finally, we relate conditional probability that the observer will give the response corresponding to stimulus j when stimulus i is presented to stimulus confusability by Luce's choice model (1963):

$$\Pr(R_j|S_i) = \frac{b_j\,C_{i,j}}{\sum_k b_k\,C_{i,k}}, \qquad\qquad (10.4)$$

where b_j is a measure of the observer's relative bias toward response j. It should be noted that although the set of confusion weights are symmetric ($C_{i,j} = C_{j,i}$), the set of response probabilities are not (i.e., $\Pr[R_j|S_i] \neq \Pr[R_i|S_j]$), in general, even when response bias is absent ($b_i = b_j$). This is true because the denominator of Eq. 10.4 will typically not be the same in the two cases, reflecting inhomogeneities in the distribution of stimuli in the perceptual space. Thus, a given distance between two stimuli, i and j, does not determine response probability in any absolute sense, but only relative to the distances of all other stimuli. These distances will usually differ depending on whether they are measured from stimulus i or stimulus j, thus producing confusion asymmetry.

The fact that asymmetry about the main diagonal in a confusion matrix may arise from spatial inhomogeneity in the perceptual space—as well as from response biases—argues against the common practice of averaging the upper and lower triangular halves of a confusion matrix to remove asymmetry. If the model is essentially correct, then such averaging removes true structure from the data rather than noise.

We recall at this point our earlier discussion of Krumhansl's hypothesis that observed metric violations in similarity-judgment tasks are due to density inhomogeneity in the perceptual space. Although we do not attempt to demonstrate the following here, it is true for this identification model that, for a given distance between two stimuli, the probability of confusion is lower when the two stimuli are located in a relatively dense region of the perceptual space than when they are located in a less dense region.

PREDICTION OF CONFUSION MATRICES: ILLUSTRATIVE RESULTS

We turn now to similarity judgment and identification data obtained in an experiment in which three observers identified visual transforms of Howard's (1977) set of eight passive sonar recordings of confusable natural and mechanically produced underwater sounds. (For details of this experiment, see Getty, Swets, Swets, & Green, 1979.) We constructed a visual display of each sound in the form of a time vs. frequency sonogram in which energy was represented by increasing darkness of the trace. Visual (Gaussian) noise was superimposed on these images with an amplitude sufficient to induce a reasonable rate of confusion errors. Each of the eight stimuli is shown in Fig. 10.1 at approximately the same signal-to-noise ratio used in the similarity-judgment task. For the identification task, the signal-to-noise ratio was greatly reduced to increase the rate of confusion errors.

The pairwise similarity judgments of our three observers were submitted to INDSCAL analysis, from which we derived a three-dimensional perceptual space. The three dimensions were found to correlate highly (.95, .97, and .83) with physical measures of mid-frequency energy, low-frequency energy, and

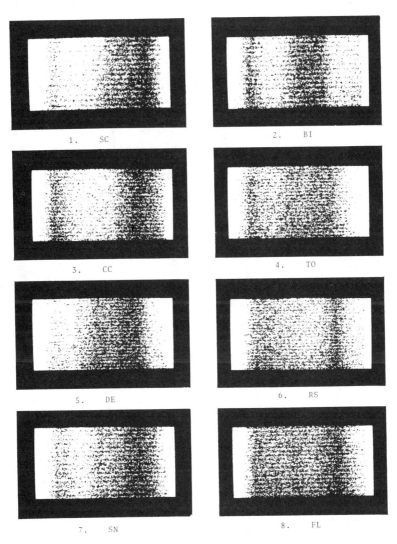

FIG. 10.1.   Visual representations of the eight underwater sounds, photographed from the display monitor. From Getty et al. (1979).

8 x 8 EXPERIMENT

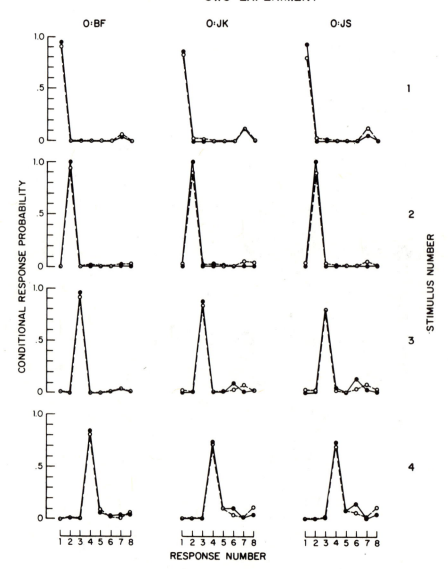

FIG. 10.2. Distribution of response probability for each stimulus (Stimuli 1 to 4 on left; Stimuli 5 to 8 on right) for each observer. Obtained distributions are given by solid lines and filled circles; distributions predicted by the model are given by dashed lines and open circles. From Getty et al. (1979).

8x8 EXPERIMENT

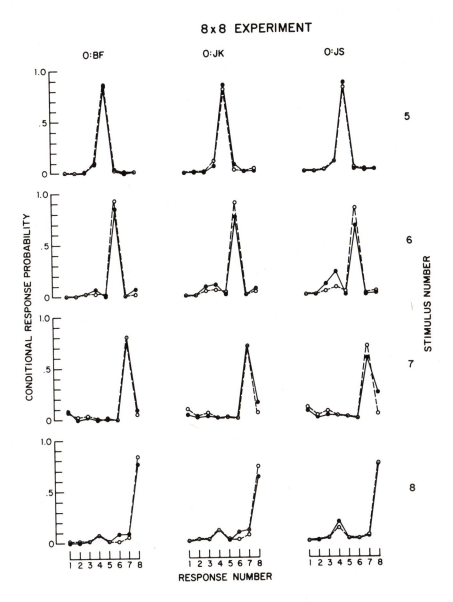

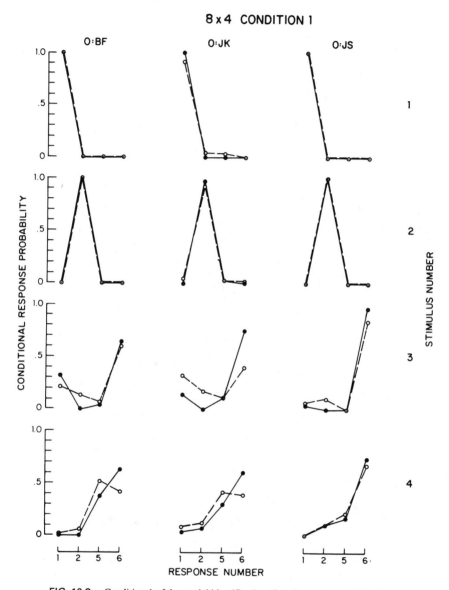

FIG. 10.3. Condition 1 of the partial identification (8 × 4) experiment: Distribution of response probability for each stimulus (Stimuli 1 to 4 on left; Stimuli 5 to 8 on right) for each observer. Obtained distributions are given by solid lines and filled circles; predicted distributions are given by dashed lines and open circles. From Getty et al. (1979).

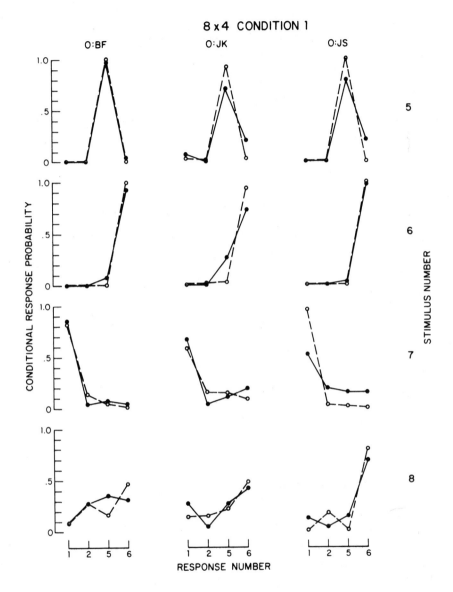

8 x 4 CONDITION 1

O:BF   O:JK   O:JS

CONDITIONAL RESPONSE PROBABILITY

STIMULUS NUMBER

RESPONSE NUMBER

image contrast. A fourth physical dimension, temporal periodicity, which is prominent in the images as alternating darker and lighter horizontal bands, did not emerge in the MDS analysis. Yet, our observers reported using it as a dimension in the subsequent identification task. We return to this point shortly. For the present, we note that the periodicity dimension was included as a fourth dimension in the model for purposes of predicting identification confusions.

On each of a series of trials in the identification task, the observers identified a very low-contrast displayed image, chosen at random from the set of eight. Each observer held a labelled reference set of high-contrast photos of the stimuli while making identification judgments.

The decision model was fitted individually to each observer's confusion matrix. Five parameters were estimated for each observer: the sensitivity parameter and the salience weights for the four perceptual dimensions. Using these estimated weights and the loci of the stimuli in the perceptual space derived from the INDSCAL analysis, we then predicted the individual cells of the confusion matrix from the decision model, separately for each observer. The observed and predicted response distributions, conditional upon presented stimulus, are shown in Fig. 10.2 for each of the three observers. The predicted matrices account for 98% of the variance in the observed distributions averaged over the three observers.

We made another, and probably more stringent, test of the identification model by determining how well it was able to predict confusion matrices arising when observers were limited to the responses associated with only a subset of the eight stimuli—a partial identification task. We ran three conditions in which four of the eight stimuli (the ''signals'') corresponded to allowed identification responses, a different set of four in each condition. In terms of the model, each conditional response distribution is determined by only four distances in the perceptual space, those between the presented stimulus and each of the four signals.

Individual confusion matrices from one of the three conditions of the partial identification task—the one in which Stimuli 1, 2, 5, and 6 of Fig. 10.1 were designated as signals—are shown in Fig. 10.3. The model was fitted to the data as before, using the same INDSCAL-derived perceptual space. Over the three observers, the predicted confusion matrices accounted for an average of 90% of the observed variance in the obtained confusion matrices. For reference, in the other two conditions of this task, the model accounted for 86% and 94% of the observed variance.

Of particular interest in Fig. 10.3 is the relative accuracy of the predicted distribution when one of the noise stimuli (Stimulus 3, 4, 7, or 8) was presented. In this case, the correct response is not among the allowable subset, thereby requiring the observer to identify the most likely alternative. In terms of the model, the distribution of response probability is determined by the relative distances of each of the four allowable responses from the location of the presented stimulus in the perceptual space.

Adaptive, Context-Dependent Weighting of Dimensions

Over the complete identification task and the three conditions of the partial identification task, we observed that the pattern of estimated dimension salience weights changed from one task to another, as shown in Fig. 10.4. Inasmuch as the same set of eight stimuli were presented in all four tasks, why should observers vary the relative weighting of dimensions across the several tasks? Although the stimulus set was constant, the requirements of each task differed in terms of the subset of signals that the observers were required to identify. We suggest that

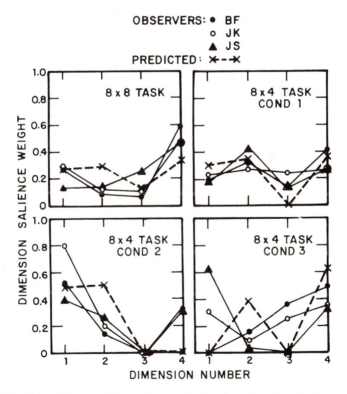

FIG. 10.4.   Estimated salience weights on the four dimensions for each observer for each condition in the complete (8 × 8) and partial (8 × 4) identification experiments (solid lines). The pattern of weights that maximizes probability of correct identification is given by the dashed line for each condition. From Getty et al. (1979).

observers are able to adjust the relative saliencies of the perceptual dimensions; the purpose of this tuning is to optimize some task-dependent performance criterion. In our identification tasks, it appears that observers tuned the set of salience weights to maximize the average probability of making a correct identification. An observer holding this criterion should have adjusted salience weights across our tasks as the allowable response set varied. For each task, we determined from the model the set of salience weights that would maximize the average probability of a correct identification. These predicted patterns, shown by the dashed lines in Fig. 10.4, correspond reasonably well with the observed patterns across tasks.

We believe that the tuning of salience weights reflected in the differences observed across the tasks is a dynamic process based on feedback of information relevant to the observer. In other work (Getty, Swets, & Swets, 1980), we have found that the adjustment process may occur gradually over hundreds of trials in an identification task.

Earlier, we suggested that the similarity-judgment task involves a particular decision process operating upon the perceptual space, a space that is invariant with regard to the task. We may suppose that the similarity-judgment process, whereby an observer assigns a number representing perceived similarity of a particular pair of stimuli, involves adaptive weighting of dimensions in the perceptual space. It is less clear for similarity judgment what criterion an observer may be attempting to optimize in adjusting salience weights. As observers are usually instructed to use all of a specified range of numbers in their judgments, one might speculate that weights are tuned to maximize the *range* of interstimulus distances in the perceptual space. That is, it may be optimal to weight dimensions such that some interstimulus distances are as small as possible whereas others are as large as possible. Alternatively, the criterion might be to make the distribution of distances as uniform as possible, thereby using all response categories about equally.

Limited Processing Capacity

The results that have been reported might suggest that the number of dimensions in the perceptual space corresponding to our set of visual patterns is quite small. The MDS analysis of similarity judgments identified a space of three dimensions that accounted for most of the observed variability. That space—and an added fourth dimension—allowed us to predict identification judgments quite well. We may suppose that the fourth dimension was available to observers in the similarity task as well but received no weight. This suggests that there may be many more dimensions in the perceptual space that were not revealed because they received little or no weight in the decision processes involved in our tasks. Presumably, other task contexts would require different patterns of dimension salience weights that might reveal other dimensions.

The fact that both the MDS analysis and decision model accounted for such a large portion of the performance variability with only three or four dimensions does argue that the number of utilized dimensions in the similarity and identification decision processes is small, and probably limited. Our view, now, is that the true dimensionality of the perceptual space reflects the complexity of the stimuli under consideration. Complex stimuli may have a representation of very high dimensionality. At the same time, we imagine that decision processes have the capacity to combine information from only a small number of perceptual dimensions and that these dimensions are adaptively selected—and weighted—in order to optimize some task-dependent performance criterion.

ACKNOWLEDGMENTS

This research was supported by a contract with the Engineering Psychology Programs, Office of Naval Research.

REFERENCES

Carroll, J. D. Individual differences and multidimensional scaling. In R. N. Shepard, A. K. Romney, & S. Nerlove (Eds.), *Multidimensional scaling: Theory and applications in the behavioral sciences* (Vol. 1). New York: Seminar Press, 1972.

Carroll, J. D., & Chang, J. J. Analysis of individual differences in multidimensional scaling via an N-way generalization of "Eckhart-Young" decomposition. *Psychometrika,* 1970, *35,* 288–319.

Carroll, J. D., & Wish, M. Models and methods for three-way multidimensional scaling. In D. H. Krantz, R. C. Atkinson, R. D. Luce, & P. Suppes (Eds.), *Contemporary developments in mathematical psychology, Vol. II: Measurement, psychophysics, and neural information processing.* San Francisco: Freeman, 1974. (a)

Carroll, J. D., & Wish, M. Multidimensional perceptual models and measurement methods. In E. C. Carterette & M. P. Friedman (Eds.), *Handbook of perception, Vol. II: Psychophysical judgment and measurement.* New York: Academic Press, 1974. (b)

Cermak, G. W., & Cornillon, P. C. Multidimensional analyses of judgments about traffic noise. *Journal of the Acoustical Society of America,* 1976, *59,* 1412–1420.

Garner, W. R. *The processing of information and structure.* Hillsdale, N.J.: Lawrence Erlbaum Associates, 1974.

Getty, D. J., Swets, J. A., Swets, J. B., & Green, D. M. On the prediction of confusion matrices from similarity judgments. *Perception & Psychophysics,* 1979, *26,* 1–19.

Getty, D. J., Swets, J. B., & Swets, J. A. The observer's use of perceptual dimensions in signal identification. In R. S. Nickerson (Ed.), *Attention and performance VIII.* Hillsdale, N.J.: Lawrence Erlbaum Associates, 1980.

Howard, J. H., Jr. The psychophysical structure of eight complex underwater sounds. *Journal of the Acoustical Society of America,* 1977, *62,* 149–156.

Howard, J. H., Jr., & Silverman, E. G. A multidimensional scaling analysis of 16 complex sounds. *Perception & Psychophysics,* 1976, *19,* 193–200.

Klein, W., Plomp, R., & Pols, L. C. W. Vowel spectra, vowel spaces, and vowel identification. *Journal of the Acoustical Society of America,* 1970, *48,* 999–1009.

Krumhansl, C. L. Concerning the applicability of geometric models to similarity data: The interrelationship between similarity and spatial density. *Psychological Review*, 1978, *85*, 445–463.

Luce, R. D. Detection and recognition. In R. D. Luce, R. R. Bush, & E. Galanter (Eds.), *Handbook of mathematical psychology*. New York: Wiley, 1963.

Miller, G. A., & Nicely, P. E. An analysis of perceptual confusions among some English consonants. *Journal of the Acoustical Society of America*, 1955, *27*, 338–352.

Miller, J. R., & Carterette, E. C. Perceptual space for musical structures. *Journal of the Acoustical Society of America*, 1975, *58*, 711–720.

Morgan, B. J. T., Woodhead, M. M., & Webster, J. C. On the recovery of physical dimensions of stimuli, using multidimensional scaling. *Journal of the Acoustical Society of America*, 1976, *60*, 186–189.

Plomp, R. Timbre as a multidimensional attribute of complex tones. In R. Plomp & G. F. Smoorenburg (Eds.), *Frequency analysis and periodicity detection in hearing*. Leiden: Sijthoff, 1970.

Plomp, R. *Aspects of tone sensation*. New York: Academic Press, 1976.

Plomp, R., & Steeneken, H. J. M. Effect of phase on the timbre of complex tones. *Journal of the Acoustical Society of America*, 1969, *46*, 409–421.

Pols, L. C. W., van der Kamp, L. J. Th., & Plomp, R. Perceptual and physical space of vowel sounds. *Journal of the Acoustical Society of America*, 1969, *46*, 458–467.

Romney, A. K., Shepard, R. N., & Nerlove, S. B. (Eds.). *Multidimensional scaling: Theory and applications in the behavioral sciences* (Vol. 2). New York: Seminar Press, 1972.

Shepard, R. N. Stimulus and response generalization: A stochastic model relating generalization to distance in psychological space. *Psychometrika*, 1957, *22*, 325–345.

Shepard, R. N. Stimulus and response generalization: Deduction of the generalization gradient from a trace model. *Psychological Review*, 1958, *65*, 242–256. (a)

Shepard, R. N. Stimulus and response generalization: Tests of a model relating generalization to distance in psychological space. *Journal of Experimental Psychology*, 1958, *55*, 509–523. (b)

Shepard, R. N. Psychological representation of speech sounds. In E. David & P. Denes (Eds.), *Human communication: A unified view*. New York: McGraw-Hill, 1972. (a)

Shepard, R. N. A taxonomy of some principal types of data and of multidimensional methods for their analysis. In R. N. Shepard, A. K. Romney, & S. B. Nerlove (Eds.), *Multidimensional scaling: Theory and applications in the behavioral sciences* (Vol. 1). New York: Seminar Press, 1972. (b)

Shepard, R. N., Romney, A. K., & Nerlove, S. B. (Eds.). *Multidimensional scaling: Theory and applications in the behavioral sciences* (Vol. 1). New York: Seminar Press, 1972.

Swets, J. A., Green, D. M., Getty, D. J., & Swets, J. B. Signal detection and identification at successive stages of observation. *Perception & Psychophysics*, 1978, *23*, 275–279.

Tversky, A. Features of similarity. *Psychological Review*, 1977, *84*, 327–352.

Tversky, A., & Krantz, D. H. The dimensional representation and the metric structure of similarity data. *Journal of Mathematical Psychology*, 1970, *7*, 572–596.

Webster, J. C., Woodhead, M. M., & Carpenter, A. Perceptual confusions between four-dimensional sounds. *Journal of the Acoustical Society of America*, 1973, *53*, 448–456.

Wish, M., & Carroll, J. D. Applications of individual differences scaling to studies of human perception and judgments. In E. C. Carterette & M. P. Friedman (Eds.), *Handbook of perception, Vol. II: Psychophysical judgment and measurement*. New York: Academic Press, 1974.

11

Feature Selection in Auditory Perception

James H. Howard, Jr.
James A. Ballas

Feature extraction plays a fundamental role in many theoretical treatments of auditory pattern recognition. At some early stage during recognition, the perceptual representation of a stimulus is broken down into a set of elementary properties or characteristics. The central role of this stage can be seen in Fig. 11.1. In this characterization of pattern recognition, the preliminary analysis stage produces a relatively unprocessed representation of an incoming stimulus. At this point, the representation is thought to contain considerable noise and redundancy. The output of this stage is then transformed by the feature-extraction stage into a relatively small set of distinctive features—the basic building blocks of the recognition process. As Anderson, Silverstein, Ritz, and Jones (1977) have noted: "Distinctive features are usually viewed as a system for efficient preprocessing, whereby a noisy stimulus is reduced to its essential characteristics and a decision is made on these [p. 429]."

Quite clearly, feature extraction involves information reduction. Some information in a pattern is retained, whereas other information is discarded. Ideally, the set of distinctive features should uniquely specify the stimulus, preserving or enhancing perceptually important differences among stimuli and reducing or eliminating perceptually unimportant differences. The significance of feature extraction in auditory recognition should be obvious. Inasmuch as the feature representation is efficient both in terms of dimensionality and redundancy, the subsequent decision process can be undertaken with minimal effort and optimal reliability. On the other hand, an ineffective set of distinctive features not only can increase the amount of subsequent processing required but, by definition, also makes satisfactory performance impossible.

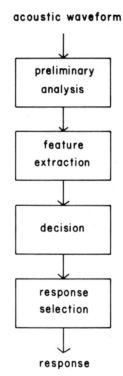

acoustic waveform

preliminary
analysis

feature
extraction

decision

response
selection

response

FIG. 11.1.   Flow diagram of a four-stage pattern recognition model.

Despite its central importance as a theoretical construct, feature extraction has not been well specified in the literature. No true psychological theory of feature extraction exists. When we say that a stimulus is reduced to its "essential elements," what do we mean? How are these crucial elementary units determined? Implicit in the foregoing discussion is the assumption that a feature tuning process exists whereby a set of distinctive features is defined. In this chapter, we focus on possible mechanisms that underlie feature tuning or feature selection in human auditory recognition.

FEATURE SELECTION PROCESSES

As outlined, the feature selection problem involves picking a set of distinctive features from the vast set of all possible features. The problem seems clear in the case of a statistician who is constructing an algorithm to classify a set of acoustic patterns. What acoustic cues or combinations of acoustic cues should be considered? Indeed, the ideal features may be some complex function of a number of more primitive spectral measurements. Given a set of preliminary measurements and the desired categorization of the stimuli, the statistician must select a set of distinctive features bearing in mind both performance and economic (i.e., "How much will the feature extraction process cc st?") considerations (cf. Meisel, 1972).

The feature selection problem for the psychologist has much in common with that of the statistician. However, instead of actually determining a set of "efficient" distinctive features for human auditory recognition (although this may be of interest in some applied contexts), it is our task to identify the features or the feature selection process that human listeners actually use.

Although a number of specific "natural" auditory feature selection processes can be proposed, two contrasting views are implicit in the literature. The first possibility is that nature has selected an optimal set of distinctive features through natural selection and built specific mechanisms, finely tuned to detect these features, into our auditory systems. The second view affords more flexibility. Perhaps, nature has built the feature selection *process* into our auditory systems. In other words, we may have internalized a set of rules and processes that enable us to establish what the distinctive features should be in any particular stimulus context. Both views can be considered in more detail.

The Property-List Approach

The first view argues that people are equipped with a set of specific feature-detecting mechanisms. In terms of auditory pattern recognition, this approach places an emphasis on the feature detectors themselves. An auditory feature extractor is, from this perspective, a filterlike device that monitors the incoming stream of sensory information for particular stimulus properties. In short, each detector is tuned to "look for" a particular stimulus property, and a set of feature detectors determines a property list for the stimulus. In the extreme, this seems consistent with previous neurophysiological investigations of single-unit responding in sensory systems. The first relevant evidence emerged many years ago from the seminal work of Lettvin, Maturana, McCulloch, and Pitts (1959) on the frog's visual system. Their pioneering research revealed the presence of highly selective neurons in the visual periphery tuned to select stimuli of particular relevance for the animal's survival. Moving edge, overall illumination, and the highly popularized "bug" detectors were among those discovered. It seems that nature equipped the frog with special detectors for virtually everything it needs to know about its visual world. Similar work soon followed, investigating feature detectors in both the visual (Hubel & Wiesel, 1962) and auditory systems (Whitfield & Evans, 1965). This research stimulated considerable speculation about hierarchical decision mechanisms where feature information is combined and recombined, ultimately leading to classification (cf. Weisstein, 1973). When extended, this line of reasoning leads to Sherrington's (1941) notion of a supreme, "pontifical" cell whose response signals the presence of a particular complex pattern. Although he opted for a more democratic system of "cardinal" cells in place of the all-knowing pontiff, Barlow (1972) succinctly summarized this approach in his specification of a "neuron doctrine for perceptual psychology."

A good example of this sort of system in human audition is the set of distinctive features and feature detectors hypothesized to underlie human speech perception (Fant, 1973). Here, a relatively small number of distinctive features have been described that may be used to characterize individual phonemes uniquely. A voicing detector, for example, would monitor the speech stream for cues that distinguish between voiced and unvoiced stop consonants. In an initial study, Eimas and Corbit (1973) used a psychophysical procedure to obtain evidence for the existence of voicing detectors, finely tuned to a relatively narrow range of voice onset times (i.e., formant onset asynchronies in the speech signal). More recent work has generalized these findings to include the psychophysical investigation of a variety of linguistic as well as nonlinguistic feature detectors in the human auditory system (Cooper, 1975).

The Process-Oriented Approach

The second alternative assumes that humans have internalized the feature selection process itself. In contrast to the property-list approach, the important "features" in a complex sound reflect whatever structure exists in the output of the preliminary analysis stage. In this sense, nature has endowed us with a set of rules and criteria for feature selection rather than with highly tuned detection mechanisms.

In arguing that the feature selection process is built in, we necessarily assume the existence of certain general principles that can characterize feature selection across a variety of stimulus and task conditions. These invariants include both the selection criteria employed and a mechanism for applying them. In the present discussion, we assume that the feature selection process attempts to reduce the dimensionality of the stimulus representation, while preserving as much of the stimulus structure as possible. An example of this approach may be seen in Wightman's (1973) pattern transformation model of periodicity pitch perception. The model assumes that the auditory system performs two successive Fourier transforms (equivalent to an autocorrelation in the time domain) to extract periodicity information from a complex tone. Inasmuch as signal periodicity reflects the frequency relations among individual spectral components, the proposed transformation analyzes the relational structure of the stimulus. Uttal (1975) has outlined a similar autocorrelational model for visual pattern detection.

Implications for Auditory Perception

The intention of this discussion is not to suggest that one or the other of these views is necessarily correct. At this point, the best view would seem to include elements of both perspectives. However, we consider these particular approaches because they occupy opposite ends on a continuum of feature selection flexibility. This difference has a number of implications for auditory recognition theory and, in particular, for recognition processes in the perception of the timbre of complex sounds. As Plomp (1976) has noted, timbre is: "that attribute of auditory sensation in terms of which a listener can judge that two steady-state complex tones having the same loudness and pitch, are dissimilar (pp. 85–86)." In other words, timbre is everything left over after we take away loudness and pitch. Quite clearly, timbre does not describe a single perceptual attribute of sound, but rather it represents a family of perceptual attributes. One would be entirely at ease in reporting that a complex sound has a high pitch or is very loud, but attempting a simple description of this sort for timbre would seem ridiculous. If asked to discuss the timbre of a sound, the listener would likely resort to a number of adjectives, "it is coarse, pleasant, bright, etc." (e.g., von Bismarck, 1974). But even given this verbal flexibility, the listener would find it difficult to describe the timbre of a complex tone adequately.

If one were to adopt a property-list approach to the feature extraction stage for timbre perception, it would be necessary to specify a list of important timbre attributes. However, it should be clear that any list of possible timbre properties or features would be very long indeed. In this case, the more flexible, process-oriented approach to feature extraction would seem most appropriate. Rather than searching for the set of distinctive features that would enable the listener to distinguish all possible timbres, in this approach we attempt to specify a process that can characterize the relations among individual components in the amplitude and phase spectra of complex sounds.

In the remainder of this paper, we examine three experiments whose findings suggest that considerable flexibility exists in the feature extraction process. In all three experiments, the features that listeners use in perceiving the timbre of complex sounds were investigated. The results of the first two experiments serve to emphasize the importance of the stimulus population in determining the timbre attributes that listeners use in comparing complex sounds. The findings of the third experiment illustrate the role of task factors in feature extraction.

STIMULUS EFFECTS IN FEATURE EXTRACTION

In the foregoing discussion, we argued that feature extraction in timbre perception may be more appropriately viewed as a structure analyzing process than as a feature detection process. In order to evaluate this hypothesis empirically, it is necessary to examine the output of the feature extraction stage and to relate this feature representation to the known properties of its input. Although the feature representation is obviously not directly observable, it may be inferred using a variety of psychophysical procedures. In particular, multidimensional scaling has emerged as a useful method for identifying the underlying psychological structure of complex sounds (Plomp, 1976). Typically, listeners are asked to provide pairwise or triadic dissimilarity judgments on the set of signals of interest. A specific multidimensional scaling algorithm is then applied to decompose the resulting subjective proximity matrix into an n-dimensional metric space in which each stimulus is represented as a single point or vector. Providing that an interpretable solution with satisfactory stress exists, it is generally assumed that the dimensions in the psychological stimulus space reflect those features that the listeners employed in comparing the stimuli. In other words, it is at least implicitly assumed that the scaling methods provide an approximate inverse to the later stages of the recognition process (cf. Fig. 11.1). If we are willing to make certain assumptions about the information available after the preliminary analysis stage, then we have the input/output information necessary to speculate about feature extraction.

In the first systematic application of these methods to audition, Plomp (Plomp, 1976) compared the timbre properties of nine musical-instrument sounds to their corresponding spectral structure. A three-dimensional stimulus space was revealed in a multidimensional scaling analysis of the subjective similarity data for these stimuli. The configuration of interstimulus distances in this perceptual space correlated highly with the corresponding distances in a three-dimensional space obtained in a physical analysis of these sounds. Although Plomp was primarily concerned with determining whether a correlation existed, for our present purposes, the specific methods used to obtain the physical space are of particular interest.

Specifically, the physical analysis was based on steady-state information that could be reasonably thought to approximate that available to the auditory feature extraction process. Recognizing the limited spectral analyzing ability of the human auditory system (Zwicker, Flottorp, & Stevens, 1957), Plomp obtained $\frac{1}{3}$-octave band level measurements for each of his complex sounds. A principal-components analysis was then performed on these spectra. The results revealed that each of the nine stimuli could be characterized in terms of three spectral attributes with very little loss of information. If we are willing to assume that the $\frac{1}{3}$-octave spectrum approximates the output of the preliminary analysis stage depicted in Fig. 11.1, then these findings suggest that the listener's feature extraction process may be somewhat similar to a principal-components analysis.[1]

This conclusion is entirely consistent with our hypothesis that the feature extraction stage in timbre perception involves a structural analysis of the stimuli. More specifically, the principal-components analysis may be thought of as a structure-preserving transformation that maps stimuli from one space into

-----

[1]It should be emphasized that Plomp and his associates (personal communication, 1978) did not refer to the dimensions extracted in their perceptual analysis as "features." Rather, as indicated earlier, they were primarily interested in determining the degree of correlation between the configuration of stimuli in the perceptual space and the steady-state spectra of the sounds.

acoustic waveform

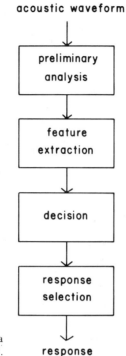

FIG. 11.1. Flow diagram of a
four-stage pattern recognition model.   **response**

another of lower dimensionality. The first principal component is simply a new
axis in the original space (in this case, the measurement space spanned by the
$\frac{1}{3}$-octave band levels) that accounts for most of the variability in the data. In other
words, the set of projections of stimuli in the measurement space onto the first
principal component has maximum variance. The second principal component is
an axis orthogonal to the first that accounts for most of the residual variance, and
so on. (In practice, the principal components are determined by selecting the
eigenvectors of the covariance matrix for the stimulus set that correspond to the
largest eigenvalues [Harris, 1975].)

In this view, then, the feature extraction process selects a subspace of the
original space that preserves as much of the variability among stimuli as possible.
It is clear that these features (i.e., the principal components) reflect the structure
of the stimulus set, and therefore we would expect the important perceptual
features to vary dramatically depending on the stimulus context.

This finding is given some generality by a similar result obtained in our
laboratory. In our experiment, listeners were asked to rate the pairwise similarity
of eight passive sonar recordings. Two perceptual dimensions were extracted
from these data using a metric multidimensional scaling procedure (Howard,
1977). The results were then compared with the outcome of a physical analysis of
the stimuli that paralleled the analysis described earlier. The $\frac{1}{3}$-octave spectrum

was obtained for each of the eight sounds. These data were then submitted to a principal-components analysis. Inasmuch as most of the variability could be accounted for by the first principal component, it was concluded that the steady-state characteristics of these sounds could be summarized adequately by a single measurement. This derived physical attribute closely approximated one of the perceptual dimensions obtained in the scaling analysis. (The other perceptual dimension revealed in the scaling analysis reflected a temporal property of the sounds and is not directly relevant to this discussion.) A closer examination of the specific signal values on this extracted dimension suggested that it summarized the overall shape of the spectra and, in particular, the degree of bimodality of the spectra. When asked to describe stimulus differences along this dimension, listeners used such terms as: "This one is more uniform"; or, "In this one, there seems to be more than one sound present."

In this experiment, as in Plomp's, it appears that a structure preserving transformation reasonably approximates the analysis performed by the feature extraction stage. Similar findings have also been reported for the analysis of steady-state vowel spectra (Klein, Plomp, & Pols, 1970). Although these experiments were conducted for another purpose, the findings are generally consistent with the present hypothesis that the feature extraction stage for timbre perception is best viewed as a structure analyzing process. Inasmuch as the principal components are simply weighted linear combinations of the more basic measurements (in this case, the $\frac{1}{3}$-octave band levels), it is clear that we could also develop a weighted property-list scheme to account for these findings. In such a system, the listener would adjust the measurement weights to develop "features" that maximally discriminate among the stimuli. Nonetheless, the objectives of this system are more naturally discussed in terms of the structure analyzing approach.

The major emphasis of this discussion is that feature extraction is both efficient in a dimensionality-reducing sense and flexible in that it readily adapts to the stimulus context. We have argued that a principal-components analysis shares these characteristics and is therefore a possible model for the feature extraction process in timbre perception. We would like to emphasize, however, that a variety of other structure preserving transformations are also adequate. For example, we could select a multidimensional scaling algorithm that would reduce the dimensionality but preserve the configuration of interstimulus distances in the measurement space.

TASK EFFECTS IN FEATURE EXTRACTION

In the experiments just outlined, listeners were simply required to evaluate relative stimulus similarity. In this situation, there are no correct or incorrect judgments. It therefore seems reasonable that listeners would employ a feature extraction transformation that preserves as much of the spectral information in the stimuli as possible. It is obvious, however, that in a classification task where performance is evaluated in terms of external criteria, the requirements of the feature extraction process would be quite different. As Figueiredo (1976) has pointed out, the performance of the entire system must be considered when selecting the optimum features in this situation. Getty, Swets, Swets, and Green (1979) have shown that observers emphasized different features in a visual classification task than they did in a visual comparison task. An experiment by Howard, Ballas, and Burgy (1978) demonstrated a similar effect in an aural classification situation and illustrates the role of task factors in feature extraction.

The stimuli investigated in this study consisted of 16 broadband noise signals that were amplitude modulated by sawtooth waves of varying frequency and attack. Four levels of modulation frequency (4, 5, 6, and 7 Hz) and four combinations of attack/decay (20 and 40 msec.) were used. Eight listeners learned to classify the 16 signals on the basis of one of two eight-category partitions. The two partitions were selected to emphasize one or the other dimension by requiring listeners to discriminate among all four levels of this dimension and only two levels of the other dimension. The two partitions are presented schematically in Fig. 11.2. Here we have labeled the perceptual dimension corresponding to attack "quality" and the perceptual dimension corresponding to modulation frequency "tempo." Clearly, the features are not of equal importance in the two partitions. Listeners in the quality group were required to discriminate relatively small differences in attack, whereas listeners in the tempo group were required to discriminate relatively small differences in modulation frequency. The confusion data from this experiment were analyzed in terms of a probabilistic model of classification.

Our model assumes that the decision stage operates on the output of the feature extraction process and classifies stimuli so as to maximize the probability correct (cf. Howard et al., 1978). An important assumption of the model is that, with feedback, listeners perform a selective tuning of their feature extraction processes. Theoretically, the tuning process determines a weighting factor for each of the two features. Selective tuning occurs when the weighting factor for one dimension increases relative to the other.[2]

Weighting parameters for each feature were estimated for individual listeners by fitting the model to the observed confusion matrices using a standard gradient technique. The weights obtained for each practiced listener are displayed in Fig. 11.3. It is evident that our listeners responded to the demands of their classification task. Listeners in the tempo group had greater weights for signal tempo than signal quality, whereas the opposite was true for the quality group. It may also be noted that no individual, with the possible exception of listener PH, maximized

---

[2]In our original presentation, we actually represent the tuning process as an adjustment in the variability of stimulus likelihood functions. The weighting factors discussed here are inversely related to the estimated standard deviations along each dimension.

TEMPO GROUP

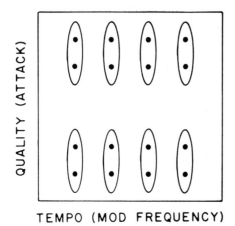

QUALITY GROUP

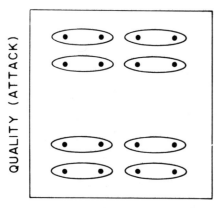

FIG. 11.2. Schematic representation of two partitions of the 16 signals into eight categories.

the weights for both features simultaneously. We interpreted this finding to suggest that, at least in the context of this experiment, the total amount of feature tuning that can occur at any point is limited. Inasmuch as we assumed that feature tuning reflects the operation of a selective attentional mechanism, this interpretation is consistent with recent limited capacity views of human attention (e.g., Kahneman, 1973).

Given an overall limit on the amount of feature tuning that can occur, we wondered what strategy the listeners used to determine how much emphasis to place on each feature. In our decision model, we assumed that listeners attempt

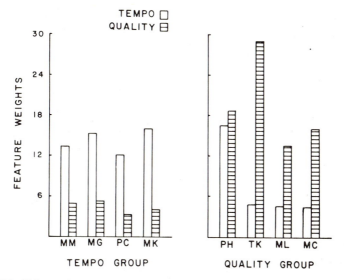

FIG. 11.3.   Estimated weighting parameters for each feature by individual listener and group.

to maximize the probability correct. Therefore, we investigated the possibility that the feature weights were also determined on this basis by estimating the theoretically optimal weights for each practiced listener. In computing these values, the sum of the two observed weights was taken to reflect the overall attentional effort expended by each listener. This overall value was then apportioned between the two features so as to maximize the average probability correct. The normalized obtained and optimal weights reflecting the relative importance of signal tempo for each listener are displayed in Fig. 11.4. Although in general the obtained weights are reasonably well approximated by the optimal values (the overall Pearson product-moment correlation, $r(15) = .98$), a small but consistent discrepancy is evident. Six of our eight listeners showed a tendency to overemphasize the more important of the two features.

Nonetheless, it is clear from these findings that listeners show considerable flexibility in the emphasis they place on individual perceptual features in an aural classification task. With practice, feature tuning processes increase the importance of both features. More importantly, for experienced listeners the tuning process appears to operate selectively with relative feature emphasis determined by a strategy that attempts to maximize the overall probability correct. Of further interest is a comparison of these findings with the results of two multidimensional scaling studies involving the stimuli that have been described. In the first, an independent group of 30 listeners rated the pairwise similarity of all 16 signals. A multidimensional scaling analysis of these data revealed that 22 of the 30 participants placed a greater emphasis on signal quality than tempo. In the

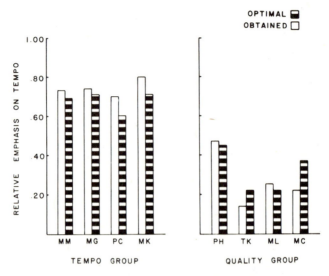

FIG. 11.4.   Normalized obtained and optimal weights for the tempo feature by individual listener and group.

second experiment, the observers from the previous classification experiment rated the pairwise similarity of the eight stimulus categories they had learned. In this case, only the category labels were provided, and no signals were actually presented. The data were decomposed into a "conceptual" space where the dimensions corresponded to modulation frequency (i.e., tempo) and attack (i.e., quality). Although we had expected the subjective importance of these dimensions to be strongly influenced by the prior classification training (i.e., tempo more important for the tempo group and quality more important for the quality group), listeners in both groups placed a greater relative emphasis on signal quality. This finding is more in line with the results of the first scaling study than with the results of the classification study. It appears, therefore, that in the similarity rating task, listeners tended to emphasize quality more than tempo, whereas in the classification task they emphasized the dimension that would lead to optimal performance. This result further illustrates the importance of task factors in determining the relative subjective importance of stimulus features.

CONCLUSION

As indicated in the introduction, feature extraction plays a central role in most theoretical approaches to auditory pattern recognition. Incoming stimuli are analyzed in terms of a set of distinctive or characteristic features that form the basis for all subsequent perceptual processing. Nevertheless, relatively little research has focused on the selection and tuning processes whereby these essential perceptual properties of stimuli are defined. In this chapter, we have considered two contrasting views of feature selection. On the one hand, it is possible that finely tuned stimulus property analyzers exist in the human auditory system. As Fant (1973) has pointed out, this property-list or detector-oriented approach is by definition context free. Some property analyzers will respond to a specific stimulus, whereas others will not. In contrast, it is also possible that feature extraction is highly context sensitive. In this latter approach, feature selection is viewed as a continuous ongoing process. The distinctive features used to characterize a particular sound emerge from a structural analysis of the more basic psychophysical measurements obtained by the auditory system.

Overall, the findings that we have outlined appear consistent with the more flexible, process-oriented approach to feature selection. In the comparative judgment task, listeners are required to evaluate stimulus similarity. Inasmuch as no specific comparison criteria are typically indicated, listeners need only know something of the structure of the stimulus set in order to make their judgments. The features identified in the aforementioned similarity rating experiments generally reflect the spectral characteristics of the stimuli. We argued that in these studies, feature extraction is most naturally viewed as an ongoing structural analysis of the low-resolution spectra extracted from the stimuli by peripheral auditory mechanisms. However, in the case of a classification task, a simple structural analysis of the stimulus set is not sufficient. In this situation, the assignment of stimuli to categories effectively changes the important structural properties of the stimulus set. Particular partitions of the stimuli serve to emphasize some stimulus relations, but de-emphasize others. We have argued that in this sort of task an additional feature tuning process occurs that adjusts the relative emphasis placed on the important structural features to accommodate the external task constraints. Furthermore, the results of our classification study suggested that the feature tuning process operates on a limited-capacity basis and that the fine-grained adjustment of feature emphasis is based on a strategy that attempts to optimize the probability correct. These findings emphasize the importance of overall performance considerations in the feature extraction process. In this sense, distinctive auditory features are tuned not only to the stimuli, but also to the decision rule employed by the listener (Figueiredo, 1976).

Before closing, we would like to offer a few caveats. First, although our conclusions were derived from the findings that have been presented, these experiments were not designed explicitly to test the issues addressed in this paper. For this reason, our conclusions must be regarded as tentative and speculative. No single experiment, for example, has enabled us to examine simultaneously the effects of both stimulus structure and task demands. Similarly, we have not addressed the detailed problem of how feature selection may operate on a trial-by-trial basis. How might the proposed structural analysis proceed in an incremental fashion? We have argued that in many cases auditory distinctive features are determined largely by the stimulus context. What external and subjective factors determine the relevant context in any particular situation? Quite clearly, the answers to these and other questions must await further investigation. Experiments designed to address some of these issues are underway in our laboratory.

Finally, it is important to remember that we are not proposing that either of the two approaches we have considered is necessarily ''correct.'' As we have indicated, these approaches represent extremes on a continuum of possible feature selection mechanisms. Although one may challenge the extreme property-list position on logical grounds (e.g., Uttal, 1978; Weisstein, 1973), a weighted property-list approach begins to resemble the process-oriented view discussed earlier. Furthermore, we suspect that it is impossible to distinguish between a modified property-list model and the process-oriented model using only psychophysical techniques. The distinction we have considered is significant because of its impact on theory and, hence, on the empirical questions that are appropriate to ask. A strict property-list model would direct us to search for evidence regarding invariant auditory feature detectors, whereas a process-oriented model would have us look for common principles underlying feature extraction across a wide range of different stimuli and tasks. Regardless of the specific view that ultimately emerges as a primary solution to the feature selection problem, it is clear that future psychological research in auditory pattern recognition must address the fundamental question of how distinctive auditory features are determined.

ACKNOWLEDGMENTS

This work was supported by a contract from the Engineering Psychology Programs, Office of Naval Research. The authors gratefully acknowledge Donald C. Burgy's contribution to this work and the helpful comments of Darlene V. Howard, Bruce M. Ross and James E. Youniss on an earlier version of this manuscript.

REFERENCES

Anderson, J. A., Silverstein, J. W., Ritz, S. A., & Jones, R. S. Distinctive features, categorical perception, and probability learning: Some applications of a neural model. *Psychological Review,* 1977, *84,* 413-451.

Barlow, H. B. Single units and sensation: A neuron doctrine for perceptual psychology? *Perception,* 1972, *1,* 371-394.

Cooper, W. E. Selective adaptation to speech. In F. Restle. R. M. Shiffrin, N. J. Castellan. H. R. Lindman, & D. B. Pisoni (Eds.), *Cognitive theory* (Vol. 1). Hillsdale, N.J.: Lawrence Erlbaum Associates, 1975.

Eimas, P. D., & Corbit, J. D. Selective adaptation of linguistic feature detectors. *Cognitive Psychology,* 1973, *4,* 99-109.

Fant, G. *Speech sounds and features.* Cambridge, Mass.: MIT Press, 1973.

Figueiredo, R. J. P. Design of optimal feature extractors by mathematical programming techniques. In C. H. Chen (Ed.), *Pattern recognition and artificial intelligence*. New York: Academic Press, 1976.

Getty, D. J., Swets, J. A., Swets, J. B., & Green, D. M. On the prediction of confusion matrices from similarity judgments. *Perception & Psychophysics, 1979, 26,* 1–19.

Harris, R. J. *A primer of multivariate statistics*. New York: Academic Press, 1975.

Howard, J. H., Jr. Psychophysical structure of eight complex underwater sounds. *Journal of the Acoustical Society of America, 1977, 62,* 149–156.

Howard, J. H., Jr., Ballas, J. A., & Burgy, D. C. *Feature extraction and decision processes in the classification of amplitude-modulated noise patterns* (Techical Report ONR-78-4). Washington, D.C.: The Catholic University of America, Human Performance Laboratory, July 1978.

Hubel, D. H., & Wiesel, T. N. Receptive fields, binocular interaction and functional architecture in the cat's visual cortex. *Journal of Physiology, 1962, 160,* 106–154.

Kahneman, D. *Attention and effort*. Englewood Cliffs, N.J.: Prentice-Hall, 1973.

Klein, W., Plomp, R., & Pols, L. C. W. Vowel spectra, vowel spaces, and vowel identification. *Journal of the Acoustical Society of America, 1970, 48,* 999–1009.

Lettvin, J. Y., Maturana, H. R., McCulloch, W. S., & Pitts, W. H. What the frog's eye tells the frog's brain. *Institute of Radio Engineers Proceedings, 1959, 47,* 1940–1951.

Meisel, W. S. *Computer-oriented approaches to pattern recognition*. New York: Academic Press, 1972.

Plomp, R. *Aspects of tone sensation*. New York: Academic Press, 1976.

Sherrington, C. S. *Man on his nature*. Cambridge: Cambridge University Press, 1941.

Uttal, W. R. *An autocorrelation theory of form detection*. Hillsdale, N.J.: Lawrence Erlbaum Associates, 1975.

Uttal, W. R. *The psychobiology of mind*. Hillsdale, N.J.: Lawrence Erlbaum Associates, 1978.

von Bismarck, G. Timbre of steady sounds: A factorial investigation of its verbal attributes. *Acoustica, 1974, 30,* 146–159.

Weisstein, N. Beyond the yellow-volkswagen detector and the grandmother cell: A general strategy for the exploration of operations in human pattern recognition. In R. L. Solso (Ed.), *Contemporary issues in cognitive psychology: The Loyola symposium*. Washington: Winston, 1973.

Whitfield, I. C., & Evans, E. F. Responses of auditory cortical neurons to stimuli of changing frequency. *Journal of Neurophysiology, 1965, 28,* 655–672.

Wightman, F. L. The pattern-transformation model of pitch. *Journal of the Acoustical Society of America, 1973, 54,* 407–416.

Zwicker, E., Flottorp, G., & Stevens, S. S. Critical band width in loudness summation. *Journal of the Acoustical Society of America, 1957, 29,* 548–557.

12 Auditory Perception: Recommendations for a Computer Assisted Experimental Paradigm

Cynthia H. Null
Forrest W. Young

To understand how complex auditory signals affect cognition, we need to investigate the way such auditory signals are perceived. This chapter proposes an experimental paradigm for continuing the work of identifying the perceptually relevant attributes of complex auditory signals.

During the last decade, there have been two new and exciting technological developments of great relevance to the investigation of auditory perception (1) the generation of artificial auditory stimuli by computational techniques; (2) the measurement of perception by multidimensional scaling.

With the technology being developed for the generation of computer music (Mathews, 1969) and speech, any auditory stimulus transducible by speakers (or headphones) can be created. All aspects of an auditory stimulus can be controlled, for example: the exact frequency of each overtone; the amplitude pattern of the overtones; the timing and amplitude for the attack, steady-state, and decay of each wave form; the phase relations between the overtones; etc. Furthermore, computers can be used to generate artificial stimuli, allowing us to formulate and test hypotheses about auditory perception much more easily than before.

However, these advances in computer sound technology are not sufficient to allow us to fully understand auditory perception, although they may be necessary. Even though they help us generate any type of auditory stimulus, they do not help us understand perception. Fortunately, there is another area of research activity that can help us understand the perception of complex auditory stimuli—psychological measurement and the development of multidimensional scaling (Shepard, Romney, & Nerlove, 1972). Multidimensional scaling (MDS) is a measurement technique that takes a complicated matrix of data and develops a picture of it that is easily interpreted by the relatively untrained human eye. The picture is called the "configuration" or "structure" of the data and is presented to the user in a Euclidean space of low dimensionality. The results of an MDS analysis are related to the data in a way that is very much like the relation between a table of distances between cities and a road map. In this case, the table of distances corresponds to the data, and the road map corresponds to the configuration. Clearly, both the table of distances and the road map present the same distance information (at least if the table is large enough), but the road map is much easier to understand. The relative ease of understanding the map as compared with the table illustrates the rationale for using MDS.

The development of MDS is especially crucial to the advancement of our understanding of auditory perception because MDS has been shown to be particularly suited to perceptual situations involving highly complex multidimensional stimuli. MDS has been centrally involved, for example, in the recent advances in taste and smell perception (Schiffman, 1971) when the substance being tasted or smelled is a very complicated multidimensional stimulus. In situations like this, a specific kind of data has been found to take maximum advantage of MDS. Just as the table of intercity distances presents information about pairs of cities (the distance between each pair), the type of data most suitable for MDS contain information about pairs of stimuli. Generally, the type of data concerns the similarity of each pair of stimuli, because it can be argued that similarity data permit the investigator to obtain an understanding of the data's structure, which is relatively free of any sources of contamination introduced by the investigator.

It would appear then, that MDS could be useful in advancing our understanding of auditory perception, particularly when combined with the computer generation of the stimuli being perceived. Indeed, investigations of timbre perception, which utilized early developments in computer music and MDS technology (e.g., Ehresman, 1977; Grey, 1975; Plomp, 1970; Wessel, 1973), show great promise in that direction. This chapter recommends an experimental paradigm that utilizes the more recent advances in computer and MDS technology (Hamer, 1978; Kriz, 1976; Takane, Young, & de Leeuw, 1977; Young, de Leeuw, & Takane, 1976).

EXPERIMENTAL DESIGN CONSIDERATIONS

Our recommended experimental paradigm has three phases. In the first, data concerning auditory perception are obtained. In the first experiment of this phase, a similarity judgment between tones is the basic datum, and data are obtained for a large number of stimuli. These two aspects allow us to obtain data that are free from two common sources of experimenter bias: (1) bias due to selection of a relatively small and nonrepresentative set of stimuli; (2) bias introduced by systematically selecting attributes on which the stimuli are rated. Thus, we can argue that the data from the first, and most basic, experiment accurately reflect the perception for these stimuli.

Inasmuch as listeners can verbally describe the sounds they hear (''This sound is very bright''), it may be important to understand how such verbal attributes are related to the auditory perception structure obtained in the first experiment. To this end, a second experiment in phase I is suggested in which each auditory stimulus is rated on several verbal attributes.

In phase II of this paradigm, a mathematical model of auditory perception is recommended. The model relates the fundamental physical characteristics of each signal to the perceptual structure constructed in phase I, relates these same physical characteristics to the verbal attributes obtained in the second experiment in phase I, and summarizes the relationship between the verbal and perceptual information. This phase differs from the others in that no empirical investigation is recommended. Instead, this phase involves a series of mathematical analyses of the perceptual, verbal, and physical information about the stimuli.

The third and final phase of our recommended paradigm involves validating the mathematical auditory perception model constructed in phase II. The mathematical model enables us to construct artificial stimuli and then to predict, from the physical characteristics of each stimulus' wave form, the specific perceptual and verbal nature of each stimulus. There are several types of experiments possible in this phase. One possibility involves constructing artificial stimuli whose complex wave forms are predicted to be perceptually unidimensional. Another possibility involves stimuli whose wave forms should have certain predictable unidimensional verbal characteristics. A third possibility involves stimuli that are predicted to be perceived as identical to the stimuli used in phase I, even though their physical wave forms are different.

DESIGN OBJECTIVES

One objective of our recommended design is to overcome a limitation present in many similarity experiments, which flows from the fact that the research is based on relatively small sets of stimuli. For very small stimulus sets (say from 8 to 12) it has been shown that MDS does not provide reliable configurations in more than one dimension (Young, 1970). This means that if we repeated an investigation that used such a small number of stimuli we could not expect to replicate the results. In fact, in order to obtain two or three reliable dimensions at least 15 to 18 stimuli must be used (Young, 1970).

A second consideration is overcoming the difficulty found in many similarity experiments of being unable to use the entire set of potential stimuli, but simply a subset. Whenever an experimenter defines a stimulus domain and then uses only a subset in the experiment, there may be criticism that the way the subset was formed biased the results of the study (Fillenbaum, 1973). If, for example, MDS was applied to a table of distances between American cities in an attempt to recover an accurate map of the United States, an inaccurate map could easily result if only cities with over 2,000,000 people were included. There are very few such cities, and their distribution around the U.S. is not representative of the distributions of all cities and towns. Similarily, if a small number of (10–15) cities were selected, the MDS dimensions may not be as veridical as those that would have been obtained had a larger (30–50) set of cities been selected. Thus, as many stimuli as possible should be included. This improves reliability as well as representativeness.

The use of as many stimuli as possible implies (due to the large number of stimulus pairs) that an incomplete judgment design must be employed. Although it would be possible to employ some of the classical incomplete designs (Torgerson, 1958) or some of the more recent noninteractive incomplete designs (Spence & Domoney, 1974), a computerized interactive procedure is superior. For example, the interactive paired comparison procedure, ISIS, developed by Young and Cliff (1972) and recently improved (Baker & Young, 1975; Cliff, Girard, Green, Kehoe & Doherty, 1977; Green & Bentler, 1979) requires the observation of a limited number of pairs (⅓ to ½) while preserving the quality of the representation of the stimuli. Another judgment limiting procedure, Interactive Similarity Ordering (ISO), uses a rank ordering procedure (Young, Null & Sarle, 1978; Young, Null, Sarle & Hoffman, in press). The subject interactively rank orders the similarity of subsets of stimuli relations to some selected set of target stimuli. The number of judgments in an ISO session may be somewhat more than in an ISIS session, but the ISO judgments appear to be faster and easier.

Although these interactive procedures help solve the representation and reliability problems, they require that the stimuli must be immediately accessible to the computer. This requirement could be met by a random access tape recorder, but we recommend digitizing the stimuli and storing the results on disk. One reason for this recommendation is that it is less expensive and more reliable. In addition, digitized stimuli are required in the construction of the mathematical auditory perception model so that a mathematical analysis of the wave form of each stimulus can be made. Finally, validating the mathematical model by constructing artificial stimuli is practical only if the computer constructs the artificial stimuli by performing the calculations dictated by the mathematical model.

In addition to design considerations centered around the nature of the stimuli, there are considerations related to procedures for interpreting the perceptual structure derived from the similarity judgments. Many MDS studies simply use informal interpretive procedures that involve looking at the configuration and trying to "make sense" of it. We prefer using multiset matching (van de Geer, 1968; Horst, 1965) and constrained MDS (Bloxom, 1978; de Leeuw & Heiser, 1980; Ramsay, 1980; Young, Null, & De Soete, in preparation) to interpret the configuration. Such procedures place the interpretation on a more objective foundation than is usually the case. Of course, these data-analysis procedures do not completely objectify the interpretation of the perceptual space because the results of any data analysis must be interpreted by the investigators. Indeed, we do not wish to objectify the procedure completely because the only way to do so would involve eliminating the investigator. However, our "objective" procedure provides the investigator with information that is very useful in guiding the interpretation, thereby increasing the accuracy of the interpretive process.

In addition to using physical information to help interpret the MDS structure objectively, this recommended paradigm also uses listener ratings of the stimuli on a number of relevant verbal attributes. Listeners, when asked, will tell you what words describe one or another of the stimuli they have been judging. But, they will not tell you that the stimuli differ in the ''amount of energy present in the third and sixth harmonics,'' even though the scientific process may find that to be the best physical explanation of some aspect of auditory perception (Plomp, 1970). Thus, to interpret the MDS configuration in ways that correspond to the subjects' intuitions, we must obtain these verbal descriptions, find out how they relate to the multidimensional perceptual configuration, and understand how they relate to the physical characteristics of the stimuli.

A final design recommendation relates to the fact that individual differences exist in auditory perception. This recommended paradigm permits the investigation of these possibilities by using the nonmetric individual differences multidimensional scaling procedure (Takane et al., 1977), as recently extended by Young et al. (in preparation), and by including individuals who, for example, vary in their sensitivity to pitch, vary in their musical experience, or vary in their familiarity with the stimulus domain being studied.

SOME EXPERIMENTAL DESIGN DETAILS

In this section, we present some details of our recommended experimental design. The overall goal of the design is to construct and validate a mathematical model of perceptual processes generated by certain auditory stimuli. As mentioned earlier, the design is broken down into three phases: In phase I, we obtain data concerning the perception and subjective labeling of the stimuli; in phase II, we construct a mathematical model of auditory perception; and in phase III, we use the mathematical model to construct artificial stimuli for which the model makes specific behavioral predictions and validate the model by testing these predictions.

Phase I: Perceptual Structure[1]

There are two experiments in phase I. The first is the fundamental experiment of the investigation—the experiment that reveals the way in which people perceive the stimuli and the way by which subjects differ in these perceptions. In this

---

[1]To simplify the discussion we will assume that an interactive paired comparison procedure like ISIS is used to collect the similarity data. Using a computerized technique like ISO would change some minor details in the procedures and data analyses described. Details on the use of ISO are available elsewhere (Young et al., in press; Young et al., 1978).

experiment, the subjects are presented with pairs of stimuli and are asked to judge the similarity of the two stimuli in the pair to each other. Note that the subjects are not told precisely what aspects of the stimuli they should base their judgments on. Instead, the subject must decide what is important. Thus, the information obtained from the subject is not contaminated by experimenter biases. (Remember: As many stimuli as possible should be included in order to minimize the possible experimenter bias due to stimulus selection.)

These two mechanisms for reducing experimenter bias create some problems, however. The first mechanism (using similarity judgments) means that the experimenter must make an additional effort to identify the characteristics of the stimuli used by the subject. The second mechanism (including many stimuli) means that there are more pairs of stimuli than can be judged and that a computerized task must be used to minimize the number of judgments.

In the second experiment in this phase, we determine verbal attributes that are related to the stimulus perception and we determine the manner in which they are involved. Inasmuch as listeners can easily describe auditory stimuli, it is important to understand how the descriptions are related to the perceptual structure obtained in the previous experiment. The data obtained in the second experiment allow us to gain such an understanding.

Experiment 1: Perceptual Structure

Stimuli. The stimuli in this experiment should be as many examples of auditory stimuli from the domain of interest as available. (We would choose a complex auditory domain that was neither generated by computer nor where the experimenter had complete control over the stimulus structure for early investigations. This preference comes from a desire to keep the stimulus selection as unbiased as possible.) The procedures place an upper limit of around 50 stimuli.

Subjects. If we wish, for example, to investigate whether or not auditory perception is related to musical sophistication, the subjects should represent a cross section of musical experience. In this case, there should be approximately 10 subjects from each of several populations. For example, one might select: (1) college sophomores who have had no musical training; (2) college music majors who have had ear training but do not have absolute pitch; (3) college music instructors who have had ear training but who do not have absolute pitch; (4) people with absolute pitch; (5) people who are tone deaf; etc. Similar procedures for defining subject populations can be followed if we are interested in other sources of individual variation.

Procedure. The subject interacts with the interactive paired comparison program while seated at a computer terminal. The stimuli could be presented through headphones or speakers. On each trial the computer selects a pair of stimuli, processes the pair through a digital-to-analog converter, and presents the two stimuli to the subject via the headphones. On each trial the subject should be able to compare the two stimuli as many times as desired. When the subject finally decides how similar the two stimuli are to each other, the response is entered via the terminal. The computer then records the response and uses it to determine which pair of stimuli should be presented next. The program selects pairs of stimuli so as to both minimize the number of judgments and maximize the reliability of the data, the subject being reinforced for judging reliably. This procedure generally reduces the number of judgments to approximately one third of all pairs. Thus, for 50 stimuli the subject is probably required to judge 450 of the 1225 pairs. Additionally, the subject is always free to terminate the session and return at a later time.

Analysis. Interactive paired comparison procedures yield two types of information: a complete matrix of Euclidean distances among the 50 stimuli and an incomplete matrix of judgments of the similarity of certain pairs of stimuli. We recommend submitting the Euclidean distances from each subject to a metric individual differences multidimensional scaling analysis and the incomplete judgment matrices to a nonmetric individual differences multidimensional scaling. Both of these analyses should be performed by the ALSCAL program (Takane et al., 1977) because it is the only program that can perform both metric and nonmetric analyses and accept missing data. The distances are submitted to a metric analysis because they are defined at the ratio level of measurement.

The analysis should be based on the individual differences model discussed most fully by Carroll and Chang (1970). This model postulates that listeners perceive sound on the basis of a common set of attributes, but that the salience of each attribute varies from listener to listener. Some listeners may find certain attributes very important, and others may find the same attributes totally irrelevant. Thus, it is not assumed that all listeners use the same set of attributes nor that they weight the attributes in identical fashions.

The individual differences model is expressed by the following equation for a weighted Euclidian space:

$$d_{ijk}^2 = \sum_{a}^{r} w_{ka}^2 (x_{ia} - x_{ja})^2, \ w_{ka} \geqslant 0, \tag{12.1}$$

where the weights w_{ka} indicate the salience of dimension a to subject k, and the coordinates x_{ia} and x_{ja} are the positions of points i and j on dimension a of the auditory perception structure assumed to underlie all of the listeners' judgments. The weights w_{ka} are elements of a matrix W of individual differences weights, and the coordinates x_{ia} and x_{ja} are elements of the multidimensional auditory perception structure matrix X. Note that the model in Eq. 12.1 implies that each individual k has his or her own private auditory perception space Y_k such that:

$$Y_k = XW_k, \tag{12.2}$$

where Y_k and X are both n $\times$ r matrices having a row for each of the n stimuli and a column for each of the r dimensions, and where W_k is an r $\times$ r diagonal matrix whose diagonal contains the kth individual's salience weights on the r dimensions. Note that the diagonal of W_k is extracted from the kth row of W, which is an m $\times$ r matrix of weights having a row for each of the m individuals and a column for each of the r dimensions. The matrices X, Y_k, W, and W_k form the basis for the mathematical model of auditory perception to be constructed in phase II of the investigation.

Experiment 2: Verbal Attributes

Stimuli and Subjects.   The stimuli and subjects in this experiment should be the same as those in the previous experiment.

Procedure.   We recommend that each subject should be asked to type a list of the aspects of the stimuli that he or she used in making judgments in the previous experiment into the computer. After the subject names as many as possible, we recommend that the computer displays additional attributes that the experimenter and the other subjects think are important. (Clearly, pretesting should be done in order to determine the list of additional attributes.) Subjects would then select any of these that they used in making similarity judgments. The computer should then present the list of important attributes, and the subject would select the single most important attribute. The subject should then be required to rate each of the stimuli according to how adequately the attribute describes the stimulus. After each stimulus has been rated, the subject would select the attribute that is next most important and repeat the task for this new attribute. This procedure should continue for several attributes.

Note that we recommend asking the subjects to generate their own list of the attributes that contributed to their similarity judgments. The experimenter should not simply present a list of attributes that he or she thinks are important and ask the subjects to rate the stimuli on these attributes (a procedure that is frequently followed in experiments of this nature). The reason this is discouraged is because it can be argued that it is a way of introducing our biases into the interpretive process. At this point, the subjects' notions of important attributes are what is of interest, and even though the experimenter has a large store of knowledge on the subject, the subjects are asked to generate their own list. However, the presentation of an additional list of attributes shown important by pretesting gives subjects the opportunity to rate attributes they may have overlooked.

Analysis.   The first step in this analysis is to obtain average ratings for each attribute. The averages should not be performed over all subjects, but should be performed over subsets of subjects that: (1) display homogeneity in their ratings for a particular attribute, or (2) have similar backgrounds (see Experiment 1). One method for identifying homogeneous groups of subjects is to perform a cluster analysis on a matrix of associations between subjects. Such a matrix could be formed by correlating ratings of the stimuli for an attribute or by summing the absolute differences in the ratings for each pair of subjects. This matrix can then be analyzed by hierarchical cluster analysis (e.g., Johnson, 1967) and subjects within a cluster can be treated as a homogeneous group.

These average attribute ratings can then be used to explain the stimulus space by the MORALS program for nonmetric multiple regression (Young et al., 1976). MORALS predicts the order of the stimuli on each dimension as well as possible by obtaining the best weighted combination of the verbal attributes.

Phase II: Model Construction

We recommend that the next task should be the construction of a mathematical auditory perception model that: (1) relates the fundamental physical characteristics of each sound to the multidimensional perceptual structure just constructed; (2) relates these physical characteristics to the verbal attributes just obtained; and (3) summarizes the relationship between the verbal attributes and the perceptual space.

The second phase differs from other phases in that no empirical investigation is warranted. Instead, a series of mathematical analyses of the perceptual, physical, and psychological information about the several stimuli is recommended. These analyses then form the basis for generating several behavioral hypotheses, which can be empirically tested in phase III.

An assumption basic to our recommendations in this phase is that the investigator interested in auditory perception, recognition, and categorization has already decided on a means for decomposing the physical wave form of each stimulus into a number of components that he or she thinks may be relevant to the psychological perception of the stimuli. Our recommendations should be valid for any method of physical analysis that results in one or more matrices of physical components for each stimulus. In the area of timbre perception, for example, the Heterodyne filter (Moorer, 1975) has been used successfully by Grey (1975, 1977) to decompose musical stimuli into perceptually revelant components. The phase vocoder (Moorer, 1976; Portnoff, 1976) has also been used in the same fashion.

Many methods for decomposing an auditory signal into components share the characteristic of decomposing the wave form into a sum of sinusoids, each of which has a frequency that is (roughly) an integer multiple of a fundamental frequency. Furthermore, each sinusoid varies in amplitude and in phase, and the decomposition is performed for each of a series of time-slices. Therefore, we represent the physical analysis as two cubes of information, one for amplitude and one for phase. Each cube is made up of p matrices (one for each partial), each having n rows (one for each stimulus) and t columns (one for each time-slice). We assume that $t > r$ and that $n > (t + r)$. We denote these amplitude and phases matrices A_p and P_p.

We recommend relating these matrices to the perceptual dimensions obtained in Experiment 1 by multiple regression, a standard procedure for objectively interpreting MDS solutions (Carroll, 1972; Cliff & Young, 1968) and by multiset matching (Horst, 1956; van de Geer, 1968), an extension of multiple regression.

At this point, it is necessary to reemphasize an assumption made earlier that the number of stimuli n must be greater than the sum of the number of time-slices t and the number of dimensions r. This assumption is a consequence of the multiset configuration matching procedure. As with multiple and canonical regression, the multiset matching procedure requires that the number of observations be greater than the number of variables. (For this application, the stimuli correspond to observations and the dimensions and time-slices to variables.) As there are not more than 50 stimuli and perhaps two to five dimensions, no more than approximately 25 time-slices can be used. Furthermore, most users of matching techniques would say that there should be less than 10 or 12 variables when there are as few observations as suggested in this study. However, it may be that the procedure chosen to decompose the wave forms will generate many more than this number of time-slices, although this depends on just what procedure is used to reduce the physical wave forms into their basic components. To circumvent this potential difficulty, 2p principal components analyses can be performed, one each of the matrices A_p and P_p. From each of the 2p analyses, a small number, s, of principal components, where $s < (n - r)$, would be retained. These s components are those corresponding to the s largest eigenvalues. The value of s is determined by criteria related to the variance accounted for and the interpretability of the components. (It is not necessary that the number of components, s, be the same for each of the 2p analyses. It could vary between, say, 6 and 12, thus keeping the total number of variables fairly small compared to the number of stimuli. Note that the restriction on the number of variables applies to the sum of the number of dimensions and the maximum number of components, not to the sum of the number of dimensions and the total number of components.) The information in the principal components should be of considerable interest in itself, because it represents the principal aspects of the physical nature of each stimuli as it varies over time.

The principal time components, then, are involved in the remaining aspects of our modeling procedure, rather than the time-slices. For simplicity, we can continue to represent the time-dependent information by matrices A_p and P_p, but these matrices are now $n \times s$ rather than $n \times t$.

The most general goal of a multiset matching procedure, stated in terms relevant to this application, is to determine a rotation of the MDS configuration X such that:

1. The first rotated dimension is, simultaneously, most like p separate linear combinations, one for each of the p amplitude matrices A_p.

2. The second rotated dimension is orthogonal to the first and is, simultaneously, most like p separate linear combinations, one for each of the p amplitude matrices under the restriction that the second linear combination for each amplitude matrix is orthogonal to the first.

3. Each additional rotated dimension is orthogonal to all preceding dimensions and, simultaneously, most like p separate linear combinations, one for each of the p amplitude matrices under the restriction that each linear combination for an amplitude matrix be orthogonal to all other linear combinations for that matrix.

4. Similar orthogonal dimensions and combinations utilize the phase matrices P_p instead of the amplitude matrices A_p. Note that the rotation based on the phase information is independent of the rotation based on the amplitude information.

Actually, the use of multiset matching in this chapter is quite a bit simpler than the general multiset procedure just described. The simplicity results from the fact that the individual differences model used to analyze the similarity judgments has a unique characteristic: The dimensions of the stimulus configuration X are not rotatable, as has been discussed by Carroll and Chang (1970). These dimensions are not arbitrary and should have a specific interpretation. Because no rotation of X need be obtained, the multiset matching procedure is greatly simplified. In particular, this procedure can be applied to each dimension x_r of the configuration X, one dimension at a time.

In this case we wish to obtain the linear combinations u_p^a of the s amplitude time components which are most like each dimension r of the MDS configuration X. That is:

$$u_p^a = A_p b_p^a \tag{12.3}$$

is obtained so as to minimize

$$\| u_p^a - x_r \| \tag{12.4}$$

where the subscript p refers to partials, subscript r to dimensions, and superscript a to amplitude. The double bars $\|$ indicate the Euclidean norm, which in this case is the sum of the squared differences between the dimension and the linear combination. It is assumed that the columns of A_p and X are normalized to have unit length and centered to have zero mean.

The problem to be solved in this special case of multiset matching is simply a series of p independent multiple regression problems, whose solution is:

$$\bar{b}_p^a = (A_p' A_p)^{-1} A_p x_r \tag{12.5}$$

where $\bar{b}_p^a$ is the estimate of the regression coefficients b_p^a in Eq. 12.3, which yield least squares estimates of u_p^a. Note that there is a separate and wholly independent regression performed for each partial p, with each regression providing s coefficients b_p^a. Note also that a parallel problem will be solved for the phase information to obtain:

$$\bar{b}_p^p = (P_p'P_p)^{-1} P_p x_r. \tag{12.6}$$

The interpretation of this analysis is fairly straightforward. For each partial we have regression weights that indicate the strength of the relationship between the partial at time component s and one of the dimensions of the auditory perception structure. If, say, the weight b_{sp}^a is large, then this means that the amplitude of partial p at time component s is involved in the perceptual organization of the stimuli. If we find, for example, that the weights for this partial's amplitude are large for the first several time components, and that they then drop off for later time components, we would conclude that for this partial's amplitude the attack characteristics of the stimulus are perceptually relevant. If this finding held for all partials, then we would conclude that the attack characteristics of the stimuli are involved in their perception.

The developments summarized by Eqs. 12.3 through 12.6 constitute our recommendations for constructing a mathematical model of auditory perception. The model itself involves only those time-component amplitudes and phases that contribute the most to our understanding of the stimulus configuration, i.e., those with the largest beta weights $\bar{b}$ in Eqs. 12.5 and 12.6. The particular procedure that should be used to determine the most important components is a stepwise backward elimination procedure. On the basis of only the important physical characteristics, we can construct a mathematical model of each perceptual dimension by calculating:

$$\tilde{x}_r = A_p b_p^a + P_p b_p^p, \tag{12.7}$$

where $\tilde{x}_r$ is the physical model of perceptual dimension x_r and where the stepwise backward elimination procedure has been used to replace the small weights in $b^a{}_p$ and $b^p{}_p$ with zeros and to recalculate the optimal values of the nonzero weights. The number of zero weights represents the parsimony of the model. Several different levels of parsimony should be tried at this point, checking each time on the predictive adequacy of the model by determining the sum of squared differences:

$$\| \tilde{x} - x_r \| \tag{12.8}$$

for each level of parsimony. The most parsimonious model, which we also judge to have strong descriptive power, should be used in the remainder of the study.

Equation 12.7, therefore, is the mathematical auditory perception model for the stimuli used in Experiment 1. Please note that this model implies a belief that auditory perception can be modeled by a mechanism that assigns a weight to each amplitude and phase distillate (for every time component) where the weight reflects the salience of the distillate to the perceptual process. The model implies that these weighted distillates are then added together to determine the final perception of the auditory stimuli. We wish to emphasize here that we do not mean to imply that auditory perception involves such a process or that there is a physiological analog of such a process. Rather, we imply that auditory perception can best be described as if there were such a physiological analog.

Additionally, we recommend using nonmetric multiple regression (Young et al., 1976) to fit the verbal attributes v_m obtained in Experiment 2 to the MDS space X obtained in Experiment 1. This is a nonmetric extension of the familiar multiple regression procedures commonly used to interpret MDS spaces (Cliff & Young, 1968), which takes into account that the attribute judgments and hypothetical variables may only be measured at the ordinal level. This procedure helps to label the dimensions of the space with the verbal attributes commonly used by listeners to describe the auditory stimuli in the study. Note that the nonmetric regression should be performed with the averaged verbal attributes from Experiment 2, where the averaging is performed in a way that preserves individual differences for homogeneous groups of subjects. This allows us to investigate whether the dimensions represent the same attributes for different subjects, as is assumed by the individual differences multidimensional scaling.

Inasmuch as we have constructed $\bar{x}$, our model of auditory perception based on physical aspects, we can also perform the nonmetric multiple regression between the verbal attributes v_m and the mathematical model $\bar{x}$. This procedure allows the investigation of the physical characteristics of the verbal attributes and allows us to construct a mathematical model of the psychological nature of auditory perception on the basis of the physical characteristics of the stimuli.

Phase III: Validation

The previous phases of our recommended investigation allow the development of a mathematical model of auditory perception. This model enables the prediction, from the physical characteristics of each signal's wave form, of the specific location of the signal on each of the several perceptual and verbal dimensions. As the third phase of the investigation, we recommend validating these predictions by constructing artificial (novel) stimuli, gathering similarity data, and analyzing the data using confirmatory MDS.

The stimuli are constructed so that their physical characteristics permit clear-cut predictions about the perceptual and psychological characteristics of the stimuli. For example, stimuli can be constructed so that their wave forms lead one to hypothesize, on the basis of the mathematical model constructed in phase II, that they will be perceived as unidimensional. Several sets of stimuli can be constructed—one set for each dimension of the MDS space derived from Experiment 1. The stimuli are constructed from the phases and amplitudes of each partial at each time component according to the mathematical model represented by Eq. 12.7.

Other sets of stimuli could be constructed so that their wave forms lead one to predict that they will have certain specific numerical ratings on the verbal scales commonly mentioned in Experiment 2. The stimuli should be constructed on the basis of the nonmetric multiple regression performed between the relevant attributes and the mathematical perception model (Eq. 12.7). Or other stimuli could be constructed involving all dimensions simultaneously. The mathematical modeling process leads us to hypothesize that these artificial stimuli will be perceived as being equivalent to the stimuli used in phase I.

The various constructed stimulus sets can then be judged by subjects similar to those who participated in the earlier experiments using the same interactive data collection techniques. That is, Euclidean distances and incomplete judgment matrices would be obtained for each stimulus set.

These matrices of distances and judgments can be analyzed in two ways. First, they can be analyzed as in Experiment 1 using an individual differences multidimensional scaling program, such as ALSCAL. These analyses should assist in determining the dimensionality of the artificially constructed stimuli. Since we have designed the stimuli with specific predictions in mind, the data should also be analyzed with a confirmatory multidimensional scaling program (e.g., Bloxom, 1978; de Leeuw & Heiser, 1980; Ramsay, 1980; Young, Null, & & De Soete, in preparation). Confirmatory MDS allows for the testing of specific predictions such as the ordering of stimuli along one dimension or the location of specific stimuli in a hypothesized stimulus space.

These analyses validate the perceptual model developed in phase II. If our hypotheses are confirmed we can be secure in our interpretation of the physical and verbal attributes relevant to the perception of the complex auditory stimuli under investigation.

CONCLUSIONS

We have presented a three phase paradigm for the study of the perception of complex auditory stimuli. Our paradigm takes advantage of computer sound technology and recent developments in multidimensional scaling. In the first phase, judgments on the similarity between auditory stimuli and ratings of these stimuli on relevant verbal attributes are obtained using computerized interactive data collection techniques. The second phase of the paradigm involves developing a mathematical model of the perceptual structure using nonmetric multiple regression and multiset matching. The final phase involves constructing artificial stimuli to test the obtained perceptual model.

Because we suggest using computerized interactive data procedures. which reduce the number of necessary judgments, the number of stimuli that can be studied is increased (to 30–50). This menas that the stimuli can be more representative of the entire domain of relevant sounds and that the results should be more replicable. Also, these data collection procedures are relatively free from the subjective biases of the investigator.

Our paradigm includes the development of a mathematical model relating the physical characteristics of the stimuli to the derived perceptual representation. We also model verbal attribute ratings. These procedures remove subjective biases of the investigator from the interpretation of the auditory perceptual space as well as allow for more complete understanding of the perceptual process. The authors are currently working on new procedures for developing the mathematical model (Young, Null, & De Soete, in preparation). The similarity judgments would be directly embedded in a subspace of the physical domain. The principal components decomposition of the physical characteristics would be eliminated by such a procedure. Also, having the perceptual representation constrained by the physical data appears to be very desireable. In the best case, at least, each of these ways of developing a mathematical model will yield the same results.

Finally, our design uses both exploratory and confirmatory MDS. Each method has advantages and these are fully used by this paradigm. We use exploratory MDS to investigate a new domain and to look for possible individual differences; then in the final phase we use confirmatory MDS to validate the auditory perception models developed in the preceding phases of the investigation. We anticipate that our empirical design and its associated data analysis will improve our understanding of auditory perception.

ACKNOWLEDGMENT

The authors wish to express their appreciation to Geert De Soete for his helpful comments on an earlier draft of this chapter.

REFERENCES

Baker, R. F., & Young, F. W. A note on an empirical evaluation of the ISIS procedure. *Psychometrika*, 1975, *40*, 413–415.

Bloxom, B. Constrained multidimensional scaling in N spaces. *Psychometrika*, 1978, *43*, 397–408.

Carroll, J. D. Individual differences and multidimension scaling. In R. N. Shepard, A. K. Romney, & S. Nerlove (Eds.), *Multidimensional scaling: Theory and applications in the behavioral sciences*. (Vol. 1) New York: Academic Press, 1972.

Carroll, J. D., & Chang, J. J. Analysis of individual differences in multidimensional scaling via an N-way generalization of "Eckart-Young" decomposition. *Psychometrika*, 1970, *35*, 238–319.

Cliff, N. Orthogonal rotation to congruence. *Psychometrika*, 1966, *31*, 33–42.

Cliff, N., Girard, R., Green, R. S., Kehoe, J. F., & Doherty, L. M. INTERSCAL: A TSO FORTRAN IV program for subject computer interactive multidimensional scaling. *Educational and Psychological Measurement*, 1977, *37*, 185–188.

Cliff, N., & Young, F. W. On the relationship between unidimensional judgments and multidimensional scaling. *Organizational Behavior and Human Performance,* 1968, *3,* 269-285.

de Leeuw, J., & Heiser, W. Multidimensional scaling with restrictions on the configuration. In P. R. Krishnaiah (Ed.), *Multivariate Analysis - V.* North Holland Publishing Co., 1980.

Ehresman, D. E. *A parallelogram model of timbre analogies.* Unpublished masters thesis, Michigan State University, 1977.

Fillenbaum, S. *Problems in use of similarity data for the study of semantic structures.* Psychometric Laboratory Report 114, University of North Carolina-Chapel Hill, February, 1973.

Green, R. S., & Bentler, P. M. Improving the efficiency and effectiveness of interactively selected MDS data designs. *Psychometrika,* 1979, *44,* 115-119.

Grey, J. M. *An exploration of musical timbre* (Report No. STAN-M-2). Stanford University, Department of Music, 1975.

Grey, J. M. Multidimensional perceptual scaling of musical timbres. *Journal of the Acoustical Society of Amierica,* 1977, *61,* 1270-1277.

Hamer, R. M. *Nonmetric interactive scaling with multiple subjects.* Unpublished doctoral dissertation, University of North Carolina-Chapel Hill 1978.

Horst, P. *Factorial analysis of data matrices.* New York: Holt, Rinehart and Winston, 1965.

Kriz, S. *The specification of digital-to-analog converters for audio.* Paper presented at the proceedings of the 2nd Annual Music Computation Conference Champaign-Urbana 1976.

Johnson, S. C. Hierarchical clustering schemes. *Psychometrika,* 1967, *32,* 241-254.

Plomp, R. Timbre as a multidimensional attribute of complex tones. In R. Plomp & G. F. Smoorenburg (Eds.), *Frequency analysis and periodicity detection in hearing.* Leiden: A. W. Sijthoff, 1970.

Portnoff, M. R. Implementation of the digital phase vocoder using the fast Fourier transform. *IEEE Transactions on Acoustics, Speech, and Signal Processing,* 1976, ASSP-24 *(3),* 243-248.

Mathews, M. W. *The technology of computer music.* Boston: MIT Press, 1969.

Moorer, J. A. *On the segmentation and analysis of continuous musical sound by digital computer* Report No. STAN-M-3. Stanford University, Department of Music, 1975.

Moorer, J. A. *The use of the phase vocoder in computer music applications.* Paper presented to the 55th Convention of the Audio Engineering Society, October 1976.

Ramsay, J. O. The joint analysis of direct ratings, pairwise preferences and dissimilarities. *Psychometrika,* 1980, *45,* 149-165.

Schiffman, S. S. A psychophysical model for gustatory quality. *Physiology and Behavior,* 1971, *7,* 617-633.

Shepard, R. N., Romney, A. K., & Nerlove, S. (Eds.). *Multidimensional scaling: Theory and applications in the behavioral sciences.* New York: Academic Press, 1972.

Spence, I., & Domoney, D. W. Single subject incomplete designs for nonmetric multidimensional scaling. *Psychometrika,* 1974, *39,* 469-490.

Takane, Y., Young, F. W., & de Leeuw, J. Nonmetric individual differences in multidimensional scaling: An alternating least squares method with optimal scaling features. *Psychometrika,* 1977, *42,* 7-68.

Torgerson, W. S. *Theory and methods of scaling.* New York: Wiley, 1958.

van de Geer, J. P. *Matching k sets of configurations.* University of Leiden, Leiden, Netherlands. Data theory report RN-005-68, 1968.

Wessel, D. L. Psychoacoustics and music. *PAGE: Bulletin of the Computer Arts Society,* 1973, *8,* 30-31.

Young, F. W. Nonmetric multidimensional scaling: Recovery of metric information. *Psychometrika,* 1970, *35,* 455-473.

Young, F. W. Scaling replicated conditional rank-order data. *Sociological Methodology,* 1975, *6,* 129-170.

Young, F. W., & Cliff, N. Interactive scaling with individual subjects. *Psychometrika,* 1972, *36,* 385–417.

Young, F. W., de Leeuw, J., & Takane, Y. Regression with qualitative and quantitative variables: An alternating least squares method with optimal scaling features. *Psychometrika,* 1976, *41,* 505–529.

Young, F. W., Null, C. H., & De Soete, G. *Principal directions individual differences multidimensional scaling: An alternating least squares approach,* in preparation.

Young, F. W., Null, C. H., & Sarle, W. Interactive similarity ordering. *Behavior Research Methods & Instrumentation,* 1978, *10,* 273–280.

Young, F. W., Null, C. H., Sarle, W. S., & Hoffman, D. L. Interactively ordering the similarities among a large set of stimuli. In Golledge, R. G., & Rayner, J. N. *Proximity and Preference: Problems in the multidimensional analysis of large data sets.* Minneapolis, MN: University of Minnesota Press, in press.

Author Index

Numbers in *italics* indicate pages with complete bibliographic information.

A

Abramson, A. S., 85, *90*
Ackroff, J. M., 28, *35*
Adams, O. S., 95, *105*
Anderberg, M. R., 131, *142*
Anderson, J. A., 181, *194*
Andrews, H. A., 147, *157*
Arnold, J. B., 66, 71, *78*
Attneave, F., 95, *105*

B

Baker, R. F., 200, *211*
Ballas, J. A., 189, *195*
Barlow, H. B., 184, *194*
Benbasset, C. A., 42, 46, 51, *59*
Bentler, P. M., 200, *212*
Berg, K., 42, *59*
Bergman, A. S., 86, *89*
Bever, T. B., 85, 86, *91*
Biddulph, R., 42, *58*
Bienvenido, G., 86, *91*
Bilger, R. C., 83, *91*
Bilsen, F. A., 9, *24*
Black, H. S., 149, *157*
Bloxom, B., 200, 210, *211*

B (column two)

Blumstein, S., 89, *91*
Bobrow, D. G., 54, *57*
Bregman, A. S., 43, *57, 89*
Broadbent, D. E., 41, *57,* 62, *77,* 80, *90*
Burgy, D. C., 189, *195*
Byrnes, D. L., 86, *91*

C

Campbell, J., 43, *57,* 86, *89*
Cardozo, B., 8, 11, *25*
Carpenter, A., 67, 68, 69, 70, 71, 73, 75, 77, *77, 78,* 167, *180*
Carroll, F. S., 86, *91*
Carroll, J. D., 164, 165, 167, *179, 180,* 203, 206, 207, *211*
Carterette, E. C., 168, *180*
Caskey, W. E., 28, *35*
Cermak, G. W., 168, *179*
Chaney, R. B., 64, 66, *77*
Chang, J. J., 165, *179,* 203, 207, *211*
Chipman, S., 110, 111, *126*
Chomsky, N., 81, *89*
Clark, H. H., 87, *90*
Cliff, N., 198, 200, 205, 209, *211, 213*
Cohen, M. M., 42, *58*

Subject Index